OEM Principles of Lean Thinking

Global Principles to Save Time and Make Money

Save time and make money in any business, anywhere in the world.

Understanding the Principles of Lean Thinking,

The OEM Way.

This Handbook comes with an **Online Course**, and a Coach, to help you along the OEM Way.

Consultants Inc.

Copyright © 2012

George Trachilis, P.Eng. CPIM

ISBN-13: 978-1475161854

ISBN-10: 1475161859

Title ID: 3845506

Copyright © 2012 Trachilis

All rights reserved.

Publishing Services

www.alphaacademicpress.com

Acknowledgements

This manual represents an opportunity for you to connect with a coach or mentor. I thought it only appropriate that I would acknowledge my mentor of over 15 years, Graham Moore, P.Eng. He was always honest with me, and time has shown me that he always had my best interest in mind.

I'd like to thank the Alberta Government in Canada for being forward thinking enough to support my company, OEM, in delivering this training to over 50 companies in the major cities of Alberta in 2007. Following the success of this initiative, the program was extended to include over 100 other companies in the rural areas of Alberta.

I'd also like to recognize my life-long friend Demetre Balaktsis for helping me create the *OEM Lean101 – Principles* online course. The course was done in an efficient and to-the-point manner. His teaching style comes across in the materials and delivers the impact that we needed. To this day, our average rating from students is still 9 out of 10.

To Bob Kerr, the consultant who first introduced the airplane simulation to me, this was the missing link that I needed to effectively communicate my excitement of Lean to others. I was finally able to describe Lean in a systematic approach and implement the concepts in every industry that I was called to help. Bob's openness for sharing is inspirational, and I have not forgotten his definition of R&D - Rob and Duplicate.

Thank you Michael Deese for creating the Airplane Simulation; what an eye-opening experience! The in-class training using the plastic interlocking blocks is enjoyable, and the learning is instinctive. The simulation is also easy to understand, and more importantly, easy to communicate.

I'd like to also thank Daniel Stanley, my publisher who put a copy of my book in my hands from the online course material. This helped me visualize the final result. In turn, I was inspired to bring this project to a close.

Finally, I'd like to express my thanks to all of OEM's clients. Without their support and loyalty, none of this would be possible.

"The OEM Lean 101 Online course provided PTI a simple to manage on-line educational tool critical to establishing a base to move forward. The education helped our organization learn to talk the same language, gain a basic understanding of the tools of lean manufacturing to build from and understand the importance of continuous improvement. All in all, the training provided a great base to build a production improvement system."

Robert Maze
Vice President of Manufacturing
PTI Group Inc.

Preface

My name is George Trachilis, Founder and President of Global OEM Solutions, Inc., and OEM Consultants, Inc. I was fortunate enough to be in a position where I could make the time to put this book together. You see… it's difficult to work on strategic work versus tactical work in any business and it is no different for me. It's difficult to work on the future when the challenges of the day are keeping us busy 8 hours more than our regular workday. The time has come to be a long-term thinker versus a short-term, results-driven individual. The OEM way is my way of doing business. I serve the consultants and recruiters in my business, and in turn they encouraged me to carve off a portion of my time so that they get the long-term benefits of sharing my business model. Thank you to all of my associates for promoting me from a "lean thinker" to an author of the lean-thinking process.

OEM is my consulting and recruiting company based in Canada, but working globally. Originally my company was integrating operations, engineering and manufacturing solutions for clients primarily in the manufacturing sector. Now, OEM has grown its offering of services to include recruiting, executive coaching, and web-based education in almost every sector you can think of. With a series of courses developed for industry called the OEM Lean 101 Online Series, my company has developed a new standard of introductory courses on productivity. Although the OEM Lean101 Principles course uses manufacturing as a basis, this book introduces the overarching mantra that it is good for anything, like healthcare, finance, construction, etc. My course comes with two coaches for every student to help them completely understand the concepts and assist them by providing direction on how to apply these concepts. OEM Lean101 – Principles of Lean Thinking course has been introduced to over 140 countries through the internet.

Regardless of whether you are a student of Lean, an expert who has been applying Lean for years, or have never heard of Lean before, you are about to be engaged on a level that you would have never thought possible. What this Handbook entitles you to is simply remarkable. Here's what you get:

- ✓ The best explanation of what Lean Thinking is about – a web-based online course on the Principles of Lean Thinking, http://lean101.ca *(coupon code in book) NO COST*

- ✓ Insight from some of the best practitioners in many industries,

- ✓ A thorough explanation of the "Airplane Simulation", used by some Fortune 500 companies to demonstrate the counter intuitive nature of "Lean Thinking",

- ✓ A Lean coach to help you by email and/or Skype as you complete the online course,

- ✓ A Lean coach in training who took the same course and is their specific experience along with their knowledge of Lean,

✓ An invitation to the Global OEM Consortium http://lean101.ca/weboffice.htm, this give you an opportunity to learn from all of the great productivity experts in world, and finally,

✓ The chance for you to coach other students as they are going through the transition from a traditional thinker to a Lean thinker.

Over the last ten years OEM has educated businesses with success, through the introduction and implementation of Lean Principles. Our expertise has kept businesses on the competitive edge of world-class manufacturing and trade. OEM is well aware that almost all businesses in the world today are subjected to the Waste of Human Potential. Through OEM's unique way of doing business and communicating with organizations, the waste of Human Potential is minimized. And it all starts with you!

I have many contributors in this book including Dr. Jeffrey K. Liker, author of the Toyota Way, Norman Bodek, known to many as the "Godfather of Lean", Mike Hoseus, co-author of Toyota Culture, and some of my Senior Leaders in Global OEM Solutions Inc. In order to engage you within these articles and the entire book, I have placed the following icons to ask questions, and give answers to some questions that may be posed. When you see these, just say to yourself, "George is asking, or, George is answering". The other icon is what I have personally added into my "personal" book of knowledge (BOK). It represents what I have learned from my experiences to be true, and I am sharing this with you in the hopes that you know it to be true as well.

When you see this icon – it represents a question I have of you (the reader)?

When you see this icon – it represents my answer.

know.

This icon represents what I know. When you see this icon, you should say to yourself, "this is George's opinion", unless you know what I know.

I Don't Know
This icon represents what I don't know. If you know the answer, please share with me in the Global OEM Consortium http://lean101.ca/weboffice.htm .

The concepts outlined in this course apply to all industries, especially the ones that need it the most, such as healthcare and government. I know that time is the valuable currency of tomorrow. Organizations poised to respond immediately to an increasingly competitive and demanding global marketplace will be successful. I would be pleased to help you on your journey to excellence. It starts with the understanding shared in this book and online course.

George Trachilis (front row) delivers training on-site for Dubai Customs in 2009. Dubai, UAE.

Why does this book exist?

This book seeks to give you the knowledge that will escalate your thinking process to new heights. This knowledge needs to be accepted, and then converted to experience by you. This book will give you an advantage as an entrepreneur, or as a practitioner of Lean in your company. It will show you the concepts used by Lean companies to make more money than their competition.

All you have to do is absorb these materials and concepts. When you register for the course that comes with this book, you will have two coaches that will help your thought process. Please use them, ask them questions, and follow their sound advice. Since most people learn from hands-on experiences, I encourage you to complete the OEM Lean101 online course which is included as part of this book. You will become engaged with the materials and if you are like 90% of my students, you will become a convert. This is the best course on lean thinking anywhere in the world.

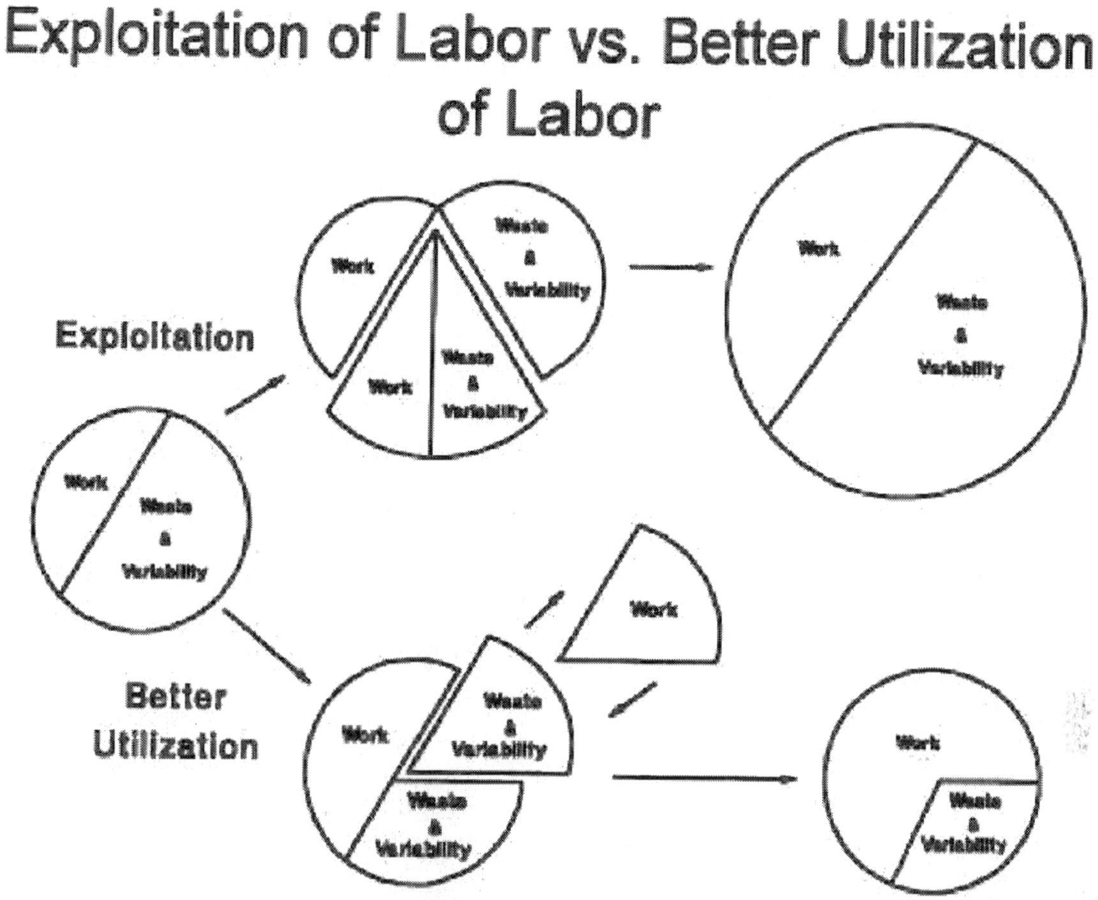

Exploitation of Labor vs. Better Utilization of Labor

The premise is quite easy. In every organization there is work being performed, and with work there is waste and variability. When organizations hire people they follow the path in the upper part of the slide shown above. They add more people which indicates more work and more variability and waste. The addition of people means the circle is larger now. The work performed (top right circle) is generally the same percentage as in the small circle on the left. This book and course will show you how to go through the *Better Utilization* path. It will show you how to do more with less. By removing waste and variability in your processes you are able to go secure more work thereby making more money. The bigger circle above and the smaller circle below it contain the same amount of work. The costs are greatly decreased in the Lean Thinking approach described by the Better Utilization approach. The concepts are simple and most companies and organization strive for this type of improvement. The secret to making this happen lies in understanding their people.

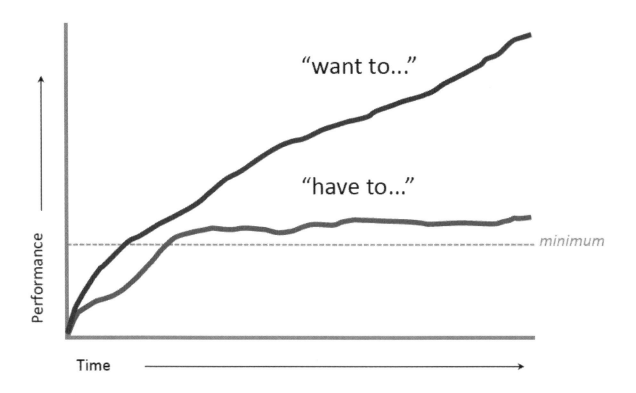

There is a huge difference between employees *wanting to* do something and *having to* do something. In organizations that depend on people, people performance is the ultimate measure. Companies make the mistake of setting up minimum requirements and then thinking that because they achieved this minimum, they are done their Lean journey. They think that they have achieved the Lean future state. This book is designed to help you close this gap between the "have to…" performance demanded by your company, and the "want to…" performance, which you know you or your employees can achieve given the support and knowledge. This book will inspire you to achieve double the performance level that you thought was possible. The experience you will gain by implementing the techniques in this book will make you an expert in your industry, able to sell your expertise to companies that need help. In my industry, manufacturing, we call this process "Lean Thinking". In Japan, they call it "Kaizen", in Greece, they are calling it "survival", and for you, you should call it the missing ingredient towards saving time, and making money.

  Why did you pick up this book and read to this point?

The OEM way of doing business should inspire you to become the servant leader that draws on the creativity and knowledge of others to boost your ability to create the right solutions for the right customers. As a child of 5 years old, you may have wanted to be the astronaut, wanting to go to space, and by today, those dreams have been sucked out of you from the people closest to you. These *dream stealers*, as innocent as they may seem, have done you an injustice.

As a general guess, 95% of the companies out there have done the exact same thing to the people that work for them. There is a ton of potential in so many organizations with absolutely no investment of money. It's the human capital that needs to be optimized today, not machines being put together in a U-shaped cell to get more productivity. It is the people being brought together with common goals that make things happen.

 Do you feel that you have much more to accomplish in life?

It's time for me to encourage dreaming once again, and having enjoyment in the process. Life is short. Don't waste another minute second guessing whether you can make money at what you love doing. Just do it! Pick up this book and engage in the learning that will assist you to become the best that you can be. Become the best person, the best manager, the best innovator, and the best thinker. Money is not the most important thing in life. Peace of mind is a lot better than money, for me anyways, and I can't seem to sit back and let life go by without showing you how I made money consistently by applying 5 simple principles. The education provided in this book, the online course, and a coach should be enough to inspire you to start your lean journey.

know.

Everyone that I have had the pleasure of coaching has expressed to me great appreciation of what I have taught them. What is clear to me is that I learned as much from them, and I am destined to die a fool.

This is my book of knowledge regarding what Lean thinking is all about. The experiences I have had in different industries will be shared, but more importantly, there are many others that have contributed with their experiences. Where I think I can guide you in the right direction, you will see another icon.

This will represent some very powerful tools in the industry that can be applied with very little effort and deliver excellent value.

If you consider yourself a "Lean Thinking" expert, and want to serve as I do (educating the world on Lean), I invite you to complete the online course (http://lean101.ca). Then contact me and convince me that you are ready to be a coach other students. The key is to encourage students of this course and book to achieve performance levels that they did not think possible. After all, we are all students, even if you are the teacher, you are learning every time you have the privilege of being listened to.

This book is not about Lean Manufacturing or the Toyota way of doing business. Enough books have been written about Toyota. What I want to make clear is that this book is about a new way of thinking. Applying this process to a way of thinking within you and your organization will generate sustainable excitement over and over again. The system becomes self-sustaining and the benefits are translated into cash. There are 257 Countries, and 145 Industries that I am currently resourcing with consultants, and coaches to assist you in your learning. Let's save time and make money together.

The 5 Principles of Lean Thinking - The OEM Way

1) Engage everyone in delivering value to your customer's future requirements.
2) Commit to Continuous Value Stream Management.
3) Target the ideal state and remove barriers keeping you from achieving it.
4) Continually increase flow by removing bottlenecks that impede flow.
5) Strive to perfect yourself, identify your purpose in life, and share it with others you trust.

As a student and practitioner of Lean Thinking:

Ask these questions of the person/organization that purchased this book for you.

1. What is our long-term philosophy? (Or, are we supposed to create it together?)
2. Where do I fit in? (Or where do you want me to fit in?)
3. How do we serve our community? (Or, how do we define community?)
4. How do you apply the 5 Principles of Lean Thinking in this business/environment?
5. How are the wastes identified in our environment? (Do we call them by different names?)
6. How do we safeguard again the Waste of Human Potential? (How are we using fresh eyes?)
7. How are you going to help me develop myself in the organization? (How can I help you?)
8. Where is a Future State Map located so I know the direction we are going?
9. How do we measure our partners? (How do our partners measure us?) How are they doing?
10. How do our partners measure us? (How are we doing?)
11. What problem-solving tools are approved for use? (What tool kit do I have?)
12. Who do I use to create a future state plan with (What is my area of responsibility?)
13. When (within 6 months) can we schedule time for the same questions to be asked and answered?

As a Leader, Owner, C-Level Executive, Vice-President, Director, or Manager responsible to implement Lean Thinking:

Ask these questions of yourself as you read through this book.

1. Do I have the right people in my organization to implement these concepts?
2. Do I have the right thought process in place to sustain these concepts?
3. Will I listen to my team when things feel out of control for me?
4. Do I trust my team?
5. Do we have a coach/mentor?
6. Do we encourage and reinforce the right behaviors?
7. Do we encourage leader's standardized work?
8. Do we measure Safety-Quality-Productivity-Cost-People throughout our organization?
9. Do we reinforce the 5 Principles of Lean Thinking throughout our organization?
10. Do we measure behaviors as they contribute to our Mission-Vision-Values?

Regardless of your answers, the first step is always education. Pick up the book and start reading. Don't hesitate to engage with the OEM team, it's our job to show you how it's done.

<u>www.oemconsultants.ca</u>

"What we have to learn to do, we learn by doing"

- Aristotle

A Forward by Michael Deese

My name is Michael Deese, the creator of the "Airplane Simulation" that is presented in Chapter 2. George and I entered into an agreement in 2007, where George added his expertise with training to enhance the simulation experience in his on-line course. This book describes what we both are very passionate about. SAVING TIME AND MAKING MONEY.

In the early 90's I was converting my manufacturing company from a traditional to a cellular environment with teams. Today, this is well known as "Lean". Back then, I needed a tool to communicate, to everyone in my organization, what these changes meant to them. They needed to know the WHAT -was going to happen, and the HOW -things were going to happen. Because of our team environment approach, I knew that things were not going to happen to them, but with them, and with their direction. I also knew that our suppliers needed to understand our new business strategy as well; otherwise they would be working against us, continually. For that reason, I created the simulation with interlocking blocks. In this book George refers to my simulation as the best in the world. I trust that he is right.

Today, it is no different. Manufacturing companies that have not converted to this thinking have gone out of business, or, are about to go out of business. Some in management are waiting for the "silver bullet" to help them out of their crises; there is not one. There are only the 5 principles of Lean Thinking that George re-iterates. The way George explains it is brilliant! His examples are priceless, and that is what makes this book a "must have".

Originally I made three sets of the simulation, kept one, and gave two to my business friends. As we talked with people, others wanted a set. I made another few sets, but the requests kept coming. I commercialized Lean Zone Production Methodologies in 1995, for the purpose of selling simulation kits to other companies that wanted to take away the fear of change from their employees. After marketing, copyrighting the materials, I built some inventory to keep up with demand.

George has introduced my simulation in this book, and also is giving away his OEM Lean101 – Principles course for FREE to those who purchase this book. I don't try to understand why, but George has a master plan. I think what George is doing is great. And with over 28 countries now introduced to the "Airplane Simulation", the demand for my kits is still growing.

I am writing this forward because George has put together a perfect mix of materials to guide you, through the confusion about how Lean Thinking is applied. Forget the fact that our backgrounds are in manufacturing, and be re-assured that this book will help you understand how to apply Lean Thinking Principles in any business, and any industry, and even in your personal life.

We should all be as passionate as George about our work. However, he continues to remind me that it is not work, when you love what you do. Great job George! I look forward to your next book.

A Forward by Bob Kerr

My name is Bob Kerr. In 2001 High Performance Solutions was trying to teach the Principles of Lean to the companies in our consortiums across Canada and I was looking for a tool that not only would get the message across, but have it stick in the minds of the participants.

We came across the Lean Zone Production Methodologies Airplane Simulation and decided that we could adapt this great tool into one that incorporated the Principles of Lean. It has been a resounding success and one that has set the foundation for many companies to build on. It is estimated that over 2,000 people and 500 companies have been exposed to Lean 101 in a live setting by our team alone. The ratings from the participants have been the highest of all of the workshops that we deliver. Using the airplane simulation has contributed to more Lean implementations than any other I know of.

Some Toronto-based companies dictated that their employees, from Senior Management to Shop Floor and Office Personnel have to have taken the Lean 101 course before beginning any Continuous Improvement initiative. This resulted in a common understanding of what Lean is and how it was going to be implemented throughout the organization. This course is not only informative, but it is enjoyable also. It teaches people to 'see' the possibilities by building airplanes using plastic-interlocking blocks while opening their minds to the possibilities of applying the techniques in their own organizations.

George has now taken this course and has brought it into the 21st Century by creating a web-based training course, thereby making it available to the entire world. His passion to make the world better through education has to be admired.

I am sure he will touch many people with his new publication and will continue to make a difference that matters. George, thank you for your great work!

Bob Kerr, Senior Partner, High Performance Solutions

George Trachilis, P.Eng.CPIM

Table of Contents

CHAPTER 1 - INTRODUCTION

This is the only book you'll ever need to understand the basics of what "Lean Thinking" is all about. Regardless of the country that you live in or the industry that you work in, Lean applies to you. You can apply it in your daily life and save time each and every day. To provide you with even more value, this book provides you with FREE access to the web-based course *OEM Lean101 -Principles of Lean Thinking*. The course materials are enclosed in Chapter 2 of this book. If you wish to further your lean education, you are welcome to join the Global OEM Consortium. You can access presentations, productivity-based materials, and listen to the most respected experts on implementing these types of changes in your life or in your business. The site is global, and as such, some of the materials will be made available in various languages.

While you are not required to take the online course, you get a unique opportunity to forge a relationship with up to two online Lean coaches. You can choose a coach that lives in your country, or choose a coach that is an expert in your industry. Choose wisely.

How does this all work?

Well, it is quite simple. At the end of this chapter you are given access to the OEM Lean101-Principles course located at http://Lean101.ca. As you make your way through the online course, you will come across a quiz at the end of each section. As you complete each quiz, the results are then sent simultaneously via email to you and your two coaches. You can get in touch with your coaches via email, Skype or our Global OEM Consortium at http://lean101.ca/weboffice.htm. Regardless of how you connect, you can be sure to get some insightful information. Your coaches are there to serve you - this is the OEM way. OEM gives back to the community by making themselves available to students of this material, regardless of the industry or country that the student resides in. OEM is able to provide coaches to every student of the OEM Lean101 - Principles course; there are enough coaches to go around. This book may inspire you enough to become one of my coaches. Let me know if you are interested after you receive your certificate.

The OEM Lean101 – Principles course comes with 6 professional development hours.

The OEM Way- Creating Relationships, Uncovering the Reality, Proving the Results

The OEM way is about creating a bond of respect, trust and truthfulness with everyone.

Lean Thinking Origins

Socrates

Socrates was credited as one of the founders of western philosophy. Philosophy in Greek (philosophia) means the love of wisdom. Another word for wisdom is knowledge. It is amazing that the man who was considered wisest of all the Greeks was quoted by his student Plato, as saying, "as for me, all I know is that I know nothing." Socrates was masterful in the development of his student, Plato who later became the founder of the Academy in Athens, the institution for higher learning.

Socrates was one of the greatest educators who taught by asking questions. This process of asking questions draws out answers from his students. Everything we know of Socrates comes from his student, Plato.

The overall purpose of Socratic questioning is to challenge accuracy and completeness of thinking in a way that acts to move people towards their ultimate goal.

know.

We need more teachers like Socrates in today's business world. In this way, we would be developing people faster than ever.

Questions about the question, I call it Mind Kung-Fu.

Socrates and the famous Socratic questioning process is used to describe a certain kind of questioning. This is where the original question is responded to by an answer, however this answer is not only in the form of a question, but the question assumes the person with the first question is correct. This forces the person who asked the first question to ask another question digging a little deeper on his or her own theory.

Turning a question in on itself is like using a student's attack against themselves. This is like playing "catch", back and forth with the student. Ask questions like this;

- What was the point of asking that question?
- Why do you think I asked this question?
- Am I making sense? Why not?
- What else might I ask?
- What does that mean?

To get your student to dig deeper into their own insight, ask these questions;

- Why are you saying that?
- What exactly does this mean?
- How does this relate to what we have been talking about?
- What is the nature of that?
- What do we already know about this?
- Can you give me an example?
- What exactly are you saying?
- Can you rephrase that so that I can understand?

To get your student to question their own beliefs, ask these questions;

- Is there anything else we could we assume?
- You seem to be assuming ... ?
- How did you choose that assumptions?
- Please explain why/how ... ?
- How can you verify or disprove that assumption?
- What would happen if ... ?
- Do you agree or disagree with ... ?

Rather than accepting the student's rationale, dig into their reasoning, ask them these questions;

- Why is that happening?
- How do you know this?
- Can you give me an example of that?
- What do you think causes ... ?
- What is the nature of this?
- Are these reasons good enough?
- Would it stand up in court?
- How might it be refuted?

- How can I be sure of what you are saying?
- Why is ... happening?
- Ask Why? 5 times, you most likely won't get past two.
- What evidence is there to support what you are saying?

To show that there is more than one viewpoint, ask the student questions such as;

- Another way of looking at this is ..., does this seem reasonable?
- What alternative ways of looking at this are there?
- Why it is ... necessary?
- Who benefits from this?
- What is the difference between... and...?
- Why is it better than ...?
- What are the strengths and weaknesses of...?
- How are ... and ... similar?
- What would ... say about it?
- What if you compared ... and ... ?
- How could you look another way at this?

If a logical statement is made, and you think the consequences can be predicted to be either desirable or undesirable, then ask;

- Then what would happen?
- What are the consequences of that assumption?
- How could ... be used to ... ?
- What are the implications of ... ?
- How does ... affect ... ?
- Why is ... important?
- What is the best ... ? Why?

know.

Problem solving skills are desperately needed in most businesses.

 The 5-Why process is one of the most powerful skills an employee can possess.

know.

If every business meeting/conversation first identified the customer and then tried to answer all of the customer's questions the meeting would be as efficient as it can get.

When you are the customer and others are overpowering your conversation (questions) ask, "Am I the customer here, can I get my questions answered?"

The 5-Why process is repeatedly asking the question why? To identify the cause of the effect. The premise is that after a certain amount of times "Why?" is asked (does not need to be 5) you get to the root cause of a problem (or effect). By understanding what that root cause is, and later eliminating it, the effect of the root cause is also eliminated.

Socrates was a master at working on developing his students and had a high respect for the communication process.

Most organizations that are Lean today use the minds of every worker to engage in satisfying the customer's requirements. Developing people should be your first priority so that your people can redevelop your processes. Driving excellence in people guarantees excellence in processes.

Henry Ford

Ford (1863-1947) was credited for the development of the assembly line technique. As the owner of the Ford Motor Company he became one of the richest and best-known people in the world. He was a genius of American industry, and ranked as the #1 most-influential businessmen of all time by Forbes.

When I first put together the online version of the Principles of Lean Thinking course together in 2006, I did what everyone with a quality background does. Standardize before making any improvements. I took materials as they were created by others, put my stories into them and delivered these materials as they were intended.

Well, as I learned more about Lean over the years, I realized that the true pioneer in the process was Henry Ford. He integrated an entire production process at Highland Park, MI, in 1913. This was a continuous moving assembly line. Parts were delivered to the workers by an assembly belt, and the timing was carefully orchestrated to ensure that the line moves smoothly. This concept revolutionized automobile production by reducing assembly time per vehicle, and lowering costs.

know.

Ford turned iron ore into cash in 41 hours. Of this, 13 hours was transportation down the Rouge River in Michigan.

He was focused on both the people and the process, consistently using standardized work and conveyance to create what he called flow production. The general public saw this as a form of an assembly line, but Henry's manufacturing engineers knew that this went much deeper.

Henry Ford first started placing fabrication processes in sequence. He even had quality checks prior to moving the parts from one step to the next. These checks were known as go/no-go gauges. In those days it was truly revolutionary. He was able to turn inventory around in his company within a few days. At the time, there was one model going down the assembly line, and by 1926 there were five body styles, and features added. There was no need for changeovers, because this was one value stream.

know.

By 1918 more than 50% of the vehicles on American roads were Ford's Model T.

Ford was a master at working on processes and had a high respect for people. He took interest in the personal lives of every one of his employees.

I Don't Know Why does a country, business, family, look for solutions outside of their own people? Edward Deming (an American) was the biggest contributor to the rebirth of the Japanese economy after WWII, with his introduction of the PDCA cycle. Americans would not listen to him.

The problem and opportunity (depending on your perspective) arose when the world wanted variety. The Model T was limited to one color.

With Ford's domination, other manufacturers found a way to provide these customers with the variety they craved. The old adage of "you can't be everything to everybody" now becomes apparent.

Sakichi Toyoda

Sakichi Toyoda (1867-1930) was referred to the "King of Japanese Inventors". His most famous invention was the automatic power loom, which was only possible through the principle of Jidoka. Jidoka (autonomous automation) means that a machine stops itself when a problem occurs. This prevented the production of any defective product. Sakichi Toyoda later sold his patent to a British firm for $150,000 which was later used to help his son found a start-up business, Toyota. The descendants' of Sakichi Toyoda have dominated the upper management of Toyota Motors.

Sakichi also subscribed and further developed the concept of 5 Whys. When a problem occurred he was able to ask the questions, and trace them back to the source (the root cause) and in this way he continually made improvements upon his inventions. Sakichi Toyoda was ranked #13 on Forbes Most Influential Businessmen of All Time.

ANSWER   Every business system today is best advised to have a "Jidoka" aspect to it. Their business system should stop producing when a problem occurs, then through methods of problem solving, fix the problem, and then start producing again.

As Kiichiro Toyoda, Taiichi Ohno, and others at Toyota became aware of the opportunity that Ford created in the early 1930s, it occurred to them that they could capitalize on this demand in which customers had a need for variety. After World War II they revisited Ford's original thinking, and invented the Toyota Production System.

The Toyota Production system is a way to describe the overall business philosophy of Toyota. One pillar of the system is called, Just-in-Time, and the other pillar is called Jidoka. There are many visuals that are used to describe the TPS system. In Japan the Toyota Production System has been credited to Taiichi Ohno and Shigeo Shingo (Toyota's industrial engineer). Today TPS comes down to two very simple concepts, excellence in product, and excellence in people.

Creating a visual that describes to the world (and your employees) how you do business is extremely powerful. It automatically identifies Do's and Don'ts regarding how to go about doing business YOUR WAY.

know.

If you had a company named ABC then the process in which you use to do business is known as the ABC Way, and the system that you create could be called the ABC PRODUCTION SYSTEM. Make it your own! Define your own principles, values! Determine success by exhibiting the right behaviors! Everything else will come, including the money.

The concept we refer to as "Lean" is described in the book *The Machine That Changed the World* (1990) by James P. Womack, Daniel Roos, and Daniel T. Jones. Later, in 1996, these principles were described to be:

- Specify the value desired by the customer
- Identify the value stream for each product providing that value and challenge all of the wasted steps (generally nine out of ten) currently necessary to provide it
- Make the product flow continuously through the remaining value-added steps
- Introduce pull between all steps where continuous flow is possible
- Manage toward perfection so that the number of steps and the amount of time and information needed to serve the customer continually falls

Lean Thinking Today

The world is always on the look-out for a cost-effective solution to their problems. China has been capitalizing on this and continues to do so. They were cheap, and that represented a solution for some North American manufacturers towards competing globally or staying competitive globally.

Well, things have changed. Today, competency will always trump cost. The thinking worker is no longer a nice-to-have. This kind of worker is a must-have in order for businesses to become more and more competitive, as their customers demand of them. The people-side of Lean Thinking has been missing in almost every implementation introducing this new (OLD) way of doing business. The focus has been on the product or the service, not on the people. The focus is now taking a shift back towards a people-first mentality. Developing people will most definitely mean continually developing your process, because in the end, people develop processes.

know.

Survival is not mandatory. You do not need to stay in business, going bankrupt is an option.

Every organization will end up choosing lean concepts whether they like it or not. They either choose to implement Lean Thinking principles or they don't. Assuming that they choose to survive, then they can do it one of two ways, through leadership, or through crisis. They are both great motivators; unfortunately one can be viewed as negative, and the other as pro-active. You choose! Are you waiting for a crisis?, or, are you willing to be a leader in driving needed change in your organization?

OEM Lean 101, the way out of the economic crisis – by Arnoud Oor, Athens, Greece

In the current turmoil of the Greek economic crisis, a lot of Greek companies are struggling to survive. They are faced with diminishing demand and serious cash flow problems. What is interesting to know is that Lean was quickly adopted due to the financial crisis of the 1950's.

During that time, the Japanese economy entered in a deep recession - very similar to the crisis that Greece is experiencing in June of 2012. The Toyota Motor Company started having serious cash flow problems.

Most of its cash was tied up in inventories for products that had no immediate demand. Under the pressure of limited cash flow and the need for lower production cost, Toyota decided to redesign its production processes. In order to reduce the need for cash, the decision was made to minimize the lead time from customer orders to delivery.

Concurrently, focus was put on reducing costs and improving the quality by driving out the waste from every step of the production process. As the situation was very critical for Toyota, these changes were done with great urgency in a short time period. With this innovative response to the crisis, Toyota managed to survive and to become the largest car manufacturer in the world.

Why is a crisis the best time to start with Lean?

During a crisis, organizations are more open to change as they realize that the ways in which they operate are simply not valid any more. This makes the required paradigm shift both easier and faster.

Lean implementations generally create very fast cash flow improvements, especially in the beginning. Lean projects require a minor investment while creating impressive cash flow improvements through significant lead time and inventory reductions.

The positive cash flow created in the early stages of the lean implementation also helps a company to finance possible investments in systems, equipment and much needed training. All of this is a good sign that will enable the implementation of productivity improvements. This again results in a further improvement of the cash flow.

Lean can be implemented in any industry

Although Lean has its origins in manufacturing, it can be implemented for any process or industry. Other examples/environments where OEM Lean implementations apply are:

- Lean Office Environment
- Lean Healthcare
- Lean Service organizations
- Lean Store design
- Lean Government
- Lean Construction

OEM consultants have an international network of Lean consultants experienced in all the above areas, making it one of the best partners to assist you in these crucial changes.

Because of the extensive knowledge within the OEM network, we at CRS Hellas decided to join the OEM network, enabling us to offer a wide range of OEM Lean services to the Greek market.

OEM Consultants in Greece

The manufacturing sector alone in Greece consists of approximately 3,500 companies that employ nearly 200,000 people and contribute 11.5% to the GDP of Greece. As a Supply Chain Director for a large multinational company in Greece, and as Partner of CRS Hellas, it has been my experience that a lot of Greek manufacturing companies are plagued with long lead times.

They also have an important part of their capital tied up in their inventories. OEM in Greece can help companies to drastically reduce the waste in their processes, which reduces their costs and improves their lead times.

I am one of the coaches living in Greece, and representing Greece when you register. I look forward to coaching you through the process of lean thinking, and applying this way of thinking in your organization. This way, OEM can make a positive contribution to the recovery of the Greek economy.

Arnoud Oor, Senior Leader, Greece, Global OEM Solutions, Inc.

Arnoud@OEMsolutions.ca

OEM Lean101 – The Italian Way – by Angelo Scordo and Team Italy

Italy has a diversified industrial economy with high gross domestic product (GDP) per capita and developed infrastructure. According to the International Monetary Fund, the World Bank and the CIA World Factbook, in 2010 Italy was the seventh-largest economy in the world and the fourth-largest in Europe in terms of nominal GDP and the tenth-largest economy in the world and fifth-largest in Europe in terms of purchasing power parity (PPP) GDP. Italy is member of the Group of Eight (G8) industrialized nations, the European Union and the OECD.

Recently Italy has entered a recession phase which is creating big trouble locally as well as at global level also. In these difficult times, Italian companies, mostly small and privately owned, face many challenges, both global and local. They need to control costs to be competitive, and at the same time free up cash flow to overcome their credit crunch. The Italian banking systems are also risk adverse, they need to become more efficient and effective especially from an organizational standpoint. They need to learn about this common language and identify better measures of the supply chain and the stronger business network that Lean creates. Businesses need to transfer knowledge and skill from the old owner to the new entrepreneurial generation. They need to innovate while keeping the "handcraft" feeling that distinguishes *Made in Italy*.

These are difficult challenges and in order to overcome them, knowledge of theory and practice are needed. Lean thinking knowledge in Italy is relatively young and almost exclusively connected to manufacturing. Theory of Constraints is pretty much unknown.

Some may say that management is an art rather than a science in Italy, which sounds appealing but sometimes prevents our companies from reaping the benefits of their efforts because of the lack of tools, methods and best practices.

On the other hand, consulting in Italy requires a lot of experience because the consultant is valued based on his or her ability to tackle practical issues. Not based on their ability to lead people and to manage complex dynamics. This is not surprising because the owner/entrepreneur experienced their business growth in this way. This is all they know, and now that the world is changing, they are either unaware of this, or simply overly focused on the products they sell and not the people that they need to develop.

OEM Consultants in Italy focus on many other business sectors, not just manufacturing, for example, the healthcare sector. This sector is mostly but not exclusively public. In the last years the healthcare is slowly adopting best practices and management approach coming from the private sectors, for example ISO 9001 is becoming more common and it is often required when bidding for big contracts. Along with a strong need to control costs the pressure to manage risk is increasing and it fosters a culture less resistant toward change. Though that decision processes in the public sector are still very slow and political-biased.

When our consulting team met after taking the OEM Lean 101 course separately, we decided to form the OEM team in Italy. We felt very lucky to be able to join our experiences and competences, since we knew from the very beginning that each one of us were masters of both the theory and the practice.

In fact, we built our experience working in both multinational businesses and micro businesses. We expand all industrial sectors, and are experts in many other business sectors (metallurgy, plastics processing, oil & gas, furniture, luxury & fashion, textile, biomedical devices, automation, and automotive). It was also quite peculiar to realize that our individual experiences had little overlap;

I, Angelo Scordo, have a technical and design experience that is quite unique.

Fabio Gambaro can count on his track record as a black belt in an extremely big and world-wide renowned company.

Luca Sarto led teams in manufacturing both in big and small companies and has a broad experience with operations.

Michela Rea dedicated her whole consulting carrier almost exclusively to Theory of Constraints methodology.

We decided to name our group Fit2compete because we would like to become the Italian businesses coaches of the future. We trust in the potential of all Italian Companies, and our role is that of a sports coach.

The coach believes in the potential of his team of athletes, as we do with the Italian companies we work with. We make them fit to compete in the local and international market.

The Italian way

Traditional consulting approach in Italy is still based on the idea of "owning" the knowledge as intellectual property. In the short term this may create dependency on the supplier (consultant) and produce results but in the long term this is not sustainable.

Coherent to OEM philosophy we want to share theory and practice and leverage the ability of the customer's resources to pursue continuous improvement. Wherever this is possible and accepted by our customers, the probability for sustainable change increases dramatically. We don't want to be embedded in the customer's day by day activities, instead we want to train, coach and bond with the customer's managers to pull the knowledge from the workers. This is the fuel that will power the engine of the company, and this change process must be taken advantage of from the very beginning.

The advantage to our approach is two-fold:

- We send a clear message as to who is leading and driving the company resources
- We don't create dependency on external consultants: in this way the change is sustainable and even if the company goes through changes, it is left with all the tools, knowledge and experience to create new solutions.

In order to do this we rely on our OEM "collective intelligence" effort on teaching materials, training system, best practices and success stories. In terms of tools we rely on powerful thinking like OEM Lean Thinking, Strategy Deployment, and Theory of constraints. We help the companies we work with create systems, and their systems are made up of tools, such as A3 problem solving, Cause and Effect diagrams, 5Why analysis, and many others. We also know how to use our suppliers effectively. We collaborate with them, and create specific solutions with our customers; NxtNote has been excellent in this regard. NxtNote is software that you can purchase, that forces the collaboration process to happen until it becomes second nature. Contact Ed@OEMsolutions.ca for information on this excellent tool.

All these thinking processes and tools help our customers to leverage and improve their understanding of their biggest problems and to develop breakthrough solutions. We ask the right questions, to get the right answers, to have our customer's understand and know what they thought they did not know (Socrates).

OEM's web-based training courses allow our customers to benefit from taking small steps. This learning is very easy to digest; they can choose to do it according to their available time.

This is particularly useful today where time is a scarce resource. Knowing that OEM has global reach is of great benefit to our Italian customers in making them more international and competitive. With their Italian ingenuity and the high level of quality we help our companies remove any barriers to be accessed by the rest of the world.

In other words we apply the concepts related to manufacturing excellence and at same time develop new solutions which are important not only for local markets but also for the global one. The future is in doing continuous improvement, and the way we respond to these future requirements is in developing systems that increasing our customer's rate of change. Sharing OEM's knowledge worldwide is a solution that we are excited at providing.

OEM inspires change by identifying clear opportunities.

We want to give our customers the best advantage possible to achieve their desired future states. Our special solutions for Italian companies include guiding them towards becoming a global player in their market, and using OEM to develop their supplier network and ensure everyone understands what it means to be an OEM Lean certified supplier.

More and more multinational companies ask their partners to certify their processes as compliant with systems like Lean Six Sigma (LSS). Take the opportunity to exploit real benefits from using LSS, and engage your suppliers to use the common language that OEM is creating within all supply chains. We help all companies that are willing to explore new ways of doing business. They should target to implement the world's best practices, and thereby use the right tools to help their business structure become robust for the purposes of creating excellence locally and globally.

Our motto is "Quick answers, proven tools, proven results"

Angelo Scordo, Senior Leader, Italy, Global OEM Solutions, Inc.

Angelo@OEMsolutions.ca

OEM Lean101 – Denmark – by Julius Paranowski

Although it's quite a small population, Denmark enjoys a strong position within the European Union with one of the highest GNP per capita and having a stable economy, and administration.

Danish companies have a very international approach and concentrate on chosen industrial sectors like shipping, oil & gas, clean-tech, pharmaceutics, green-energy, agriculture & processing, construction and others. There are few large Danish global corporations like Maersk/A.P.Møller, Novo-Nordisk, Vestas, Carlsberg, Danfoss or Lego and a high number of small and medium size companies very eager to maintain excellent business operations.

Denmark is also a popular place for many foreign companies and corporations. This guarantees a broad complexity of products and services. Since we have high costs for human resources, running and maintaining a business is only possible by outsourcing of manufacturing, and/or highly automated production processes.

In this demanding environment, Lean thinking became one of the important tools for optimizing the operations and organizations during the last twenty years. Many organizations implemented Lean elements with outstanding how the results would improve their positions. However, some companies failed to benefit from Lean to a similar extent due to different reasons, e.g. rapid change in the business context, wrong choice of the tool-set or unbalanced focus on the Lean elements and need for their development.

OEM Consultants are in Denmark to help organizations in Lean understanding and implementation (or re-implementation). We tailor Lean solutions using leading state-of-the-art knowledge, education methods, Lean tools and experience in order to help our clients excel in the global market.

Julius Paranowski, Senior Leader, Denmark, Global OEM Solutions, Inc.

Julius@OEMsolutions.ca

I thought it would be appropriate for you to know how some of our consultants across the globe joined our consulting team. Now I invite you to take the next step, and register for the online course that was developed. It will give you more interaction than you would ever get from a book. All of the material in Chapter 2 is presented in this online course. It is simple, and concise. If you have at least 10 years of experience implementing Lean, and you know that you want to be a coach to other students, then please identify yourself early in the process.

To register for the web-based OEM Lean101-Principles course, do the following:

STEP 1 - Go to http://lean101.ca/signup2.asp (don't let $399.00 CAD scare you, it's free with the code)

STEP 2 – Enter a country or industry coupon code (located in the Appendix of this book)
Then, fill out all of the information.

STEP 3 - Click on the Continue button at the bottom of that page.

Enjoy the Journey.

We have countries going broke today. Greece is just one of them. Spain and Italy are now in the spot light, and I suspect Portugal is not far behind. At the time this book is being published, the only solace that Greece has is that Spain and Italy are in worse shape. We need to learn how to share knowledge and money throughout this little planet. It's clear to me that the rich will try to get richer, and the poor will end up having to find creative ways to keep from getting poorer. Everyone competing with low cost labor must make the decision to become artisans once again.

 Why do you think that everyone must become skilled at a craft once again?

We need to find a need and fill that need better than our competition. Sometimes our customers think they know what they want. It is our job to dig a little deeper and identify what they may not have identified as a need. This need may be known or unknown to them, articulated or unarticulated by them. Identify a need that only we can fulfill and all of a sudden, we are in an excellent position to make money.

We need to be creative with the skills that we have so that we may produce what our customer's want, and need. We must find a way to develop ourselves continually in the craft that we choose to be the best in the world at. My craft is finding the best people for the job.

 What is your craft?

My company, OEM, is about the 3R's, relationships, reality, results. Let me give you some reality. *The Avengers* movie made over $1 Billion in less than 19 days.

There are two interesting things here, one some organizations know how to tap into the wallets of others to make money, and two, we are willing to pay for the entertainment value that we receive. The reality is that we (humans) need to escape reality at times. We need to find ways to enjoy ourselves. Creating your own future is one of the most fulfilling experiences that you can receive out of life.

Why don't you create a future that energizes you?.

I will say that we usually need support, and encouragement. That is why this book has been put together. OEM is here for that support. Now, is the time. While our economy is spiraling into a sink hole, we somehow find $1 Billion dollars to give towards being entertained. I know, it was a great movie. Life can be that way too. It can be the best movie of all, one in which you are the playing the starring role AND at the same time directing the movie.

Imagine if we were entertained at work, imagine if we enjoy ourselves at work, and imagine if we were willing to pay to learn. Implementing lean thinking and enjoying ourselves at work is what it is all about. Get the creative juices going and creating our own future. You will have the encouragement by my coaches and together we can make a new future happen for you, one in which you are excited to go to work every day. A job that involves understanding your customers better. For many of us self-employed, that customer could anywhere. For many of you, you may want to become a consultant after reading this book, and why not. You will understand what most companies do to fail their employees. You will understand what is missing in most businesses to make them the best in their industry. You will understand the OEM way of doing business. You will also understand why 95% of all companies fail to achieve the results that they can only get by using the knowledge of every worker pulling in the same direction. Not only do businesses fail to get the results, the initiatives they try to implement fail.

> 70 % of all change initiatives fail.

Why? Why do 70% of all initiatives fail? What initiatives have failed in your company?

By applying Lean Thinking principles, the right way, the results are certain.

What is the right way of implementing Lean?

You don't need to go much further than knowing that it starts with education. You need to be educated on the topic. In this industry, all experts will agree that implementing Lean is like pealing an onion. When you start eliminating waste, there is only so far you can see. Just like an onion, there is a natural layer that you should peal away to. Then, after that layer is gone, you are able to see the next layer, and so on. That is what the journey is about. One layer at a time. From one current state to the next current state. They key is to make sure you create the next current state, don't sit back and let it happen to you. Make change through leadership not crisis.

Everyone likes immediate results, we don't want to wait. We don't have the patients or the long-term thinking. It's time to apply just a few basic principles that will give us the short term results along the road to long-term gains. Welcome to the OEM Lean101 – Principles of Lean Thinking methodology.

CHAPTER 2 – THE OEM LEAN 101 PRINCIPLES COURSE

Module 01

Section 01 - Lean Thinking

As our associates and professionals in the industry are talking about Lean and getting very excited about it, they all realize that they can apply it in their own workplace, at home, or any place where they can go and apply processes.

My personal background in the manufacturing business has been in production, scheduling, and plant management. Usually, when we want to make improvements it is to a department or a process itself, not on the whole. It is when we start focusing on the whole that we see large improvements for a company.

We started realizing that we were spending money in the wrong places, when we should have been eliminating potential bottlenecks in the manufacturing process. Lean Thinking allowed us focus on the whole, while providing a methodology for people to get trained and to see things differently.

The principles of Lean Thinking have been around for a number of years and will be around in the foreseeable future - it's hard to disagree with the amount of productivity improvements that are gained from applying it.

> **LEAN THINKING**
> * Applies universal principles
> * Focuses on the whole
> * Changes your thinking
> * Is based on the tried and true

Many have gone to investigate why and how Toyota Motor Co. became the most successful company in the world. In 1996, Jim Womack and Dan Jones authored the book Lean Thinking, which provided us with the 5 Principles of Lean Thinking. While the overall concept is very simple and extremely effective, a large number of companies and organization in the world have yet to adopt it.

> Lean is based on history.
> 90% Reduction on lead times

If you've visited an Emergency Room lately, you will have noticed that the wait time is usually outrageous, regardless of the urgency. People get frustrated and despite that you still end up waiting for hours. The reason for this is the lack of information.

> Less information creates frustration.

Hospitals put in a light system, allowing patients to see where they stood in line, relative to others regarding priority. If a person came in with a severe condition, no one got frustrated because of this system. They could see that this person was on their death bed. As a result, all hospitals adopted this technique.

> 90% reduction in work-in-progress.

A former colleague of mine, Bob Kerr, went deep sea fishing in the middle of the Atlantic Ocean. To help them improve the fishing company's process, he proposed to implement Lean Thinking. They initially thought that it wouldn't work there.

> Lean is **effective in any system**.
> Lean is **focused on the whole**.

He drew a map of their process and what he found was that their fishing capacity had nothing to with the size of their net or any other obvious factor. It just had to do with the motor on the boat. Every time they had a big load, the motor would give in. As they would try collecting more fish, the motor couldn't handle the load. By mapping everything out, Bob figured out the weak link in this system. When he pointed this out they started bringing in less fish, but more frequently. At the end of the day, they brought in more fish overall. Lean Thinking applies to all sorts of industries.

> 40% increase in productivity.

Section Key Points

• Lean Thinking was a book written by Jim Womack and Dan Jones.

• Womack and Jones studied the Toyota Motor Co. practices and came up with 5 universal principles for positive change within a system.

• Lean is based on over 6 decades of the 'tried and true' methods. It applies strategies that improve upon any process.

• A lack of relevant information leads to a greater amount of waste within a system.

• Lean principles effectively apply to any system of processes, and, in every work environment.

• Lean focuses on a company's systems as a whole in order to diagnose the root causes of waste.

• Lean utilizes simple to understand concepts to minimize/eliminate waste, and, to make improvements.

• Lean trains people to see things under a new light, and, to think differently about how they can function effectively in their workplace.

Section 02 - Defining Value

There are five principles to Lean Thinking. The first one, *Define Value from the Customer's Perspective,* is actually the most important. When we say 'define value', we really mean the activities that the customer cares about. If you brought your external customer into your facility and asked them, "What activity would you be willing to pay for?", you would know what value added was to the customer. Non-value added activities are the ones that the customer is not willing to pay for.

A customer can be external, somebody buying a product or a service, or an internal customer within an organization. Anybody helping you put that product together further downstream of the process is also a customer. They are an internal customer in this case.

Any activity that the customer cares about is a value-added activity. In contrast, a non-value added activity is one that the customer doesn't care about. It may not be done right the first time and therefore the customer is not willing to pay for it. However, there are non-value added activities that are necessary – the third criterion that these activities fall into. These non-value but critical activities at this point are necessary, yet wasteful, we can't eliminate them, but we can reduce the time they take. The non-value added activities are a target for elimination - not just to be minimized but completely eliminated.

> **DEFINING VALUE**
> - Value from the customer's perspective
> - External vs. internal customer
> - Value Added, Non-Value Added and Non-Value Added but Necessary

> The customer determines value.

> Rework adds to customer cost.

We said that if a customer is willing to pay for something, that indicates that there is value associated with it. When I was working with PAL Manufacturing, I asked a group of employees if they had ever done a rework. What do you think they answered? Yes, of course. However, is the customer willing to pay for the rework?

No, the customer ends up paying for the rework, but it is built into the cost. No matter what the customer's perspective is, you have a company to run and your costs are built into it.

You charge the customer the lowest price you can and try to stay competitive. At the end of the day, you have to absorb those costs.

> 70% improvement in space utilization.

We want to identify and define value from the customer perspective. Three categories identify and define value, and all three must exist.

> **A - VALUE ADDED**
> 1) The customer cares about it.
> 2) Done right the first time.
> 3) Has to change the item.

The first category is value added. Value added is defined as having three criteria. The first criterion is that the *customer cares about it*. The second one declares that the customer cares about it but it also *has to be done right the first time*. If you are doing it the second time around, you are not adding value because it could have been done right the first time around. The third criterion states that it *has to change the item* while going through the process. These three criteria must be met in order for an activity to be considered as value added.

> **B – NON VALUE ADDED BUT NECESSARY**

Is payroll a value added or non-value added activity? Payroll is non-value added but necessary. That means that we have to minimize the amount of waste in such an activity, but right now we cannot eliminate it because we deem it necessary.

> **C – NON-VALUE ADDED (not necessary)**

In all other cases, activities are non-value added and unnecessary; these have to be completely eliminated out of the organization.

Section Key Points

- The first principle of Lean is the most important one. A company must strive to determine value from the customer's perspective.

- If a customer is willing to pay for a step in the process, it is a strong indicator that company should attach value to it.

External Customer:
One who buys your product and/or service.

Internal Customer:
One who downstream in your internal process and is between you (the employee) and the external customer.

- Companies which lack a sound knowledge of Lean feel that they must build rework expenses into the customer's cost.

- 3 Categories for Defining Activities:
     - Value Added
     - Non Value Added
     - Non Value Added but Necessary

- An activity is considered as Value Added when:
     - The customer cares about it
     - It's done right the first time
     - It changes the item going through the process

- The Non Value Added but Necessary category is defined as activities we wish to reduce. We cannot eliminate them from a process because they are still considered essential to the system.

Section 03 - Percentage of Waste

In this next section, we are going to be talking about the percentage of waste during the entire process. As we go through each of the steps, we will break them down into smaller fragments, analyze them and think about each of them as a verb starting that process.

> **% OF WASTE**
> - Break into smaller steps
> - A 'verb' starts each process.
> - Define as Value or Non-Value Added.
> - Keep the customer's perspective.

For example, 'wait' is a verb that starts the process - wait for the material or cut. 'Cut' would start a process, as in 'cut a raw material' for example. As you break down each of these pieces and define whether they are value or non-value added you'll be able to answer questions from a customer's perspective, such as "am I willing to pay somebody to wait for material?"
The answer is very clear.

> Use a customer's perspective.

> Activities must change the item.

At PAL (Princess Auto Limited) Manufacturing, the value added is found in the cylinders that they make. In this case, what is the customer willing to pay for? A cylinder consists of a shaft, a tube, and seals. What does the raw material look like? A twenty- foot length of metal, which has to be cut by someone. When it is cut, value is being added. The same goes with the welding operation, the drilling, etc. - all these add value because you can see that the item is changing.

> 90% improvement in quality.

Can you guess the percentage of activities that add value to a typical non-lean manufacturing shop floor?

The answer is *only 5%*!

> Manufacturing – 5% VA Activity.

> The biggest obstacle is change.

This is sad considering how high manufacturing costs are. This means that 95% of the activities are non-value added from the customer's perspective. When you start a company, we get used to doing things in a way that makes sense at the time. Then years go by, we get comfortable, we don't want to change, and we end up building up waste from the customer's perspective, and we don't know how to change it. We actually are not able to see the waste in the process. Ultimately, this translates to higher costs to the customer.

> 60% reduction in unplanned downtime.

> Office Activities are only 1% VA Activity.

We mentioned earlier that only 5% of manufacturing activities add value. What about in a typical office environment? It's only 1%!

> *Make it Lean!*

Section Key Points

- When you are trying to determine what activity is Value Added, use a customer perspective.

- When you are defining the activities within a process, think of them as small steps. Use a 'verb' to start each sentence that describes an activity (e.g. run).

- Some examples of operations that change an item going through a process and add value are: the cut, the weld, the drill, the tap, etc.

- Only 5 % of all the activities in a non-lean company add value from a customer perspective.

- North American companies are lagging behind other nations when it comes to their knowledge and implementation of Lean. Generally, our cost of our products is higher due to waste and non-value-added work.

- The biggest obstacles to a Lean implementation stem from people's fears. Most of us are afraid of, and resistant to, change; we prefer to stick to our comfort zones.

- When we resist the positive changes identified by the Lean process, we remain blind to the wastes that the customer sees.

- 1 % of all activities in a non-lean office environment add value from a customer perspective.

Section 04 - The Waste of Overproduction

Sometimes, finding value in a process is almost like finding a needle in a haystack. Instead of trying to find the needle, we look at the haystack to see what it is made up of. By defining waste as being the haystack, we come up with 7 forms of waste that we need to eliminate. These are overproduction, waiting, transportation, inappropriate processing, unnecessary inventory, unnecessary motion, and defects.

SEVEN FORMS OF WASTE
- Overproduction
- Waiting
- Transportation
- Inappropriate Processing
- Unnecessary Inventory
- Unnecessary Motion
- Defects

We strategically start with the first waste: overproduction. This prevalent symptom is found in manufacturing and office environments. As soon as we see overproduction as a waste, we see a ton of inventory as what is visually there because of that overproduction. Overproduction is the waste that contributes to every other waste and for that reason it is the first one that we review.

Overproduction
Producing more/sooner than the Internal or External customer needs.

"What do you mean the design's been changed!"

Consultants Inc.

> **OVERPRODUCTION**
> Producing more/sooner than the
> Internal or External customer needs.

In the 1980s, Michael Dell wanted to establish the best and largest supplier of computers in the world. He revolutionized the computer industry by cutting out the middleman and selling directly to the customer.

> Focus on quick product delivery.

He actually produced a lot of computers, because he wanted to fulfill his strategic goal and dream: to be the biggest supplier. The issue that he faced was overproduction. As technology advanced at a very fast pace, the overstock couldn't be sold for the same price. In the end, as the components ended up costing him more than what he could sell them for, he started losing money.

> Overproduction is not a solution.

> Overproduction cannot meet all needs.

> It costs money to carry inventory.

Overproduction almost cost Michael Dell his company in the early eighties. As Dell computers were made to order and according to their wishes, the component inventory increased like crazy.

Inventory costs money. In the financial books, inventory may show up as an asset. But storage costs, including rent, heating/cooling, electricity, etc. all cost money.

How do you think Dell computers are produced today? They are made to order, and Dell is still a major manufacturer of computers. In fact, production is higher than it originally was, satisfying more customers and yet with inventory levels reduced down to 72 hours' worth. Production is done according to the customer demand.

> Produce according to demand.

> Lean carries less inventory.

By producing on demand, which completely differs from the initial strategy, Michael Dell is way more successful.

The lower your inventory is, the better your customer service is, as long as you are doing it right and thinking Lean.

> ***Less is Lean!***

Section Key Points

There are seven forms of waste:
1. Overproduction
2. Waiting
3. Transportation
4. Inappropriate Processing
5. Unnecessary Inventory
6. Unnecessary Motion
7. Defects

- The first waste is Overproduction, i.e. producing more/sooner than the Internal or External customer needs. This waste happens to contribute negatively to every other waste. That is why it is mentioned first.

- Excess amounts of Inventory are a visual indicator that overproduction is prevalent in a company.

- The Dell computer company recognized early on that the customer equates good service with quick product delivery. The company set to the task of providing each customer with what they wanted in the shortest time possible.

- Dell made the mistake of choosing overproduction as a method of being able to deliver on time. The issue was that the mix was too diverse and Dell could not possibly configure to every customer using non-lean manufacturing methods. Also, the products became obsolete before he could sell them all.

- It costs money for a company to carry inventory. Costs range from storage, insurance, obsolescence, theft, damage, etc.

- Today Dell has very little carrying cost - they carry 72 hours' worth of inventory, a strategic amount. They also produce according to the customer demand.

- Carrying more inventories does not result in the ability to provide better customer service. Lean suggests that carrying less inventory and responding to customer demand in a timely fashion is a better solution.

Section 05 - The Waste of Waiting

> **WAITING**
> Long periods of inactivity for people,
> information, machinery or materials.

A lot of people spend a lot of time on quality. And of course this makes good sense: the better quality product you deliver, the happier a customer is. In the past, you would *try* to get quality by doing things right the first time and that made a lot of sense. Nowadays, a lot of companies get it right the *first time*.

Waiting
Long periods of inactivity for people, information, machinery or materials.

"The parts were supposed to be here yesterday!"

When you remove time out of a given process, you are doing the right thing. Waiting is one of the biggest factors around removing time out of a process. Finding out why you're waiting, and then doing something about it.

Our focus is to open up our eyes to waste. Waiting is just another waste that we have to identify and eliminate completely. If we look at retail, an obvious example is waiting to get the stock on the shelf.

> Stick to the customer perspective.

> Eliminate customer wait time.

What happens when a customer comes in, and he or she is looking for something but can't find the item? An employee has to look for it on the computer if they have an inventory management system, or directly in the retail area, then in the back if it hasn't been found. Think of what the customer could be doing instead of waiting while the employee looks for the item. As we eliminate the waiting, we actually increase the ability for the customer to shop for more. In manufacturing, if a machine goes down, we have to wait for the machine to become operational again or for a backup. At one of my former client's plant, a CNC machine was down for two or three months!

> Waiting costs companies money.

It actually held us up quite a bit and the related costs were quite high. This could have been prevented. If there is no backup, but the process is done right, we actually get operators to work very closely with their machines, as if they were married to them - they are tasked to do regular maintenance checks.

> We all tend to cause waste.

Sometimes we are waiting for machinery, people, and processes. For this reason, we have to go after this waste like there's no tomorrow.

> Eliminating waste is worthwhile.

> *Lean is quicker!*

Section Key Points

- The waste of Waiting is defined as long periods of inactivity for people, information, machinery or materials.

- A lot of companies spend money on quality. In the past quality meant doing things right the first time. Removing time out of a process is a clear indication that you are 'doing it right'.

- As we focus on saving time in a process, the waste of Waiting is a central target for companies to go after - i.e. finding out why an internal customer is waiting and then doing something about it.

- Companies must become attuned to the waste of Waiting and try to eliminate it out of their processes.

- Remember to always think from the customer's perspective when you try to identify the waste of Waiting - i.e. you need to eliminate the customer wait time.

- In the retail example, a customer is waiting for support in order to find an item. They are being withheld from the Value Added activity of shopping for products.

- The best solution to machine breakdowns is to build regular maintenance checks into your processes. Preventative measures eliminate people's tendency towards ignoring the warning signs.

- Creating routines that people follow are an effective way to prevent waiting from occurring in the future.

Section 06 - The Waste of Transportation

> **TRANSPORTATION**
> Excessive movement of people,
> information or materials.

Of all the wastes, I personally enjoy eliminating the waste of transportation the most. I enjoy communicating it to others because transportation waste is usually large and can be identified visually. When we are talking about transportation, we are talking about the transportation of material, information, or even people from one place to another so that they can do the job.

Transportation
Excessive movement of people, information or materials.

"I had to go across the street!"

The waste in transportation can be mapped out using a system which has been around for a long time: the Spaghetti Diagram.

> Spaghetti Diagram.

This diagram basically follows a person, product, or information from where it comes to where it goes, and how many times it crosses back and forth.

> Map charts the transportation path
> process flow.

On a map, every step taken by a person gets drawn as a line, from one place to another, allowing us to calculate distances traveled.

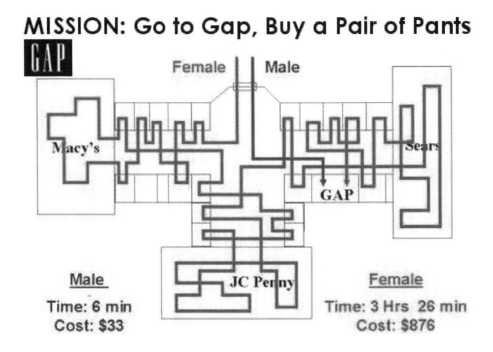

Some time ago, I was a plant manager. One day, we decided to follow the journey of an order from the time a customer placed it. From the sales person it went into our order entry system. Then a print-out landed on my desk, which made it to engineering, then purchasing but came back to engineering. Why do you think that happened? The information wasn't recorded right.

> Do things right the first time.

We followed an order, by the time it had gone through all of the required steps, it had traveled 3 kilometers!

> Eliminate the unnecessary steps.

Many people's hands touched this sales order.

> Determine the VA & NVA steps.

Would you consider this activity Value Added? Not at all. Then it finally got out to the shop floor. It first went into a saw, after which the item had to be placed onto a rack. From the rack, it went into tube drilling.

Once the drilling was performed, the item had to be taken to the rack again. As the product went through 3 other Value-Added steps it had to be placed on a rack between each operation!

> Reduce the amount of travel.

As it finally arrived to the inspection area, the whole floor was covered with inventory. Then the item passed by quality control, it then went into yet another rack and from there, and it finally went into assembly where they actually started putting the product together.

Section Key Points

- The waste of Transportation is defined as excessive movement of people, information or materials.

- It is easy to see the waste of Transportation and to visually communicate it to others; a spaghetti diagram is used.

- A spaghetti diagram charts out the process flow and allows us to reduce/eliminate wastes of Transportation.

- In the office example, the order was followed as it was being processed. It was exposed that the order traveled a distance of 3 km before it got to the VA part of the process.

- Companies must learn methods that assist them in determining whether parts of a process are Value Added or Non-Value added.

Section 07 - The Waste of Inappropriate Processing

> **INAPPROPRIATE PROCESSING**
> Using the wrong set of tools,
> procedures or systems.

Across this manual, I talk about hidden wastes, because we can't see them. Many of the wastes, such as inappropriate processing, are hidden from the people who are executing the tasks. As we find ourselves in situations where the same things are done over and over again, no one can imagine doing them differently.

Inappropriate Processing
Using the wrong set of tools, procedures or systems.

"Bigger is not necessarily better!"

When somebody new comes in, their 'fresh eyes' perspective allows them to see things we maybe shouldn't be doing - call it a customer's perspective. We have to ask dumb questions. Dumb questions are great; these help us uncover the inappropriate processing that goes on.

Going back to our company example earlier in this chapter and remembering that it had a big pile of inventory. The material was received in 16 foot lengths although they actually needed 15 ½ feet. The welder had to get a hold of the material, proceed to saw off 6 inches before performing his own task. As a result, welding was considered as a bottleneck at this company.

> Look for errors in the process.

I asked the following question "why are you purchasing material from a vendor at 16 feet, when you could be bringing it in at the right length?" What do you think the answer was when I asked the owner of the company? "We brought it in at the right length, what are you taking about George, who told you this? And who's cutting that material?" We ended up looking for the enemy within, which is the wrong way to go.

> All of us become blind to waste.

If and when we uncover waste, we should celebrate that we found the problem, not try to find out who caused it. In this whole process we were able to identify all of the waste. It had nothing to do with people - it's the process we were after.

Let me give you an example of waste over at PAL Manufacturing. Cylinders come in different lengths and have variables such as stroke, bore, etc. How many different part numbers do you think we had for the cylinders? There were 625 part numbers, each of which had its own bill of material. They weren't using their software correctly. When we looked at the variables, and created proper bill of materials, we managed to organize and combine as many part numbers, reducing the bill of materials (BOM) count down to 25.

> Eliminate the NVA operations.

They were managing 625 BOMs when they could have been managing 25 – a perfect example of inappropriate processing.

> *As right as Lean!*

Section Key Points

- The waste of Inappropriate Processing is defined as using the wrong set of tools, procedures or systems.

- Inappropriate Processing is hidden to the people that are doing it. People engage in behaviors for a certain length of time and then they can't imagine doing things differently - they enter a comfort zone.

- New hires bring 'fresh eyes' to their workplace. They see things more objectively and provide a customer's perspective. These individuals should be viewed as a valuable resource.

- All new processes should be questioned at every step in an effort to try and understand whether they are being processed appropriately. Look for errors in the process and eliminate the root-cause of those errors.

- We all become blind to waste over time. The goal is not to lay blame, but rather, to celebrate that we found the waste. In this way we are uncovering the NVA operations in a process and eliminating them.

Section 08 - The Waste of Unnecessary Inventory

> **UNNECESSARY INVENTORY**
> Excessive storage and delay information or products.

Of all the wastes, inventory is the one practitioners' talk the most about. You do need a strategic amount of inventory in your company. Everything above and beyond that amount is unnecessary inventory and that is what our focus is all about. On the balance sheet of a non-lean company, inventory is sitting in the column called assets, which is somehow confusing when we look at it from a lean perspective.

Unnecessary Inventory
Excessive storage and delay of information or products.

"We're running out of room. We need to expand!"

We really need to think of excess inventory as being very wasteful, otherwise we will never get rid of that asset from our balance sheet. As we go into the inventory discussions and start looking at how it impacts us, think about inventory even in your own home. It collects; it's like a magnet. The more you hold on to it, the more it collects. And there are many reasons why a lot of companies have gone bankrupt in manufacturing. And one of those causes is excess inventory which ties up cash.

Today, Dell has inventory in their system. They need a strategic amount of inventory. Therefore, anything that is above that strategic amount is unnecessary inventory.

> Determine a strategic amount.

Would you say the strategic amount of inventory for a given company is high or low? It can be high on some items, and low on others.

> Be aware of inventory costs.

What does inventory cost us today? Way too much. We need to know exactly how much inventory costs us in order to help reduce it and to save money.

> Reduce the amount of inventory.

The most important thing to remember about inventory is that it is a symptom of the real problem. You can reduce the inventory but to keep it reduced, you must eliminate the cause of the problem that created the inventory in the first place.

> *Lean is smart!*

Section Key Points

- The waste of Unnecessary Inventory is defined as having more information or products than your system requires.

- A company needs to have strategic amounts of inventory. Everything above this amount is Unnecessary Inventory.

- Inventory has a tendency to collect. Determine what your strategic amount is and keep it at that level. No more, no less.

- Many companies have a difficult time responding accurately to the question, "How much is it costing your company on a monthly/daily basis to hold on to inventory?" "Lots," is not a good response to this question - be aware of inventory costs.

- Lean encourages practices that reduce the amount of inventory in a company. This means that you must have eliminated the root cause of holding excess inventory. This results in saving money and more importantly increasing productivity.

Section 09 - The Waste of Unnecessary Motion

> **UNNECESSARY MOTION**
> Any motion above that does not add value to the theoretical minimum

The waste of unnecessary motion gives you a lot of opportunity to get creative. Companies usually go through and identify things that are dumb, dirty, and dangerous and generally eliminate them by decreasing human labor, and automating by putting a robot in place.

Unnecessary Motion
Any motion that does not add value to the product or process.

"There's got to be an easier way!"

In situations where you have someone leaning over to get tools, reaching up to get supplies, and unnecessarily moving materials or machinery, creative methods are found to eliminate these unnecessary motions out of the entire process. Companies implement systems like 5S. The operator gets involved, first of all by seeing it, and is tasked to eliminate it. He or she eliminates all unnecessary motion by using a few guidelines.

Let's consider a shop floor in manufacturing as the simulation environment for this section.

> All movements should be minimized and must add value.

We have a 45 degree rule. If materials and tools are not within 45 degrees in front of you either way, they are in the wrong spot. This is a 90 degree zone so that you do not have to turn your head. We also use a strike zone. If it's not between your knees or your shoulders, then it's too high or too low. We get very strategic about where the tools need to be for everyone to do their job. Think about how this improves the health and well-being of the operator. This is a real win-win.

> Keep items near point of use.

The 5S system is a workplace organization system. A respected consultant and partner in my group, Othmar Furer, worked in Singapore as a supplier to Yokogawa in 1985.

> 5S – Work place organization.

Toyota would not let his company become a supplier unless it implemented 5S as one of the foundations of their system. 5S comes from 5 Japanese words that start with the letter "S". I am sharing the English conversion of these words for obvious reasons. While the Japanese formalized this process, it was first developed by Henry Ford back in the early 1900's.

> **1. SORT**
> Sort through all items and sort out those unneeded.

The first "S" is sort. As we walk into a given area, we are talking about sorting through what is necessary and unnecessary for inventory or tools, and removing those unneeded items to a different area, a red tag holding area. From there, the unneeded items get disposition. This means some items are thrown-out, some get cleaned up and get placed elsewhere, and some go to auction and get sold. Regardless, they are no longer where they are not needed.

> **2. SET IN ORDER**
> A place for everything, and everything in its place.

The next "S" is set in order. We organize everything in the area in order for all things to be where they need to be. This includes equipment, inventory, information, and work instructions.

Before we are done with Setting in Order, we ensure that we have put lines, labels, and sign boards on the floors and walls. This way everyone knows what work is being performed in the area, and where the workspace ends and the aisles begin.

> **3. SHINE**
> Clean everything and use cleaning as a method of inspection.

Third "S" is shine. We keep the place clean. Cleanliness is a way of inspecting in the future.
As we are keeping it clean, we can make sure that everything is where it needs to be, i.e. material and tools are in place. We are also making sure that if we run equipment that we inspect during cleaning. This inspection can eliminate downtime for that equipment by finding the problem before it happens.

> **4. STANDARDIZE**
> Create standards for the first 3 S's and make them obvious through visual techniques.

The fourth "S" is Standardize. Based on what was achieved with the first thee S's, we develop best practices and try to standardize to that level. We develop standards for Sort, such as having a monthly "red tag" event, where all employees are tagging items that are not needed. We standardize Set-in-Order by creating color coding standards, and agreeing upon how to locate tools, and information for the entire organization. And finally, we standardize Shine; we ensure that there is a cleaning cart available when it is time to clean the area. We show pictures of what the standard is, and expect everyone to follow it.

> **5. SUSTAIN**
> Sustain the gains through self-discipline.

And the fifth "S" is Sustain. This is where more companies fail more than anywhere else. We need to maintain the change we made by sustaining these improvements. Less than 10% of companies that start with 5S stay with it. The fact is it never ends when you start. I suggest that you get a copy of Norman Bodek's book, "How to do Kaizen" to learn how to sustain.
By joining my Global OEM Consortium http://lean101.ca/weboffice.htm, you will be able to see his webinar explaining the process.

Selecting a Team for 5S:

Selecting the area to start the first 5S is important as it will be your benchmark for future 5S projects. You should be able to initiate major improvements which should be not too difficult but challenging; it needs to be a win-win for both the company and the employees.

The most important part is the selection of the 5S-Team:

- The team members need to be team players,
- They should be willing to make changes,
- Ideally, they have been exposed to 5S before,
- They will not be afraid of promoting novel ideas in a meeting.

You can't always pick an ideal team. In one company the heat-treatment area was picked for a showcase 5S-Area. It was selected because it was a bottleneck and also had a large number of safety issues.

One of the employees felt that too much time and money was spent on 5S. He also felt that 5S was simply a waste; the funds could have been better used for the upcoming new labor contract. Since he was a key employee in the department, he needed to be on the team. Our first priority was to make sure the improvements on the line would make his job easier. We installed a scissor lift for the operators, thereby eliminating the very awkward work position. This also improved the quality of the work because of a better sightline. We also improved the task lighting, installed a shelf - for commonly-used tools, and eliminated over 40 safety issues.

After completing 5S on that line John was the biggest supporter for the 5S system and for Lean because we took his needs into account first.

Othmar Furer
Shareholder, OEM Consultants Inc.

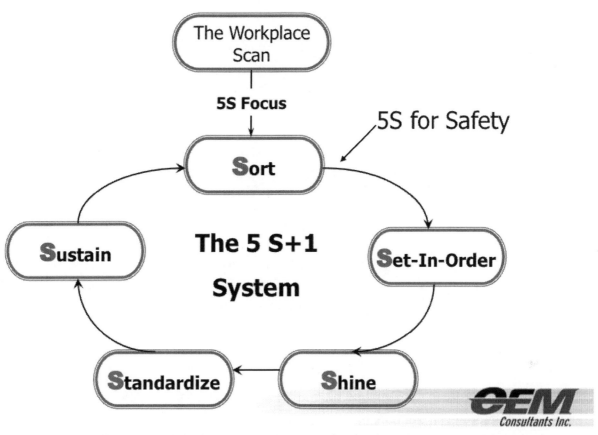

5S+1 or 6S is a workplace organization and standardization process that works.

The most critical part of this process is the workplace scan. This is the time where all of the workers in the area are called together and create a list of the current conditions and the desired conditions. By asking the workers what they want to see, a shared vision is created. Management gets what they want, more efficiency. And, the workers end up owning the changes.

During the SORT stage, all of the employees in the area were asked to fix yellow tags on surfaces and areas where a safety problem existed. Then those safety issues were logged on an area map and categorized. As each issue was resolved, a different color sticker was placed above the old sticker, indicating that the safety issue was gone. By placing red tags on items that need to move to the red tag holding area, and yellow tags on the items that represent a safety issue, everyone in the area starts to recognize that they are responsible for their area. Employee ownership is the most critical factor in a successful 5S initiative.

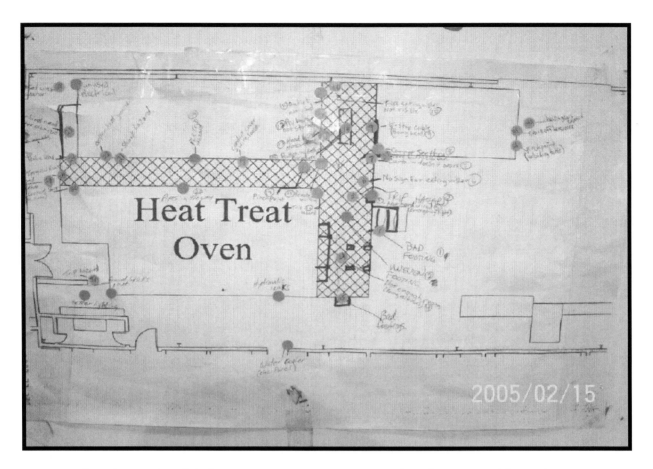

Logging each safety item on an area map ensures that they are not forgotten.

The 5S System is a set of universal principles and activities that sustain high performance in companies in any industry. An uncluttered, well-organized and understandable workplace is an essential foundation for efficient, low-inventory production, total quality management, total productive maintenance, or any other advanced change initiative or improvement approach.

The 5S Program is a systematic approach that organizes and standardizes the workplace. It promotes safety, good housekeeping, improved workflow, better product quality, reduced inventory waste, and above all puts people in control of their work areas.

It is not possible to be a world-class company without being organized. The 5S System is widely used across North America and has proven to be very successful. It is a program that improves safe working conditions while addressing many employee concerns.

5S represents the most basic process in manufacturing in which the employees are continually thinking about the maintenance of their workspace. By thinking about 5 words that start with the letter "S", each employee is able to communicate clearly about the new process that they are helping to implement.

By applying the 5S's it helps them continually ensure that their work area is maintained to a standard that allows anyone else to "jump in" and do the designated work in that area without a lot of searching for tools, and information. You can find presentations on 5S in the Global OEM Consortium site that was set up for all OEM consultants and enthusiasts. Go to http://lean101.ca/weboffice.htm and become a member.

5S is very applicable in our home lives. As I show you a picture of each stage of the 5S's, think about how it applies to home life. One clear indicator that I get when implementing 5S is that someone from the team comes up to me and says, "George, I did it. I went home and 5S'd my garage, it is awesome." This is when I know they got it, when they start applying it to the area that they hold most sacred.

SORT

Can you imagine finding anything in these drawers? What about at home, or at work? Can you always find what you are looking for, e.g. information on a computer, or ingredients in your kitchen? If you can't, it can be sorted in a better fashion. You should only keep what you need in that area.

SET IN ORDER

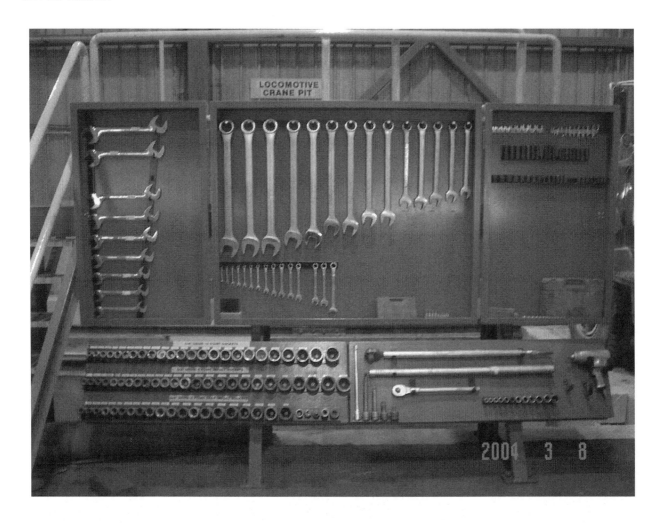

If I know that I want a tool board, I use a little trick that to get the right size board manufactured. I place all of the tools on the floor first. I then move things around, as I would like to see them. Then I get the measurements for that tool board. In this way, I ensure the right size of board is made to hold all of the tools.

SHINE

The biggest benefit of doing Shine is that how you can isolate where a leak may be coming from, for example. By painting the floor, you are able to root cause the problem and eliminate it, thereby fixing the problem.

STANDARDIZE

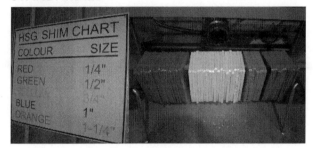

In this scenario, standardizing saved this company a lot of money. By ensuring shims were color coded, the operators rarely made the very expensive error of using the wrong shim. Color-coding is a very valuable technique, as long as you don't forget to back up the color scheme with words for those that are color blind.

SUSTAIN

The best way to sustain is to build an environment for it. Pictured above is the Hyundai plant in Ulsan, South Korea. When I was there, I was impressed with the one-point lessons, and the work instructions that were standardized in the area. Sustain is very much about appreciating the human being who works beside you. This concept of the boss at the top working for all of their employees in the plant is a very good one. I would gladly state that I work for each of you.

The reality is that I do not. I am forced to strive for my business goals like everyone else, and let's not forget personal goals. We all work for one another, when we have a shared goal. Where I can help you I will, and I suspect that you will too, reciprocally. This is the beauty of the world we live in. Other than the stress that we put on ourselves, we are all here to help each other make our way through life's challenges. That is my firm belief.

While I do not speak Korean, my tour guide did. He had worked with the leaders of this Hyundai plant for many years. This is why the doors were opened for my visit. Respecting each other is what it is about. So out of respect I tell you this. Forget the notion that you as a manager work for all of your employees. Also forget the old paradigm that your employees work for you. It's your job to be a leader and energize people around you. Only by showing them what a leader is will they be in a good position to mimic you. That is the only way to ensure things are sustainable.

Section Key Points

- The waste of Unnecessary Motion is defined as any motion that is more than the theoretical minimum to perform a task that completes a product or process.

- Companies have identified activities that are 'dumb', 'dirty' and 'dangerous'. Generally, these have been eliminated through automation and robotics.

- Examples of Unnecessary Motion are: leaning over to get tools; reaching up to get supplies; moving materials unnecessarily through a plant; etc. Lean has identified creative ways of moving things together and thereby eliminating unnecessary motion from an entire process.

- 5S is a workplace organization system based on a Lean system for workplace organization. It aims at getting the operator involved in seeing unnecessary motion and then eliminating it. All movements must be targeted for reduction.

- The 90 degree, Strike Zone, and Point-of-Use rules are examples of how 5S ensures that tools and materials are in the right spot.

- The term 5S refers to 5 Japanese words that start with "S". These are translated to be Sort, Set in Order, Shine, Standardize and Sustain. A sixth "S" is Safety.

- Less than 10% of companies that start with 5S - stay with 5S. It is a system that needs to be maintained in order to be effective. If you stop, you inevitably slip back to a wasteful state.

Section 10 - The Waste of Defects

> **DEFECTS**
> Errors, Frequent errors in paperwork,
> product quality or process problems,

This particular waste, the waste of defects, is very obvious to everybody. When we have a defect, it means the product doesn't work or the service doesn't work and the customer will let you know about it, and maybe not in a nice way.

Defects
Frequent errors in paperwork, product quality problems etc.

"Of course it's taking a long time!"

Companies tend to think that they solved the defect related problems but they don't really know whether they did or not. And that's where most of the other problems come by. There might be more than one root cause to a problem. Defects are rarely measured to ensure that they are gone. Making sure that they are gone forever, and stay gone forever should be the real goal.

One of the most effective tools when it comes to eliminating defects is called the 5 Why process. It involves asking Why something is a defect 5 times.

To give you an example, if cylinders coming out of a machine are defective, we will start by asking why they are coming out defective. If the answer is that they leak, and then being more specific asking, why is there a leak? After some testing, it is determined that they all leak at the port weld area. So the next question would be, Why do they leak at the port weld? This would happen until we finally reach the root cause of the problem. It may be that we asked Why 5 times, or more, or less. The number of times is not important. What is important is that we know what the root cause is, and we begin the process of eliminating that cause from being a factor again in the future.

> **Prevent occurrences of defects.**

At PAL Manufacturing, the entire team created a future state map. It turns out that after the meeting one of the managers pulled me aside and told me that we were not ready for implementation. The QA Manager said, "George, it's not going to work, because we have defects coming off of our CNC machine". Was I concerned? Very much so.

> **Get to the root cause.**

I told them to get to the root cause of the defects, since they hadn't done that yet. We started root causing with the inspector: why we have the defects, why things aren't working the way he expects them to, why the product isn't coming out exactly right.

> **Keep asking why until you know.**

What we found out is that three years ago, when they had originally bought the CNC machine, somebody actually changed the original manufacturer's nozzle to a different one. For three years they had one person programming that machine, and all the programs were no good. Three years' worth of programs went in the garbage when we root caused where the problem was coming from and we started from scratch. I ask you again, are we looking to blame people? No. As much as the urge may be overwhelming know for certain, that as soon as you start blaming people, your Lean initiative comes to an abrupt end.

> Don't just find and repair defects.

No, we actually need to celebrate that we found the problem. We found the problem, we eliminate it, and we're moving forward. This is the key, and finding the defects is one way of saying that we were able to get a little deeper, give the reason why it hasn't worked, why we couldn't do things a certain way and how to get rid of defect.

> **_Lean cuts to the root!_**

Section Key Points

- The waste of Defects is defined as any error in paperwork, product quality or any problem that prevents us from doing it right the first time.

- Defects are obvious forms of waste. When you have a defect, the product/service doesn't work and the customer is not pleased.

- A defect is a sure sign that something is wrong with our process.

- An effective tool for discovering the root cause of a problem is the "5 Why Analysis". We ask the question "Why?" five times. With each "Why" that we ask, we become more specific with our quest. As we become more specific, we eventually get to the root cause of our problem.

- Root causing our defects is an important practice. Remember that we are not looking to blame people. We are looking to get rid of the symptom called 'the defect' by getting to the root cause of the problem in our process, and eliminating that cause.

Section 11 – Waste of Human Potential and the Waste of Complexity

What is the waste of untapped human potential? Untapped human potential is not getting the ideas out of the people that work in the area. And this doesn't have to be just at work.

2 More Wastes

- ## Waste of Human Potential

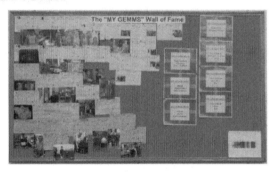

- ## Waste of Complexity

Employees might go home and run a business on the side which might grow into a multi-million dollar business. Can you imagine if you had that talent working for you? Why didn't you let them help you run your business?

> Encourage the sharing of ideas.

Untapped human potential is about getting those ideas out of the group and implanting them as a system that we will want to abide by. People who have been working for a company under six months should be considered the most valuable employees in the company. Why would I say that?

> Ask new hires for their thoughts.

Fresh eyes are the reason why. As managers, we don't go up to our employees that have been here under six months and say to them, "What stupid things do you see that we are doing as a company, that we should stop doing?" You have to say it that way, and don't forget, wait for an answer. Definitely remember not to say it this way, "what stupid things are *you* doing" it can come across as if you are reprimanding the employee, especially if he or she is still on probation. Good luck trying to get an answer from them.

> ## K.I.S. – Keep It Simple

To keep it simple is an art that everybody should get back to, and I don't care what business they are in or what job you are doing. We tend to make things very complex. A colleague of mine was working as a VP of manufacturing. He was approached by one of his managers who said, "We've got this product that has a shelf life of one year." That means that the product was no good one year after that date of manufacturing. They had this uncanny ability to ship some of the most recent items to the customer, leaving older inventory to expire. This cost them money. They came up with an elaborate system which consisted of getting everything barcoded when it came off the production line, prior to being placed onto a rack. When a customer order would come in, a pick list would be generated, telling them the order in which items would be manufactured.

As a result, the oldest item in the facility would then be packed and shipped out, every time. What do you think the ticket price was for that improvement? By the time they would get the computer in and have the whole system up and running, it would cost $100,000!

> ## Ask frontline people for help.

"We should practice what we preach; let's ask our people ask what kind of system we really need," the VP said. One of the team members said to leave it with them for two weeks. They came back after two weeks, and the VP immediately asked, "Before I go even further, what's it going to cost me?" What do you think the cost was? A mere $25. He said "how did you do that?" The team lead said "it is simple; we got masking tape; when the product comes off the end of the line, we take masking tape and put a date on it. We've reserved a spot in the warehouse for this stuff. And we actually put it in sequence and we pick, by the oldest date, and we get it out to the customer, and it never fails." So what was the $25 for? Masking a tape and magic markers, that was it! We have a way of making everything more complicated than it actually is...

Here's a picture of PAL Manufacturing before:

You can see a lot of racks; there is a waste of inventory and a waste of motion. They actually had to bring a forklift in to get items out, which caused waste of inappropriate processing. Not to mention, this stuff couldn't even be put together as the shafts and tubes on this rack were of the wrong size.

After they were done with their improvements, this is what the area looked like:

It's very impressive and the credit goes completely to the people in that area. They did a fabulous job and I take absolutely no credit for their ability to work together as a team and make it happen. Somebody mentioned "We made no changes to the lighting; adding just a coat of paint made a big difference."

Section Key Points

- The waste of Untapped Human Potential is defined as not getting the ideas out of people that work in an area. Our frontline teams are best suited to providing solutions to the problems of waste.

- Ask new hires for their thoughts; they have a "fresh perspective". The question should be, "What dumb things are we doing today that we can improve upon?"

- The waste of Complexity is defined as making things more complex than they need to be. Keep it Simple (K.I.S).

- Sometimes, the best solutions to problems are also the most cost efficient ones. You don't necessarily need high tech solutions to low tech problems.

- When you become good at "flushing out" the wastes within a system the results are dramatic.

Module 02

Section 01 - Second Principle of Lean Thinking

> **IDENTIFY THE VALUE STREAM**
> - Draw a Value Stream Map (Current State)
> - Identify the Material Transformation Process
> - Draw a future state map
> - Develop the action plan

The 2nd principle of Lean Thinking is to identify the value stream. In order to do this, you really need to know what a value stream is. It is all of the VA and NVA activities that deliver a product/service to the customer. One way to do this is to draw a map. We call this a value stream map; it helps identify all those activities as well as the processes to deliver the product or service.

We really don't want anybody to have any reason for *not* doing the value stream mapping process. Value Stream mapping is a paper and pencil exercise. We start with the material transformation process first.

The first step in the value stream is to draw the existing process. We start with the customer. Then we identify the material transformation process by drawing the process closest to the customer (i.e. where the product is being delivered) and work our way upstream through the process. As we are going through it and calculating relevant information, we ask people what they think about the material transformation process and what the challenges are. We will also include the inventory levels and information flow on the map.

> Draw the existing process

We are now ready to create the future state map. We are now brainstorming and looking for ways to eliminate the non-value activities.

The future state map answers the following question: "what would the process look like if we were able to eliminate some of these Non Value Added (NVA) activities?" That alone is a very powerful tool. Just asking "what if?" and following the question by drawing a new map, one that is not limited by the current rules. The action plan connects the current state and the future state.

Although the skill for drawing value stream maps is a course onto itself we will introduce you to some of the concepts and icons needed to run through a case study and simulation of this process. Our goal with value stream mapping is to provide a communication platform between organizations, utilizing a standard language. If you have two cross functional teams doing mapping within an organization, each team must be able to look at the others' map and understand what is happening.

The second principle of the 5 Principles of Lean Thinking is to identify the Value Stream.

Identify the value stream.

In retail, the value stream starts with the external customer. When a customer comes into the store value should be generated. The value stream refers to all activities, value added or non-value added that satisfy the customer's needs. Going back to the PAL manufacturing example, they have many different products so we have a little bit of a challenge. We said that cylinders were going to be the pilot value stream for them, not compressors, washers or anything else. It allowed us to focus on getting the job done for that product group. When we consider retail, what do you think we are picking as a value stream? Is it *every* item in the store? It is not.

> ## Select a value stream wisely.

For this retail store, promotional items are what we are going to be focusing on.

> ## *Take Lean baby steps!*

IDENTIFY YOUR VALUE STREAM

Section Key Points:

- The 2nd principle of Lean Thinking is to identify the value stream. A value stream is all of the activities, VA and NVA that delivers a product/service to the customer.

- One way used to identify the value stream is by drawing a value stream map; this is a paper and pencil exercise. Before we draw the map we must choose a product/service to focus on (e.g. a cylinders for manufacturing, promotional items in retail, etc.).

- In a value stream map we start with customer information first. Then we draw the material transformation process second. We draw the process starting with the step closest to the customer and work our way upstream through the process to the supplier. Then we place inventory-level information between these process steps, and finally draw the information flow on the map.

- Along the way we ask people in the value stream what they feel the challenges are. We then brainstorm for improvements and draw a future state. This map answers the question, "What would the process look like if we were able to eliminate the NVA activities?"

- The action plan is a list of activities to be used in order to transform our company from its current state to the future state. Our goal with value stream mapping is to communicate amongst our organizations, utilizing a standard language.

Section 02 – Mapping your Value Stream (Part A)

Customer/Supplier	This icon represents the supplier when in the upper left, the usual starting point for material flow. The customer is represented when placed in the upper right, the usual end point for material flow.
Dedicated Process	This icon is a process, operation, machine or department, through which material flows. Typically, to avoid unwieldy mapping of every single processing step, it represents one department with a continuous, internal fixed flow path.
Data Box	This icon goes under other icons that have significant information/data required for analyzing and observing the system. Typical information placed in a data box underneath factory icons is the frequency of shipping during any shift, material handling information, transfer batch size, demand quantity per period, etc.
Work cell	This symbol indicates that multiple processes are integrated in a manufacturing work cell. Such cells usually process a limited family of similar products or a single product. Product moves from process step to process step in small batches or single pieces.
Inventory	These icons show inventory between two processes. While mapping the current state, the amount of inventory can be approximated by a quick count, and that amount is noted beneath the triangle. If there is more than one inventory accumulation, use an icon for each. This icon also represents storage for raw materials and finished goods.
Shipments	This icon represents movement of raw materials from suppliers to the receiving dock(s) of the factory, or the movement of finished goods from the shipping dock(s) of the factory to the customers.
Push Arrow	This icon represents the push of material from one process to the next process. Push means that a process produces something regardless of the immediate needs of the downstream process.
Supermarket	This is an inventory supermarket (Kanban stock point). Like a supermarket, a small inventory is available and one or more downstream customers come to the supermarket to pick out what they need. The upstream work center then replenishes stocks as required.
Material Pull	Supermarkets connect to downstream processes with this "pull" icon that indicates physical removal.
External Shipment	Shipments from suppliers or to customers using external transport.

> ### *The Online course includes a short film that illustrates Value Steam Mapping*

When was the last time you went out to buy a car and found exactly what you wanted? Because of the vast number of options most customers end up compromising, like buying a color they don't want or buying a sound system they don't need.

Why do modern non-lean factories manufacture an abundance of product that sits as inventory, yet they don't have exactly what the customer wants? Not having exactly what the customer wants isn't a new problem.

Mass production was typified by buying the biggest presses available to stamp out huge volumes of parts. Mass production lowered individual piece prices and this was great when there was unlimited demand but not so good as the demand dipped. The problem with mass production thinking is that people are focused on optimizing pieces of the system instead of looking at the whole value stream.

A value stream map follows the flow of raw material, inventory and information within a factory or all the way to the final customer. Value stream mapping, a tool developed by Toyota, is now being adopted all over the world. Mike Rother and John Shook, two Lean entrepreneurs, made the mapping technique widely available through their teaching and books.

This tool allows you to diagram your current value stream, identifying the bottlenecks that prevent you from making what your customers want when they want it. Finally, it helps you develop a vision of what your future lean picture should look like.

Even companies that work hard at implementing Lean Manufacturing get caught up in creating islands of excellence. Creating a cell or reducing changeover time is not the same thing as creating a Lean value stream. Before making any improvements, it is important to know why we need to make the change. What if the improvement just makes the machine run more, building even more unnecessary inventory? With a value stream vision, you know what to improve. It allows you to become more flexible and reduce inventory in the process.

Value Stream improvement looks at the whole business as only senior managers have responsibility for the entire business; they must lead value stream mapping and steer the improvement action plan needed to reach the future state.

Section Key Points

- Mass production is about lowered individual piece prices and this was great when there was unlimited demand but its significance dwindled as demand dipped. The problem with mass production thinking is that people are focused on optimizing pieces of the system instead of looking at the whole value stream.

- A value stream map follows the flow of raw material, inventory and information within a factory or all the way to the final customer. Value stream mapping is now being actively adopted around the world.

- Creating a cell or reducing changeover time is not the same thing as creating a lean value stream. Before making any improvement, it is important to know why we need to make the change.

- Value Stream improvement looks at the whole business since senior managers must have overall responsibility for the entire business, they must lead value stream mapping and steer the improvement action plan needed to reach the future state.

Section 03 – Mapping your Value Stream (Part B)

Many companies are familiar with process maps but value stream mapping is different because it focuses on the material and information flows central to a production system. There are a few things different in a value stream map. One is that we are able to visualize a closed circuit of information coming back from the customer to the supplier. Another difference is that we have the material transformation process that the product undergoes until it reaches the customer. Finally we have the inventory levels shown and how the inventory travels through the process. This, combined with a timeline at the bottom of every value stream map makes this map a very powerful tool in communicating where we are, and where we want to be in the future.

Henry Ford was drawing process maps back in 1914, including the steps, the amount of time, and the distance between the steps. Process maps are not the same as value stream maps. Value stream mapping takes process mapping to a new level. For instance, process maps only have push arrows to indicate that material and/or information is PUSHED from one station to the next. VSM utilizes PULL icons and supermarkets, which become evident as methods to prevent over production.

> ### *Getting Started with the Mapping Tool*

Let's get our mapping started. First you have to select the product family that you are going to map.

> **Getting Started with the Mapping Tool**
> Product Family
> Draw Current State Map
> Draw Future State Map
> Implement an Action Plan

The easiest way is to target one of your largest customers and pick out a product or product family that you ship to the customer. The value stream map always starts with your customer. In this case, the map is for ACME Stamping, a fictional company. The part is a steering bracket produced for the customer identified as State Street Assembly.

$$\text{TAKT Time} = \frac{\text{Available Work Time}}{\text{Customer Demand}}$$

$$60 \text{ Seconds per Part} = \frac{27,600 \text{ Seconds per Shift}}{460 \text{ Pieces per Shift}}$$

All the data in a value stream map is based on the customer's TAKT time. TAKT time is the heartbeat of the market, the voice of the customer in operational terms coming back to you. It equals to the available work time divided by the customer demand. With an available work time of 27,600 seconds per shift and customer demand at 460 pieces per shift, TAKT time is 60 Seconds. In this example, the ideal value stream would be for all processes to be producing one part every minute with no waste in the process. We know this does not currently exist, but we need to strive for perfection, continually.

This current state map shows where ACME Stamping is today, which reveals obvious opportunities for improvement. One of the biggest 'ah-ha' moments in value stream mapping comes when you draw a timeline at the bottom of a map to show the amount of value added work being performed on the product. The lower Timeline shows the actual time spent on the product where the product is transformed to what the customer wants. This is the value-added time (VAT), which in Acme's case is 188 seconds. The upper timeline is the most revealing; showing that the product lead time (PLT) is over 23 days. The best way to visualize this is that if you placed a "red dot" on a coil coming from Michigan Steel Company, and followed that red dot as the coil converts to a stamped part, then welded, then assembled, you would find that over 23 days would have passed before the red dot got shipped to State Street Assembly.

Current State Map: ACME Stamping

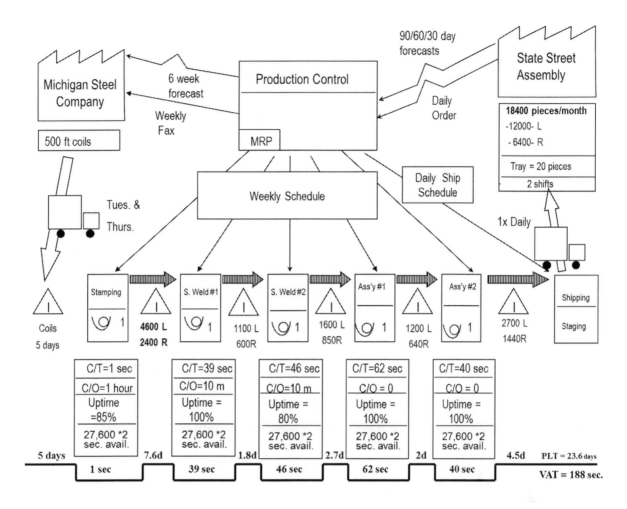

Each value added step at ACME is shown as a process box. Traditional non-lean manufacturing improvements have focused on squeezing out mere seconds from these processes. Lean manufacturing focuses our attention towards eliminating all activities that are of no value, or wasteful. Value stream mapping helps us to identify this waste. The reduction in time will be a RESULT of eliminating the waste. That is why lean manufacturers do not focus on eliminating time (the measure), but eliminating the waste (the root cause of excess time spent).

Value Stream mapping is divided into:

> *Material Flow*
> *Physical Transformation Process*
> *Information Flow*

By mapping the information flow you develop an understanding of why inventory is being created. In the Case of ACME Stamping, like many companies, has individual operations that are scheduled by production control based on a weekly schedule. Individual operations build according to the schedule, regardless of whether the next operation really needs it. Drawing a current state map gives you a high-level view of waste in your system. When mapping, do not get caught up in unimportant details. Make each map as simple as possible. Use paper and pencil, go to the factory floor, and collect key information and just DO IT. Most value stream maps can be done within hours. For collaborate value stream mapping, sticky notes can be used. Today, *NxtNote (Ed@OEMsolutions.ca)* has automated the sticky note process and made collaboration between teams even easier.

> **Getting Started with the Mapping Tool**
> Product Family
> Draw Current State Map
> Draw Future State Map

After measuring and identifying waste, put the current state map aside. The next part is the enjoyable and creative part of value stream mapping as you develop a future state map for your Lean system. The final stage of your value stream mapping is developing and implementing an action plan to achieve the future state.

Value stream mapping provides its own set of icons for designing the future state. Most traditional process mapping leaves out such concepts as pull systems and supermarket style storage areas. The super market is an inventory location that holds the proper level of strategic inventory. Think of strategic inventory as that which is needed to assure FLOW.

Customer & Vendor Facility Icon

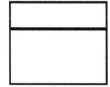

Value Added Steps are illustrated as Process Boxes

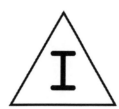

Inventory is drawn as a triangle or in the original Toyota Model, a tombstone representing dead material.

Transportation, a necessary but non-value added activity, is shown as a truck.

A push arrow illustrates traditional product movement. This is where a product is made and pushed to the next process whether it needs it or not.

A leaner approach is the pull arrow represented by a circular arrow.

Super Market

Instead of Inventory stockrooms, lean manufacturing uses a supermarket concept. Each supermarket has a small, well-managed inventory where employees can pick only what they need, which is what is available in the supermarket.

| Go See | Kanban Post | Triangle Kanban |

These 3 icons represent ways of controlling material and information so that flow can be achieved. With these tools you are ready to create your future state vision.

The ACME Stamping map starts with the customer and the TAKT Time but we now place an emphasis on how the product flows through the system: we see supermarkets, Kanbans, pull systems and frequent deliveries of product to the customer.

The future state map predicts that the production lead time has shrunk from over 23 days to 4.5 days and the processing time has been reduced by a few seconds. Once these improvements are implemented, ACME can be much more responsive to changes in customer demand, hold far less inventory, and free up floor space for future business.

Section Key Points

- To start mapping you have to select the product family that you are going to map. The value stream map always starts with your customer. Target one of your largest customers and pick a product or product family that you ship to the customer.

- One way used to identify the value stream is by using a value stream map; this is a paper and pencil exercise. Before we draw the map we must choose a product/service to focus on (e.g. cylinders, promotions, etc.).

- Drawing a current state map gives you a high level view of the waste in your system. When mapping, do not get caught up in un-important details. Make each map as simple as possible. Use paper and pencil, go to the floor, get estimates of key data and just DO IT.

- Value Stream Mapping incorporates its own set of icons. The standardization of these icons allows you to use this universal language to communicate to others that know how to create Value Stream Maps.

Section 04 - Case Study – The Mock Company, Drawing the Current State Map

The Mock Company VSM

(Current State)

Let's draw the current state map of the company by working backwards through the system. By backwards, I mean from the customer, upstream to the supplier.

We begin with our customer icon.

After putting a title and date on the top of your paper, take your pencil and place the customer icon at the top right corner. As we create the map, try to observe the way the material and information flows. **Material flow** identifies the movement of physical product through the value stream. Material flows from left to right on your paper, it flows from the supplier to the customer. **Information flow** shows sources of data that tell a process what to do or produce. Information flows from right to left on your paper, from the customer upstream to the supplier. Be mindful of the **Material Transformation Process** in which raw materials are transformed as they make their way downstream in the process. The transformation may convert raw materials into subassemblies and eventually into the final product.

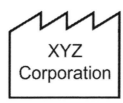

Outside Sources

This is identified in our map by an icon that represents a material source. This type of icon can be used to show a customer, a supplier or an outside manufacturing process.

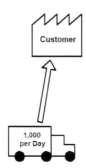

The customer demand is presently 1,000 pieces per day. It is shown in the truck icon. The arrow between the truck and the customer represents another material movement icon used to represent a shipment of finished goods. The frequency is important as it translates the customer demand into terms your company can understand and guide its internal operations towards achieving.

The arrows moving from right to left represent information flow.

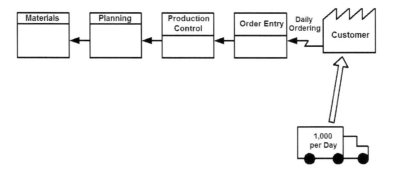

The customer sends in daily orders and they are processed. This row of boxes represents the flow that the information takes in translating a customer order into an internal shop order.

Each process box represents the best description that you have as to where the information goes. All processes must always be labeled. The boxes are also used to describe departments, for example production control. In this case study, orders go through order entry, then production control, then planning, and then materials.

The zigzag arrow, as seen in the diagram above, is represents an electronic information flow, e.g. Electronic Data Interchange (EDI).

The straight arrows represent manual information flow. For example, a production schedule or shipping schedule, this is communicated on paper (manually).

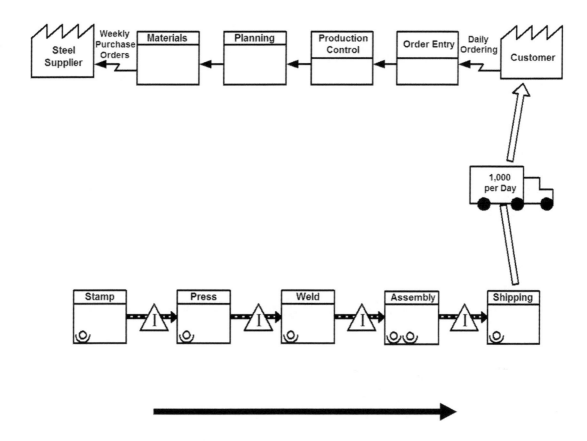

We are going to follow some of the material flow through the plant; we have added various manufacturing processes to the bottom of the map going from right to left. Always work your way upstream, from the customer towards the supplier. It should be obvious that the material flows from left to right, as the arrow above indicates, however when mapping make sure you place your process boxes on the map from right to left. This technique of PULL is also utilized in Lean construction, where we start from the end (right) and pull trades into action via hand-offs.

Operator

An operator for a given process is represented by the icon above. If a process requires more than one operator (see Assembly area in the map), additional icons are added accordingly, or a number can be placed beside the icon.

Movement of Production Material by PUSH

This arrow represents the movement of production material by push. This means that material that is produced and moves forward before the next process needs it. This is usually based on a schedule.

The triangular icon represents inventory between each of the operations. The inventory count must be noted. When we walked the process in the Mock Company, we found the follow amounts of inventory between the processes:

- Between stamp and press we have 1,500 pieces,
- Between Press and Weld, 1,750 pieces,
- Between Weld and Assembly, 2,000 pieces,
- Between Assembly and Shipping, 2,000 pieces.

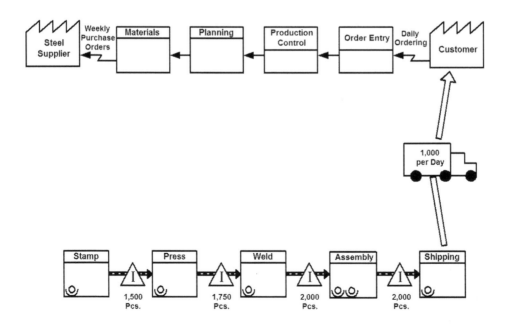

The steel supplier is shipping weekly. The truck shipment is two coils. Each coil represents 1,500 pieces.

Data boxes are used below each of the operations to record information relating to a manufacturing process, department, customer, etc. The next step in our case study is to gather the information for each of the operations. We want to include as much meaningful information as possible in these data boxes.

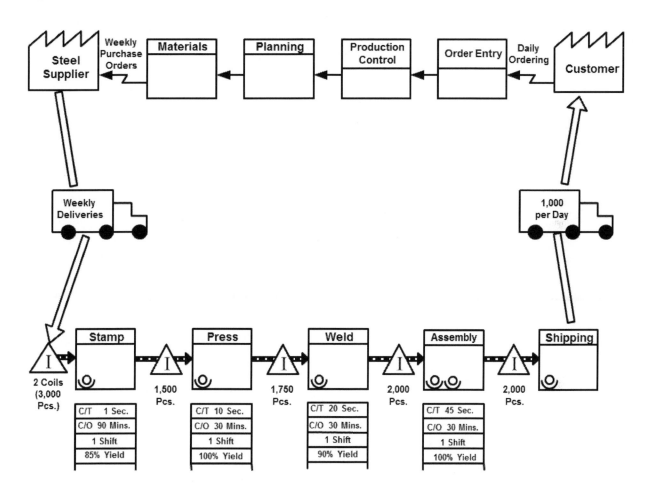

Let's focus in on the data box for the Stamp Operation. The cycle time (C/T) specifies how frequently an item or product is goes through a process as timed by direct observation. This is also known as the time it takes to get a good part after another is completed in the process. It can also represent the time it takes an operator to go through all of his or her work elements before repeating them.

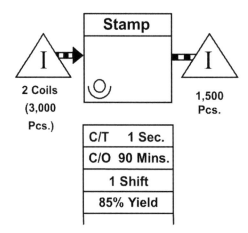

Changeover (C/O) occurs when production has to be stopped for a piece of equipment in order to be refitted for producing a different item. For example, the installation of a different processing tool in a metal working machine, different color paint in a painting system, a new plastic resin and mold in an injection molding machine, loading different software, and so on. Changeover time specifies how long this takes between the last good parts from the previous run of parts, to the first good part in the next run of parts.

The third piece of information in this data box lets us know that we are running 1 shift.

The yield measures the percentage of material that is accepted by the downstream operation as being "good" or acceptable without rework. This implies that whatever is left over is scrapped.

As we compare the data across all of the operations, we make the following observations:

- The cycle time for stamp is 1 second; Press = 10 seconds; Weld = 20 seconds; Assembly = 45 seconds,
- The changeover times are: Stamp = 90 minutes; Press = 30 minutes; Weld = 30 minutes; Assembly = 30 minutes,
- Yields are Stamp 85%; Press = 100%; Weld = 90%; Assembly = 100%.

At this point we know that planning gives a weekly schedule to Stamp, Press, Weld, and Assembly, which is adjusted daily. This is represented by an information icon (Weekly Schedule) and some manual information flow arrows.

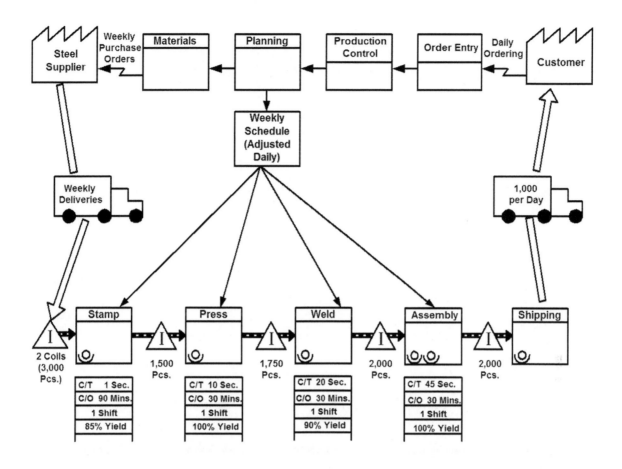

The Mock Company does some daily expediting, during which they gather information from each of the operations. They check inventory levels and adjust schedules.

The "eye glasses" represent "Go See", an information icon that symbolizes the scheduling function, or production control. This information is fed back to production control and then planning as indicated by the dotted arrows and then schedules are adjusted accordingly.

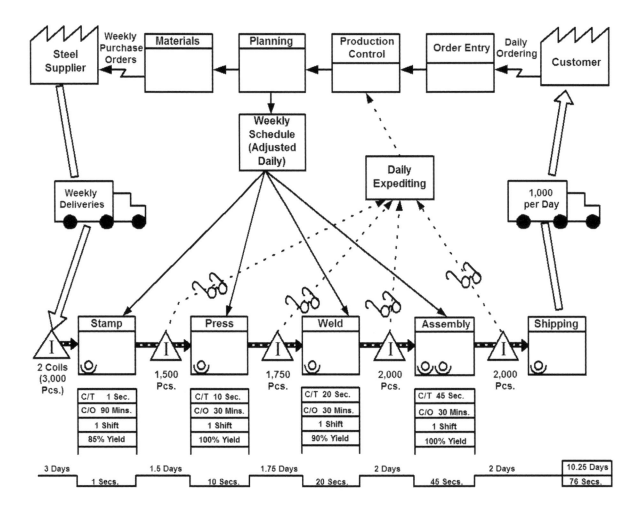

The graph along the bottom of the map (see above) looks at the value added time and the production lead time. Lead time is the time required for one piece to move all the way through the value stream from start to finish. By looking at this graph, we can determine the Percent Value Added time for this Product Line.

FACT: The percent VA time in most non-lean manufacturing processes is 0.02%

A value stream map can be created for every business. The icons may be different, the process boxes will be labeled differently, and the information in the data boxes below collect different information, but it applies. Value stream mapping has been applied to product development, healthcare, dentistry, retail, government, and many other businesses that consider time to be a competitive factor for their success. Time is the ultimate measure of determining whether you are working towards a more lean system. But remember, we do not focus on eliminating time; we focus on eliminating waste, which will result in reducing the time it takes to produce a product.

Section Key Points

• Material flow identifies the movement of physical product through the value stream. Information flow shows sources of data that tell a process what to do or produce. As items flow through the system we observe the material transformation process, during which raw materials travel through sub-assemblies to eventually be transformed into the final product.

• Data boxes are used below each of the operations to record information regarding a manufacturing process, department, customer, etc. This data helps determine what changes can be made in order to improve the value stream.

• Cycle Time (C/T) specifies how frequently an item or product is completed by a process as timed by direct observation. It also represents the time it takes an operator to go through all of his/her work elements before repeating them.

• Changeover (C/O) occurs when production has to be stopped for a piece of equipment in order to be refitted for producing a different item (e.g. installation of a different processing tool in a metal working machine). Changeover time specifies how long this takes.

• The Yield refers to the percentage of material that is transformed into a usable product. This implies that whatever is left over is discarded. Generally, we refer to the discarded material as scrap.

• Lead Time (L/T) is the amount of time required for one piece to move all the way through a process or value stream - from start to finish. By looking at a Lead Time graph, one can determine time spent on VA and NVA activities.

Section 05 - Evaluating the Current State

Current State Map for the Mock Company

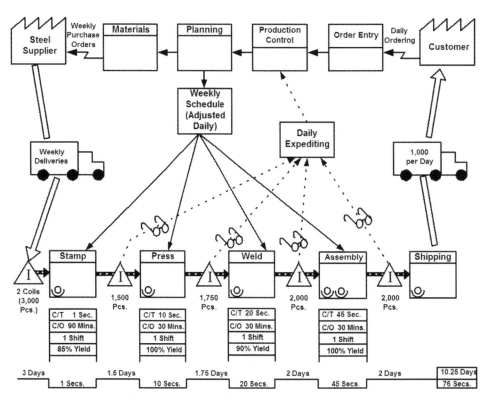

The current state map allows us to come to a conclusion about Non-Value Added activities present in our organization. This is most effective when everybody is involved. Some of the most significant information will come from the operators themselves, especially when that person is a new hire. As stated earlier, they bring fresh eyes to the situation. Also remember that the customer's perspective needs to be kept in mind as you highlight the wastes in your system. Here is an example of how this is done:

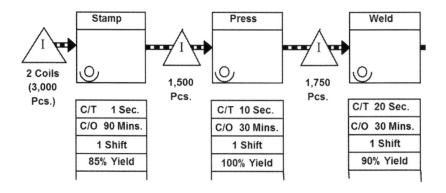

From the above 3 processes, what do you think one type of the waste is?

Evaluation of material waste due to scrap

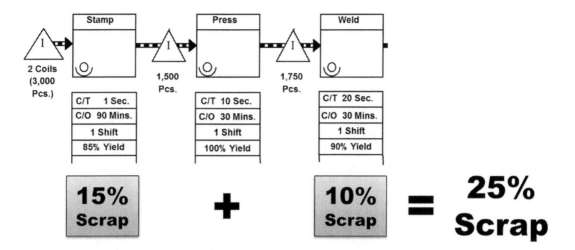

We can see from the stamping operation that an 85% yield results in 15% scrap, and welding with a 90% yields 10% scrap. This is about 25% in the entire process. This is 25% scrap that the customer does not want to pay for. Scrap represents the waste of defects.

> **SCRAP = COSTLY WASTE**
> - Cost of wasted materials
> - Cost of wasted time/labor
> - Cost of waster opportunity
> - Cost of freight

Most of us recognize that scrap is a waste of material. With this kind of waste, let's take a look at stamping. Stamping has an 85% yield which means 15% of it is scrap. The time spent producing that scrap is also a waste. We waste our labor and more importantly we incur a lost opportunity to produce a good product. Thus, this scrap has associated to it a lost opportunity cost. Looking further back in the process, as the material is not used the freight that we spent on that material is also a waste.

> **HARD TO SEE NVA ACTIVITIES**
> - We can't see 50% of all waste.
> - New employees are more objective

Many Non-Value Added activities are virtually invisible to us as we're working in the details of the process. Statistically it has been shown that we cannot see 50% of the waste. That is why when we have a new employee in the process; we need to ask him or her what "dumb" things we are doing today, in order to see what we need to improve upon. By doing this and making that inquiry we are able to identify even more waste.

> **THE SCRAP REPORT**
> - Stamp/Weld Operator
> - Supervisor/Manager
> - Quality Assurance
> - Materials/Accounting
> - Production Control
> - *The list goes on...*

It's not always easy to identify all the waste within a company. In our example above, which is very close to another real life example, the scrap report took the Stamp and Weld operators 10 minutes daily to fill out. It then went to the supervisor who compiled all of the data in about half an hour. From there the information traveled to quality assurance which aggregated daily figures into a report for their monthly meeting.

Naturally, everyone gets concerned about the scrap report which ends up in the hands of production control which has to accommodate for more materials because of the scrap process. This has a snowball effect on every single person in the organization that is given access to the report and then proceeds to make adjustments. The real problem is that no one is focused on doing something about the scrap itself. This is a real issue for most organizations as they tend to spend many hours measuring things instead of using the same time and manpower to fix things.

> **2 FULL TIME PEOPLE**
> - 16 Hours/Day
> - Non-Value Added

Just to report this kind of waste takes two full time people. This means 16 hours per day and if we don't do anything with the reporting and that time and manpower is also waste. That is why value stream mapping is a very important tool to identify waste, so we can see it, and do something about it.

Let's change our focus now and identify how much inventory is between the processes. We want to know if there is excess or not, so we actually go out and count the inventory. Looking at the diagram below, you'll notice that there is quite a large amount of inventory

Current State Map

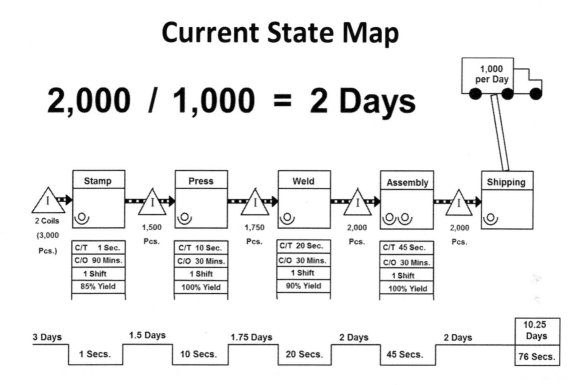

How do we know how many days of inventory we have in the system? If we have 2,000 pieces of inventory between assembly and shipping and we ship 1,000 pieces per day to the customer, so we have two days of inventory. It's as simple as that. Inventory represents waste in time.

As we analyze the process for value added time, we use information from the data boxes. We consider stamping to be a Value Added activity. In this instance, its Value Added time is 1 second, the cycle-time, and we consider the cycle-time value added time. As we sum all of the amounts up, we end up with 76 seconds of value added time over a period of 10.25 days.

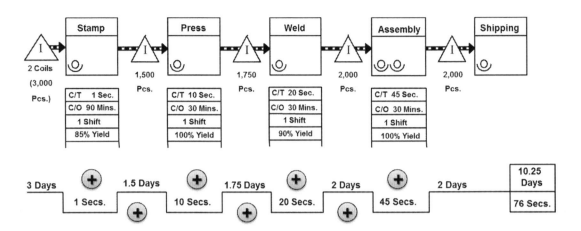

This may be a little difficult to grasp if you are looking at it for the first time. So here is that "red dot" scenario again. If we followed a red dot that we placed on the coil at the beginning of our process, it would take 10.25 days for that red dot to get to shipping. Now imagine that we only consider these processes of stamp, press, weld, and assembly, value added processes. This red dot would have 76 seconds of value added to it. This is terrible. I could not believe this when I first saw a value stream map.

The value added time as a percentage is calculated as follows;
Convert the 10.25 days to seconds. There are 60 seconds in a minute, 60 minutes in an hour, and 8 hours in a workday. In this way, our workday is equal to 60*60*8= 28,800 seconds. Multiply that by 10.25 days and you get 885,600 seconds. Now the shocker, take 76 seconds and divide that by 295,200 seconds and you get 0.026 % value added time. Notice we used 8 hours in a day (we could have chosen 24 hours) regardless of what you use keep it consistent. This way, improvements are always measured the same way.

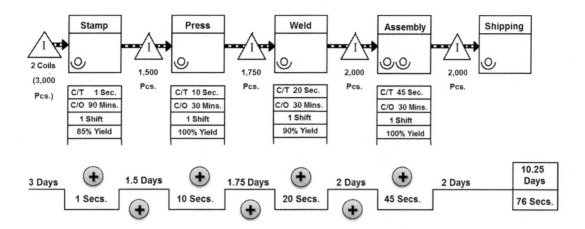

This is a small number, so I tested the knowledge with a real company, over and over again. The average that I have experienced is 0.05% value added time.

The following picture is of the actual PAL Manufacturing value stream map. PAL Manufacturing supplies stock cylinders to over 30 retail stores in Canada, and also engineers cylinders to customer order. To simplify the map we decided to map both custom and standard cylinders since the main components of the cylinder are the shaft, and the tube. The shaft and tube come together in assembly where the cylinder is tested to the final customer specifications. For the steps to make the tube we have cutting, we have tube drilling, base plate welding, port weld, machining, final weld, and cylinder assembly. As we totaled it up and calculated how many seconds of value added time there was, we got a number of 39.7 days and we estimated that there was 1800 seconds (30 minutes) of value added activity.

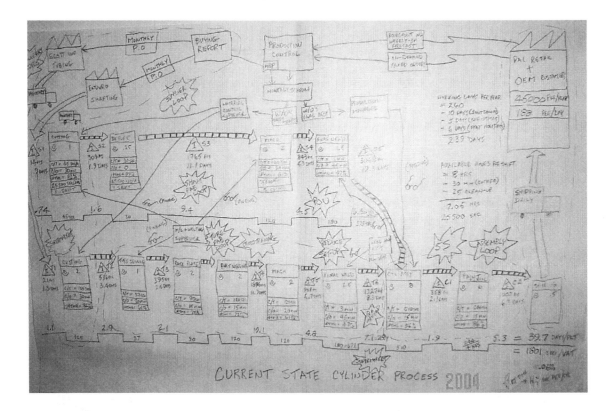

CURRENT STATE CYLINDER PROCESS 2004

When we did the math, it ended up that value was being added to the cylinder only 0.06% of the time. Incredible! However, I want to point out that the biggest "ah-ha" was that we had 843 shafts, and 1327 tubes that comprised of the inventory before assembly. Of this inventory, because one shaft goes with one tube, we assumed that we could put together 843 cylinders for the customer. The fact is that we only had 110 cylinders that could be matched. The inventory was mostly made and sitting there without regard for the customer. The MRP (computer) system helped create this Push disaster, and people in this process of pushing work through the shop did not see the waste.

Lean Engineering is an interesting concept, and very applicable here. During the excitement on the shop floor, the engineering team wanted to make improvements as well.

When we mapped the information flow, and learned that most of their engineering time is dedicated to managing customer specified cylinders, we focused in that area. It turned out that we could take 625 bills of material and reduces them to just 25. So we did! Amazingly enough, the concept of Lean implies that whatever you do, the result should be that you have done it quicker the next time. This elimination of 600 bills of materials saved the team over 50% of their engineering time.

We have a great opportunity to make improvements, please enjoy the simulation that follows as all of my implementations on Lean Thinking start with this incredible example that gets everyone thinking the same way, regardless of the industry.

If you decide to educate your company using the "airplane simulation" make sure to purchase a kit from Visionary Products. They are sure to give you a discount and welcome you as another owner of this powerful educational simulation.

> **Lean is on time!**

Section Key Points:

- A Current State Map allows us to come to a conclusion about NVA activities present in an organization. This is most effective when everyone is involved. Some of the most significant information will come from the operators themselves.

- Knowing how much inventory is between workstations is very important. This information assists in determining whether or not there is too much inventory in the system. To calculate the days of inventory one takes the amount of inventory, convert it to an equivalent shipped item, and then divide by the number of pieces shipped to the customer per day (on average). This gives us the days of inventory between stations.

- VA and NVA times are shown on the lead-time graph. The lead-time graph shows the theoretical minimum we call perfection. Continually achieving the future state will gradually bring the company closer to perfection.

- It is the customer's perspective that needs to be evaluated when determining wastes in the system. These wastes must be eliminated if they are deemed to be NVA and unnecessary.

- Most people are not aware of at least 50% of NVA activities, because they are too close to the process. It is a good idea to use new hires to spot the wastes in the system.

Section 06 – Sky-View Information Sheet

Sky-View Airplane Company

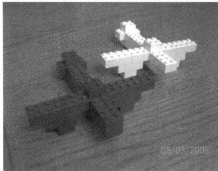

Here is a sample of the high quality airplanes they build:

A "Lean" Simulation

By switching from the Mock Company case study to the *Sky-View Airplane Company simulation*, we can see theory being put into practice. For practical purposes, the simulation uses interlocking-plastic blocks to mimic airplane components. Let's first start off by providing some background information on the Sky-View Company. This will help you understand the steps that will follow during our simulation exercise.

The Airplane simulation was developed by Visionary Products, Inc. (www.visionaryproducts.biz)

Sky-View produces a high quality product. But it has large inventories and a history of not being able to deliver on time. Currently the company is trying to deliver 10 airplanes per day consistently. This has been a challenge.

The Sky-View Airplane Company is currently negotiating a large contract which requires that we guarantee a delivery of 24 airplanes per day. The president of the company is asking his direct reports to help him guarantee 24 airplanes per day. This means that in negotiating this contract, they will need to work on deliveries and increase their production.

SVAC is considered a 'traditional' manufacturing operation, which uses quarterly sales forecasts that drive their MRP system. A Master Production Schedule (MPS) is generated through the available information and weekly spreadsheet schedules are prepared and delivered to Workstations 2 and 4. As situational changes occur in the plant, daily adjustments to the schedule are made.

For those who are unfamiliar with the term MRP system, it stands for Materials Requirements Planning System. This consists of taking sales forecasts and putting them into a computer program. The program then computes using a planning process; what the raw material, manpower requirements and other capacity requirements are. This type of information is then used to schedule the facility; schedule make parts, and produces a schedule identifying when to buy parts.

Daily orders are received from customers and a daily shipping schedule is given to the shipping department, which must ship an average of 10 airplanes per day.

Expeditors conduct daily checks at Workstations 2, 3 and 5 to ensure parts are available to meet the customer's requirements. The information gathered is then fed back to the scheduler.

Sky-View Industries (SVI) is the main supplier of parts to SVAC. SVAC gives Sky-View Industries a monthly forecast of their requirements and sends them purchase orders that will cover them for the following week's production. Sky-View Industries is within 5 miles of SVAC and can deliver any day of the week. SVAC decided that it would take deliveries of parts on Mondays.

SVAC has decided to adopt a 'Lean Thinking' strategy to try to improve their deliveries and reduce their cost of running the company.

The following additional information is available:

- It is assumed that all of the critical components required to build the aircraft are brought into the plant from Sky-View Industries.

- At this point SVAC has decided to concentrate its initial efforts on their assembly plant.

- The parts coming into the plant are spot checked for conformance to specifications.

The Airplane simulation was developed by Visionary Products, Inc. (www.visionaryproducts.biz)

In our simulation, the critical components of the Aircraft are represented by interlocking-plastic blocks which are stored in raw materials bins and placed somewhere inside the plant.

- The plant operates on a one-shift basis of 8 hours with a 30-minute lunch break and two 10-minute coffee breaks. For our simulation we run it for 8 minutes, and therefore each minute represents one hour in real life.

- At present a lack of skilled people has prevented them from operating additional shifts.

- There are no extra shifts available.

There are four assembly operations, one inspection operation and a shipping operation:

1) Assembly of Primary Wing/Airframe Section

2) Assembly of Two Wing Sections

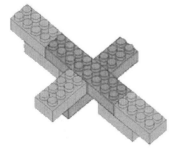

The Airplane simulation was developed by Visionary Products, Inc. (www.visionaryproducts.biz)

3) Assembly of Large Section of the Tail

4) Assembly of Nose, Fuselage, Cockpit, Tail and Wheels

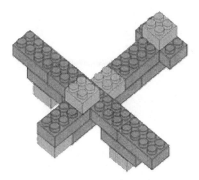

5) Inspection and Quality Control

6) Information Gathering and Shipping

Additional information:

- A "Set-up" or "Changeover" is required at Assembly Operation #3.

- The current plant effectiveness is at 80%.

The Airplane simulation was developed by Visionary Products, Inc. (www.visionaryproducts.biz)

<table>
<tr><td>SKY VIEW AIRPLACE COMPANY
• Traditional manufacturing set-up
• Produces a high quality product
• Has large inventories</td><td>THE CHALLENGE
By using the principles of "Lean Thinking" we will explore improvements that will make our customers successful by achieving deliveries of 24 airplanes per day.</td></tr>
</table>

This is an exciting new opportunity for Sky-View Airplane Company and they are eager to meet the challenge head on.

Section Key Points

- The traditional manufacturing operation employs quarterly sales forecasts to drive the Material Requirements Planning (MRP) system.

- The MRP process has the input coming from the sales forecasts or orders. The computer calculates the requirements from a planning point of view. This assists in planning the raw material requirements, human resource requirements, and other capacity requirements.

- The production schedule is reviewed daily and new schedules are created to reflect any changes. Any new information is then relayed to the operators.

- At this time Sky-View Airplane Company (SVAC) receives weekly deliveries of raw materials. The supplier is in close proximity to SVAC.

- SVAC has decided to adopt lean thinking principles. This means that they want to improve deliveries and quality of the finished product. They will do what is required to incorporate a lean manufacturing system.

Section 07 - Airplane Assembly

Sky-View Airplane Company

A "Lean" Simulation

The following is the airplane assembly layout:

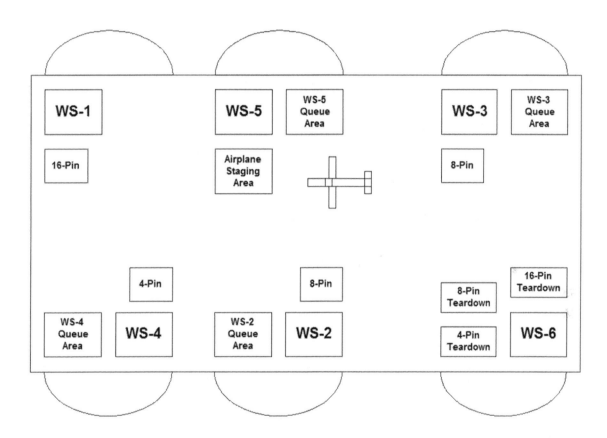

The Airplane simulation was developed by Visionary Products, Inc. (www.visionaryproducts.biz)

Operation 1 – Primary Wing/Airframe Section

2 – 16 pin blocks are required at Workstation 1. These are assembled at Workstation 1.

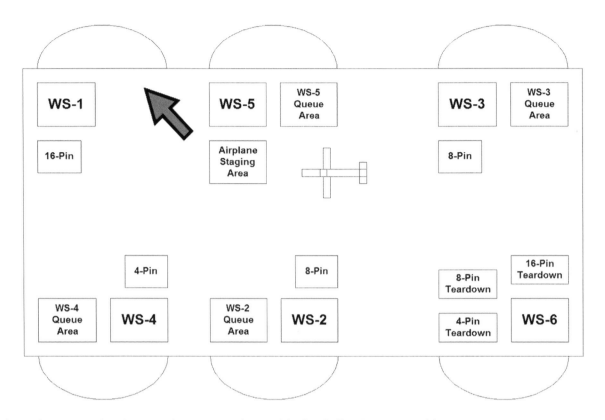

When the operation is complete we end up with the following assembly:

At this point, the plane moves to workstation 2.

Operation 2 - Assembly of Two Wing Sections

Five 8-pin blocks of raw materials are added to the assembly.

The operator adds components to the wings and to the front section of the nose.

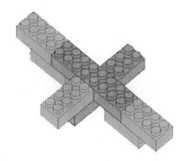

The assembly now moves to workstation 3.

Operation 3 - Assembly of Large Section of the Tail

Three 8-pin blocks of raw materials are added which constitute the tail section.

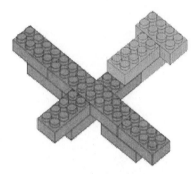

Once the tail section has been added the operator checks the plane for length using a checking fixture. The plane now moves to workstation 4.

Operation 4 - Assembly of Nose, Fuselage, Cockpit, Tail and Wheels

The operator installs the section under the nose, installs the fuselage, and adds a cockpit, the remaining part of the tail and the wheels using 6 four-pin blocks of raw material.

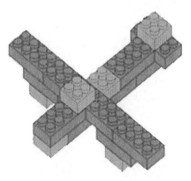

Operation 5 - Inspection and Quality Control

Operation 5 is a checkpoint, where the assembly undergoes stringent quality control. The operator checks various stress points.

The Airplane simulation was developed by Visionary Products, Inc. (www.visionaryproducts.biz)

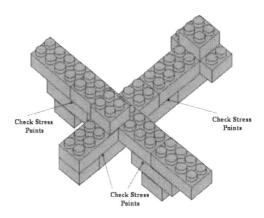

If a crack in the frame is detected, the aircraft is reworked.

When the plane passes all QC tests, it is sent to workstation 6, which is the shipping area. All planes that arrive at Workstation 6 are considered *shipped*.

Operation 6 - Information Gathering and Shipping

The operator counts and records the number of planes that are shipped. These planes are then torn down in order to prep for the next part of the simulation. *The teardown is of no significance to the data being gathered.*

Note that at Operation 3, there is a changeover required. The company makes a white plane whenever a customer puts in a special order.

When a white plane arrives into the queue area of workstation 3, the operator must change the checking fixture (which checks length).

The Airplane simulation was developed by Visionary Products, Inc. (www.visionaryproducts.biz)

The operator must take the tape off the top and bottom of the green fixture.

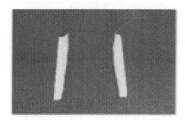

He must then pick up the green fixture and take it to storage. The green fixture is temporarily replaced by the white fixture back at workstation 3.

They must then tape the white fixture down and measure the length of the white plane.

Once this is done, the process is repeated, this time from the white fixture back to the green one again.

When the green fixture is back in place, it is business as usual until the next special order of a white plane.

Finally, there are two engineers who check for performance and record the relevant data. Both engineers use a stopwatch to make their observations.

The first engineer checks for the following cycle times:

- the time of construction at workstation 1,

- the delivery of the assembly or assemblies into the queue of workstation 2,

- The cycle times of movement into each of the subsequent workstations.

The second engineer checks the lead time, which is the period it takes to move from the beginning of assembly at workstation 1 to the end as a plane goes into the queue at workstation 6. Remember, every minute of our 8-minute day in the simulation represents one hour of an 8 hour day.

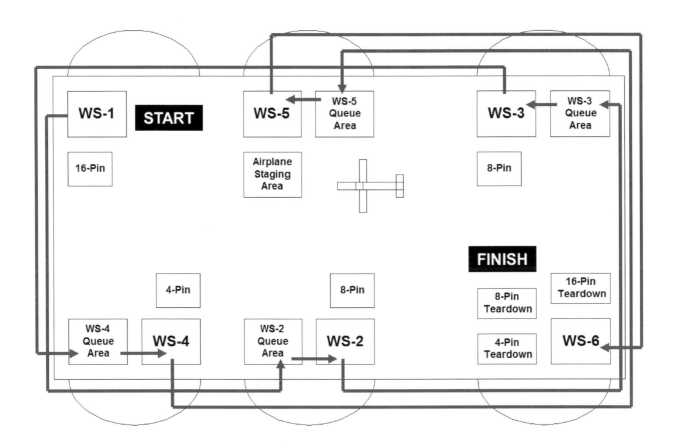

The Airplane simulation was developed by Visionary Products, Inc. (www.visionaryproducts.biz)

Section 08 - Rules of Engagement

> **DAY 1 – RESOURCES**
> - 4 – Assembly Stations
>   - ➤ *At Station WS-3 there is a need for setup*
> - 1 – Inspection Station
> - 1 – Shipping, Tear-down and Recoding Station
> - 2 – Industrial Engineers

Let's get familiar with the rules of engagement for Day 1.

The resources in the simulation will remain the same for the next three days. Workstations 1 through 4 are assembly stations. We have one operator for each of these stations. At workstation 3, we have a need for a setup. Workstation 5 is an inspection station. We have one inspector at this station. Workstation 6 is for shipping, teardown and recording where an operator records relevant information. We also have two industrial engineers. They calculate the cycle time and lead time through the process using a stopwatch.

We build in batches of 5, because our computers determined that economic order quantity (EOQ) is five. With that number, we hope our cost per unit is less. Batches must remain together through to final inspection. This means that the product must be built and transported from one station to the other, right through to workstation 5, then brought to workstation 6 for delivery.

Operators themselves must deliver the batches to the next operation. They cannot move the planes across the table because of safety concerns. They have to get up out of their chairs and deliver the product to the next station.

> **DAY 1 - INSTRUCTIONS**
> - Build in batches of 5.
> - Batches must remain together through final inspection.
> - Operators deliver batches to next operation.
> - Operators must procure their own parts.
> - Operators must maintain a steady rate of production.

The Airplane simulation was developed by Visionary Products, Inc. (www.visionaryproducts.biz)

Operators must procure their own parts. When they run out of parts, they must go to material stores and bring back what they need to their stations. Operators must maintain a steady state of production. That means that after an operator delivers the appropriate structure to the next workstation, he or she gets back to work and production continues on the next plane.

- At operation 3 a set-up has to be done.
- Inspector must identify quality problems and set them aside but cannot communicate with the operators.
- Tear down operator will gather the data to measure how production is performing.

At workstation 3 a set-up is required; we also call this a changeover. We try to do this very consistently each time so that the quality of the product remains the same. We need to go through a standard operating procedure with very specific rules on setup so that the time and product quality are taken into account each time. The inspector must identify quality problems and set the planes aside. They cannot communicate with the rest of the plant, which is not unusual in this type of environment.

At workstation 6, the operator handles the shipping, tear down and recording. That operator considers the product shipped at that point in time. The information needed for daily production numbers is recorded at this time. This feedback is given to production to indicate how well they are doing.

Section 09 – Generating the Current State Map for Start of Simulation

Before we start our simulation, it is important to be able to visualize the entire business. For this reason, we are going to create a Value Stream map prior to starting the simulation. The first thing you do when creating a value stream map is draw the customer on the right hand side with their requirements as of today. In this instance, the requirements are 10 per day, I know the new contract calls for 24 planes per day but if we don't understand our current state, there is no way we should be experimenting with our future.

After placing the customer icon on the right hand side of our over-sized piece of paper, we start to identify the current requirements from our customer. Then we work our way upstream from the customer to our shipping department. We identify how we ship to our customer. Then follows all of the assembly processes (5 through 1), then upstream of that to our supplier. Our observations of our inventory levels in the past are averaged as shown below. We also have 60 sets of parts in the warehouse, which gets put on the map as well.

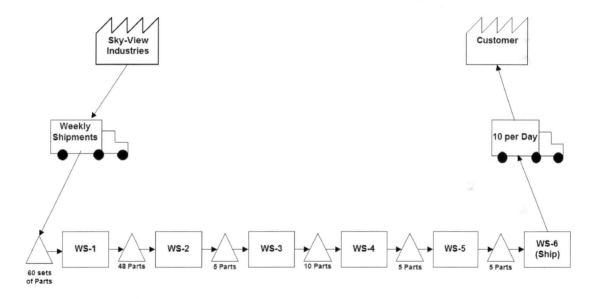

We also get weekly shipments from SVI (Sky-View Industries) and we show that as information that we place on the truck icon between the supplier SVI and us, SVAC. We average 60 sets of parts in our warehouse so we use the average.

Cycle time represents the number of seconds that it took to do one operation at workstation one for one part. As you know we run based on our MRP systems recommendations of making 5 airplanes each time. We have to take the time related to making 5 airplanes and divide that by 5 to get the cycle time (C/T) per airplane.

We are interested in the value added time for one airplane so we add up the cycle times in each of the assembly stations to get this total value-added time..

At workstation 3, we have a change over time. We indicate that separately, and do not consider it as part of our cycle time. We can now put this information on a graph to better analyze our production. Looking at other relevant information in map, we see that our utilization for the company is 80% (given to us from the data). This implies that our productivity level is about 80%.

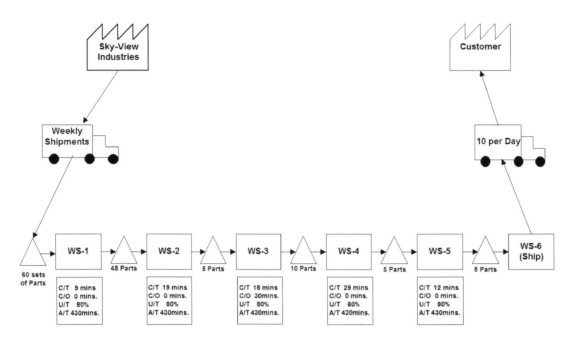

Our available time is 430 minutes out of a day. If you're wondering how do we came up with 430 minutes, it's 60 minutes per hour x 8 hours/day = 480 minutes/day, minus (30 minutes for lunch and two 10 minute breaks) 50 minutes/day = 430 minutes/day.

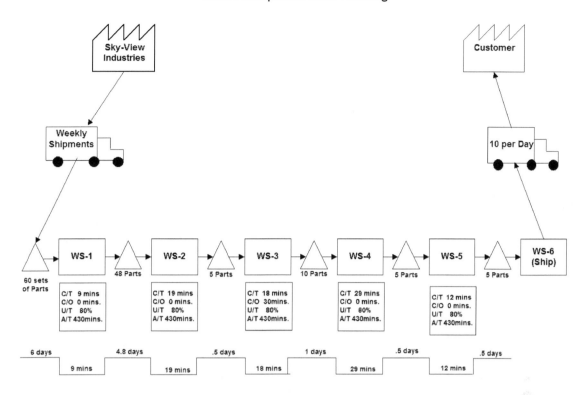

We've identified how much value added time we are spending on these particular planes. With the inventory levels as stated, we convert that into number of days of supply.

Is there any value added at workstation 5? Quality is important for the customer, so you'd be inclined to say yes. Even if we did it right the first time, does the customer care about it? In this case, yes. The customer expects the inspection process to happen and recognizes that they must pay for this. In most companies, inspection is not value added, we would classify it as a type 2 waste – Non-value-added but necessary. If we don't inspect here, we could be passing on defects to the customer. The US Air Force and the Canadian Air Force want the inspection done for their records and for obvious reasons.

The Airplane simulation was developed by Visionary Products, Inc. (www.visionaryproducts.biz)

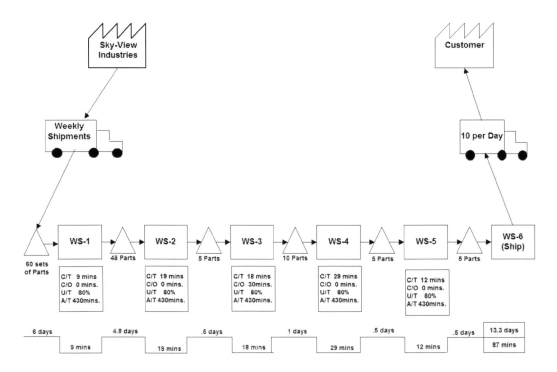

It is time to convert the date to meaningful information. If I were looking at a value stream map I would always look at the bottom line. The bottom right hand corner in this case. It tells the whole picture. Here is how to interpret this.

First, we convert our entire inventory to "days of supply". For example, given that we produce ten planes per day and we have 5 parts (airplanes) on hand, we have half a day of inventory. At ten parts between station 3 & 4 we have one day of inventory.

With 48 parts between station 1 and 2, we have 4.8 days of supply. In our system, we have quite a few days of inventory when you add it up and take a look at the value added process.

The available supply is 13.3 days and we have a total of 87 minutes of Value Added Time. To get a percent value added time – convert the 13.3 days to minutes, then take 87 minutes and divide that by the 13.3 days (in minutes), then multiply by 100. It is a small percentage, more on this later…

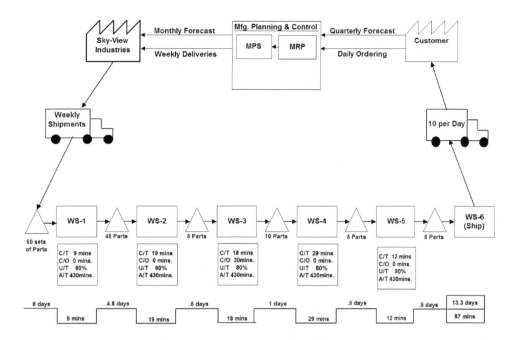

The value stream map does not end with the material flow. We are actually looking at the information flow as well. We get quarterly sales forecasts from the customer, along with their daily orders. It all goes into our MRP System; we then send a monthly forecast to our supplier, along with weekly deliveries, amounting to a weekly schedule.

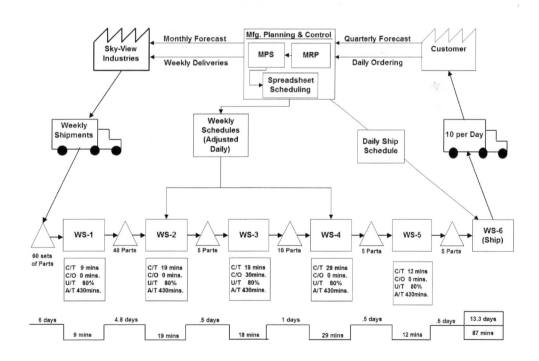

If you remember, we have daily checks at Workstations 3, 4, and 5. We use "Go See" icons (glasses) to remind us to perform daily checks at those workstations. Is this wasteful? Of course, the customer does not care about checking inventory.

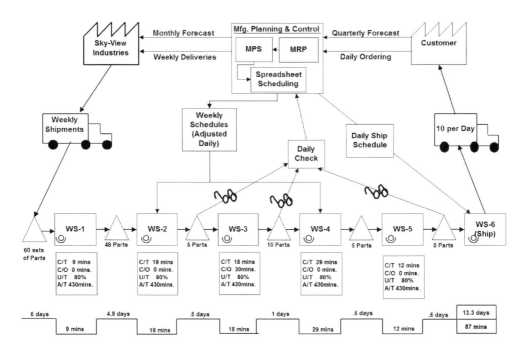

This gives us a concrete idea of how we are doing business today. It also provides us with an understanding of how much inventory we are sitting on, how it is flowing towards shipping to support the output of 10 planes per day. Having developed an understanding of our business is important; this should be done before we start making improvements.

Section Key Points

- Every Current State Map is started with information on the customer. Then the delivery characteristics to the Customer, then going through the product transformation flow from the customer, upstream to the supplier. It is not a complete loop yet until the information flow is defined and closes the loop.

- The Current State Map shows only what is happening today. It must be a true reflection of the current activities. Any identifiable improvements or changes needed must be reserved for the Future State Map.

- In our example we note that there is an inspection process. In most cases this is considered a non-value added step because the customer expects a quality product and is willing to pay for the extra inspection, it is value-added. In this case, SVAC is happy to know that inspection is mandatory as there has been the occasional quality problem in the suppliers' material.

- In calculating TAKT time, one must use only the available working minutes per day, not the total number of minutes in a shift. The design of the future state must be as close to reality as possible.

- A value stream map includes the material transformation process, the information flow, and information on material movement. The most revealing part of the map is the bottom right hand corner, where you can determine the percent of time value is being added.

Section 10 – Day 1 (Part A) - Start of Simulation

A day in the life of Sky View Airplane Company. It all starts with observation. Before you go through a Plan-Do-Check-Adjust process, you should observe. In this simulation, Day 1 represents an understanding of the current state of SVAC. After an 8-minute simulation we understand what some of the problems are. For purposes of the simulation, one minute is equal to one hour of SVAC time, and one second represents one minute of SVAC time. So let's get started in our 8-minute day. Remember, we have 2 engineers, so one will measure the cycle time, and the other will measure the overall lead time.

Timer at 00:00 - Event – Production starts

Operator 1 will complete his first batch of 5 and deliver into the queue of workstation 2 in good time. This workstation has the smallest workload and experiences the fastest cycle time. This results in overproduction. A fast cycle time is a smaller number.

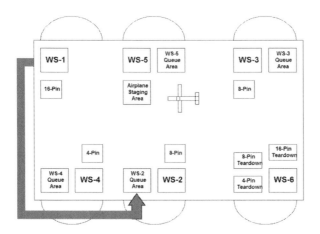

Timer at 00:51 – Event – First batch of 5 received in WS-2 Queue

Operator 2 takes more time to complete his assemblies. This will result in a slower time or longer cycle time than that of Operator 1. Before operator 2 can complete the work, inventory starts to build-up between Workstations 1 and 2. This reinforces that there is an imbalance in the workloads, and the waste of unnecessary inventory represents this.

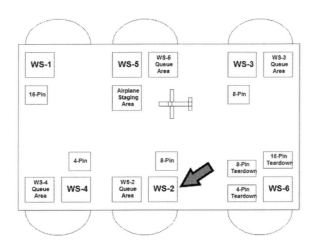

Timer at 01:26 – Event – Operator 2 moves work-in-process inventory to Operator 3

Operator 2 delivers into the Queue of Workstation 3. You will note that all of the operators are experiencing the waste of transportation.

The waste of transportation occurs each time an operator delivers the work-in-progress batch into the queue of another workstation. It also occurs when they go and get more raw materials from stores, which are located a fair distance from the point of use.

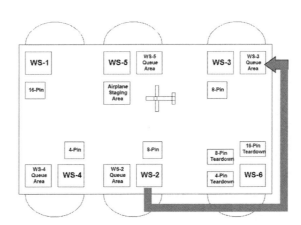

The Airplane simulation was developed by Visionary Products, Inc. (www.visionaryproducts.biz)

Timer at 02:34 - Event – First batch of 5 received in WS-3 Queue

Operator 3 must deal with extra responsibilities – this will result in the slowest cycle time amongst all the workstations. One extra responsibility is checking the planes for length.

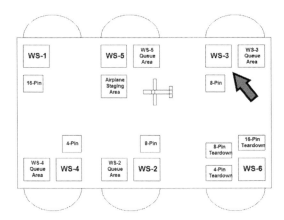

Timer at 03:00 – Event – Start of Changeover (C/O)

Operator 3 must also do a set up (changeover) of fixtures during this first batch – the white plane fixture is located some distance from the point of use. The extra responsibilities and transportation required of this operator will result in some inventory buildup between Workstations 2 and 3.

Timer at 03:48 – Event - First batch of 5 received in WS-4 Queue

Operator 3 completed the first batch and delivered it into the queue of Workstation 4. The operator at Workstation 4 has been waiting a long time for the first batch to arrive from Workstation 3. Just ignore the plant accident that occurs during this drop-off.

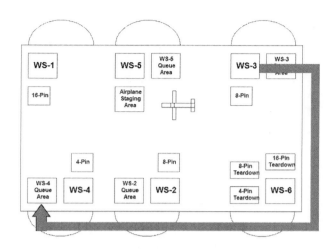

Timer at 05:08 - Event – Defect noticed at Workstation 4

The occurrence of some defects in airplane construction noticed at Workstation 4 adds to operator 4's cycle time.

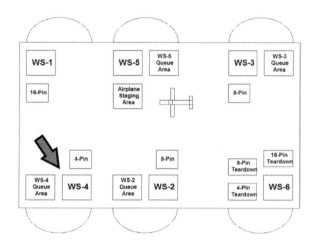

Operator in WS-4 is still working to assemble the nose, fuselage, and cockpit, when all of a sudden; a whistle blows at exactly 6 minutes (6 hours) into our Day 1 of assembly.

Timer at 06:00 – Event – Whistle blows

At the 6-minute mark the clock stops. We are now 6 hours into the SVAC workday and the inspector at Workstation 5 has not received any planes yet. The operator at Workstation 6 has not started working either. They have been waiting patiently….

The simulation continues in the next section.

The Airplane simulation was developed by Visionary Products, Inc. (www.visionaryproducts.biz)

Section 11 – Day 1 (Part B) - Scrap Cost Calculations

We have a little over 2 minutes left in our simulation. For purposes of discussing potential scrap costs – each operator counts how much inventory is in their area, and in the queue of the next workstation. The clock then starts up again.

Timer at 06:33 - Event - First batch of 5 received in WS-5 Queue

Workstation 5 has received the first batch of 5 and is in the process of inspecting them.

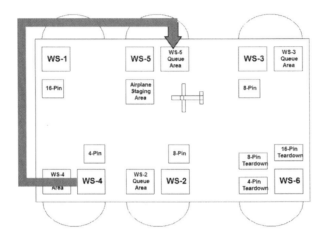

In the final minutes of the simulation this team has predicted that they will complete the batch of 5. This is nowhere near the expected shipment of 24 the customer wants. However, our understanding is starting to deepen as to why.

Timer at 07:08 - Event – Defective airplane noticed

The inspector at Workstation 5 declares one of the airplanes as defective. As a result only 4 planes make it to shipping before the 8 hour day is over.

Timer at 08:00 - Event – Whistle blows – the day is over.

The team has shipped 4 airplanes by the end of Day 1. As soon as the airplanes arrived in WS-6 we considered them shipped.

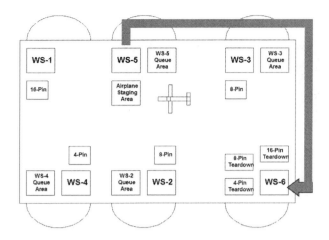

Timer back at 6:00 – Event – Raw materials failed our inspection process.

Let's talk about scrap. Let suppose we have a customer ordering an airplane.

Airplanes are expensive and must meet the specifications of the customer. In this case, the customer only wants a certain type of steel to be used. This particular type of steel does not repel lightning as well as other types of steel.

The company's engineers test this steel regularly because the suppliers send the wrong material from time to time.

This inspection happens at 2:00 pm, which is 6 hours into the 8-hour shift.

In this case, let's assume that they received a bad batch of steel. All of the airplanes that were produced during this shift would not meet the customer's specifications.

How much would it cost us to tear them apart and rebuild them? As the wrong steel was used, what is the exposure to this problem?

> **EXPOSURE**
> **Sum of each …**
>
> (Number of Assemblies) X (Cost Per Assembly)

The Airplane simulation was developed by Visionary Products, Inc. (www.visionaryproducts.biz)

The exposure is calculated by multiplying the number of assemblies by the cost per assembly. It makes sense for us to say that in order to minimize the potential scrap cost the amount of inventory in the plant should be kept as low as possible.

Now let's take a look at what our scrap exposure is for the Sky-View Airplane Company. This table shows all of the scrap cost calculations.

Sky-View Ariplane Company
Scrap Costs Calculation

16 Pin Costs $10,000.00	8 Pin Costs $5,000.00	4 Pin Costs $3,000.00

Day 1		Scrap									
		16 Pin			8 Pin			4 Pin			
	Sub Assy's	Parts per Assembly	Total Parts	Cost	Parts per Assembly	Total Parts	Cost	Parts per Assembly	Total Parts	Cost	
Workstation 1	22	2	44	$ 440,000	0			0			
Workstation 2	9	2	18	$ 180,000	5	45	$ 225,000	0			
Workstation 3	6	2	12	$ 120,000	8	48	$ 240,000	0			
Workstation 4	0	2	0	$ -	8	0	$ -	6	0	$ -	
Total Sub Assy's	37										
				$ 740,000			$ 465,000			$ -	

Total Scrap Cost $ 1,205,000

The first step is to count the number of assemblies between WS-1 and WS-2. We count all of the assemblies that are either finished in WS-1 and in the queue of WS-2. Remember, this was done at 06:00 into our simulation. At the time we only had inventory up to WS-4, none of the inventory made its way to WS-5 as that point in time.

Each piece of interlocking-plastic block in our assembly has a cost. The 16 pin pieces are $10,000 each. The 8 pin pieces are $5000 each and the 4 pin pieces cost $3000 each. The number of assemblies between WS-1 and WS-2 is 22 at 2 parts per assembly it is equal to 44 parts. Each of these parts are 16 pin parts so there are 44 parts at $10,000 each for a cost $440,000.

We can do similar calculations for each finished sub-assembly. We can see the high cost of the assemblies between the workstations 3 & 4. At the six-minute mark there are no assemblies between work stations 5 & 6 yet. The total cost for the 16 pin assemblies is $740,000

The total cost for the 8 pin assemblies is $465,000 / the total scrap cost is calculated to be $1,205,000.

If SVI were to send us the wrong kind of steel, the manner in which we produce airplanes in Day 1 costs our company $1,205,000 in scrap. It makes sense that we should keep the number of subassemblies between workstations as low as possible.

Section Key Points

- Engineers must test this steel regularly because occasionally, the suppliers send the wrong material. Sometimes after inspection, at 2.00 pm, a bad batch of steel is discovered. This means that all of the airplanes we had produced during that shift did not meet the specifications.

- Our exposure to scrap is: Sum of the number of assemblies x the cost per assembly.

- If SVI were to send us the wrong kind of steel, the manner in which we produce airplanes in Day 1 would have cost our company $1,205,000 in scrap. It makes sense that we should keep the number of subassemblies between workstations as low as possible in order to minimize the cost of scrap.

- There are no inspection points until the airplane reaches Workstation 5.

The Airplane simulation was developed by Visionary Products, Inc. (www.visionaryproducts.biz)

Section 12 – Day 1 (Part C) - Inventory Carrying Costs Calculations

On the subject of INVENTORY...
There's a Carrying Cost.

Carrying cost is a measure usually expressed as a percentage of the cost to hold inventory. Simply put, inventory that sits in the plant has a cost associated to it. This cost is a result of:

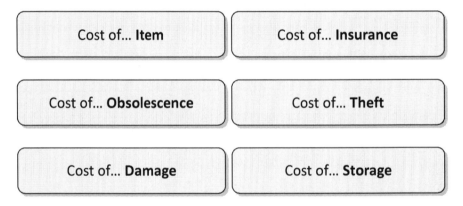

Cost of... **Item**	Cost of... **Insurance**
Cost of... **Obsolescence**	Cost of... **Theft**
Cost of... **Damage**	Cost of... **Storage**

It is extremely important that every company associate inventory as a liability, and not as an asset. Many companies perform year-end inventory counts. Sky-View Airplane Company is no different.

Let us assume that the company uses a bank for financing. If the bank were to charge SVAC for the risks that it takes in financing their inventory it would go about it in a very thorough manner. The bank would calculate what it needs to charge on the overall annual inventory tied up by the company. They would count material or physical inventory between machines, processes, or activities waiting to be processed. The bank charges 24% interest per year on the carrying costs for your inventory. This means it charges 2% per month. We use this number for purposes of making our point, inventory costs money. If we don't associate a cost to the inventory, we won't consider it a problem, and inventory levels above a strategic minimum, should be considered a problem.

The assumption is that the amount of inventory does not fluctuate too much. As long as this system remains the same, this count is a valid measure with which to determine your monthly average.

We calculate the carrying cost by multiplying the inventory value by 2%, so at the end of day 1, we stopped after 8 hours of work.

At this point we ask ourselves, what if that were the amount of the inventory at the end of the month. We assume that this is true and complete our carry cost calculations.

And our count becomes the amount we use to represent the physical inventory at the end of the month. For example, the amount could be $250,000 worth of inventory. Multiply that by 2%; our inventory costs become $5000 per month. So in some ways that 2% is the cost of borrowing money from the bank.

Let's take a look now at the inventory carrying costs for Sky-View operations. This table shows all inventory carrying cost calculations. That is for Work in Progress.

Sky-View Ariplane Company

Inventory Carrying Costs Calculation (WIP)

| 16 Pin Costs $10,000.00 | | 8 Pin Costs $5,000.00 | | 4 Pin Costs $3,000.00 |

Day 1		Inventory									
		16 Pin				8 Pin			4 Pin		
	Sub Assy's	Parts per Assembly	Total Parts	Cost		Parts per Assembly	Total Parts	Cost	Parts per Assembly	Total Parts	Cost
Workstation 1											
	25	2	50	$ 500,000		0			0		
Workstation 2											
	7	2	14	$ 140,000		5	35	$ 175,000	0		
Workstation 3											
	9	2	18	$ 180,000		8	72	$ 360,000	0		
Workstation 4											
	6	2	12	$ 120,000		8	48	$ 240,000	6	36	$ 108,000
Workstation 5											
	0	2	0	$ -		8	0	$ -	6	0	$ -
Workstation 6											
Total Sub Assy's	47										
				$ 940,000			$ 775,000				$ 108,000

Total Inventories $ 1,823,000

Carrying Cost per Month (2%) $ 36,460

Our first step is to calculate the amount of inventory between WS-1 & 2. There are more assemblies now because we have completed the last two hours of our workday. Once again we count all of the finished assemblies in WS-1 and in the queue of WS-2.

As we said then each Lego piece in our assembly has a cost. The pin cost remains the same as in the earlier calculations.

The Airplane simulation was developed by Visionary Products, Inc. (www.visionaryproducts.biz)

We calculate the cost of assemblies in the same fashion as in the scrap table.

Thus, in this example the total cost for the 16 pin assemblies is $940,000. For the 8 pin assemblies the cost is $775,000 and for the 4 pin assemblies, $108,000 giving a total inventory cost for stock between WS-1 to WS-6 of $1,823,000.

At 2% per month, this works out to be $36,460 per month. This means that the manner that we are doing business on day one costs our company $36,460 per month for the inventory carrying costs. It will be our goal to reduce the amount of inventory that sits between our work stations. This in turn will bring our costs down which will make us more competitive.

Section Key Points

- It is a fact that when Inventory levels are reduced, problems that were previously hidden become exposed.

- Carrying costs are a result of the cost of Inventory, Insurance, Obsolescence, Theft, Damage, and Storage.

- Carrying costs are calculated based on the amount of inventory (represented in $) multiplied by the monthly % charged that we have assigned it based on our experience.

- Carrying costs are calculated on all inventories, not only the work-in-process (WIP).

Section 13 - Gathering Data Determine SVAC Future State Requirements.

$$\text{TAKT Time} = \frac{\text{Available Time}}{\text{Customer Demand}}$$

Let's graph out our findings to give our engineers some numbers to work with. And then we are going to develop what is called a TAKT time. TAKT is German for the word 'beat'. So it is the beat of the drum, or beat of the market (the customer). How many planes does our customer want? They want ten right now. 24 if we can guarantee the 24. We have to translate the Customer's requirements into our organization. So today, we get 10 planes out per day, what does our TAKT time need to be? In the future, if we want to get 24 planes per day, how many planes do we need to get out per minute? Maybe a better question is: how many minutes does it take to get a plane out?

So let's look at how we calculate TAKT time. Let's use PAL Manufacturing as an example.

The demand for cylinders was 45,000 per year. When we looked at it, we said we had 480 minutes available per shift, we were running two shifts, giving us an available 960 minutes per day. What we want to do is get 200 cylinders out per day. If we could get 200 cylinders per day, we would have no problem in attaining the goal for the year.

If we can do this every day, we know we can easily produce this number of cylinders per year.

- Available Time per Shift = 480 mins.
- Number of Shifts   = 2
- Total Available Time   = 960 mins.
- Customer Demand   = 45,000 units/year

- TAKT Time = $\dfrac{\text{Available Time}}{\text{Customer Demand}}$

The TAKT time is simply the available time we have during the day divided by the customer demand.

In this case, we have 960 minutes available in the day, divided by the daily 200 cylinders, and that turns out to be one cylinder every 4.8 minutes. So that is what our TAKT time is. Knowing TAKT is critical to helping us balance the work between stations. Each station's cycle time must be below the TAKT time.

The Airplane simulation was developed by Visionary Products, Inc. (www.visionaryproducts.biz)

Let's calculate our TAKT time for the Sky-View Airplane Company.

In our day, we have to calculate the available minutes; you get a paid 30-minute break, and two 10-minute breaks. That leaves us 430 minutes per shift. So the 24 is the planned number of planes we need to get out in a day. That means we need to get a plane out every 17.9 minutes. If we need to get a plane out every 17.9 minutes which means our cycle time per plane needs to lower than 17.9 minutes. If it is higher (or a bigger number), then we have a bottleneck in our system.

TAKT TIME = 17.9 minutes per airplane.

I am going to ask the engineers to give me the cycle time to get a plane through the system. At WS-1 - how long did it take for 5 assemblies to be completed? The observations over the entire day were taken into account, not just the first batch of 5 planes. In order to make this simple, our engineer said it took 27 seconds to complete the first 5 airplane assemblies in WS-1. We place that number in the "C/T (sec) for 5 Planes..." column. Then since we are looking for the cycle time for one airplane, we divide it by 5. This ends up being 5.4 seconds per assembly in WS-1.

Initial Airplane Production

Workstation Number	Cycle Time	TAKT Time	C/T (sec) for 5 Planes...
1	5.4	17.9	27
2		17.9	
3		17.9	
4		17.9	
5		17.9	

$$\text{TAKT Time} = \frac{\text{Available Time}}{\text{Customer Demand}}$$

$$= \frac{430}{24}$$

$$= 17.9$$

That means that on a per plane basis it is 5.4 seconds on average to get a plane from WS-1 to the queue of WS-2. This number is below the TAKT Time; therefore, we can guarantee that we can meet our customer's demand in this workstation.

Remember that for WS-3 we need to include the set up time. We need to plug in all of these numbers.

Initial Airplane Production

Workstation Number	Cycle Time	TAKT Time	C/T (sec) for 5 Planes...
1	5.4	17.9	27
2	18.6	17.9	93
3	27	17.9	135
4	18.8	17.9	94
5	12	17.9	60

TAKT Time   =   Available Time
                    Customer Demand

              =   430
                        24

              =   17.9

TAKT Time Calculations

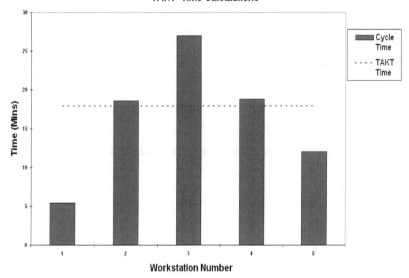

The Airplane simulation was developed by Visionary Products, Inc. (www.visionaryproducts.biz)

Section Key Points

- TAKT is a German word which refers to the beat of music. It can also mean cycle, rhythm or repetition time. Sometimes it refers to the baton of an orchestra leader.

- TAKT Time is the desired time between units of production output, synchronized to customer demand.

- The concept carries backward through a process stream. Ideally, every step synchronizes with the final output. TAKT Time is fundamental to Lean Manufacturing. The TAKT time is the available time we have during the day divided by the customer demand.

- Part of the TAKT time calculation is to know how many units you want to produce on an annual basis. This will allow you to calculate the daily production quantity.

- Cycle Time is the total elapsed time to assemble a unit from the start of one process to the end of the same physical process. (Note: Cycle Time is not the same as Lead Time).

- The engineers calculate the cycle time. In this simulation it took 27 seconds to get 5 planes through WS-3 into the queue of WS-4. At this time, we are not meeting the cycle time required (or TAKT time) to satisfy the customer demand.

Module 03

Section 01 - Flow & Pull - Pull System Example

We want to take this opportunity to talk about Day 1 and understand the current state of the business. Usually, it takes an average of 6 weeks to get to this point with a company. We help the team understand the principles of lean thinking in order to design a future lean system. They need to see and understand the complexities and the root cause of the problems they are facing today.

In doing this, the entire team puts together a future state design. They are pretty excited about it because it makes a lot of sense. And why shouldn't it, they created it. They need to get out there and just do it. As they are doing this, they can't forget the golden rule of involving everybody that is affected by change. We always have some forces working against us and change is a force to be reckoned with. My suggestion is to just do it, but keep the people side very high up on your priorities.

> **MAKE THE PROCESS FLOW**

Make the process Flow is the third principle of lean thinking.

In our example, think about the retail side, how do you make the process flow? How does the customer come in and get what they want. What do they do? Let's look at the manufacturing side.

In manufacturing we identified the value added time at the bottom of the value stream map. Making the process flow means that the company gets as much waste out of the process. The immediate goal should be to go for the big things that shrink the production lead time as much as possible.

The rule of thumb is FLOW where you can, and PULL where flow is not currently possible. Flow implies that you are able to remove all – or as many – obstacles that impede value getting to the customer. Flow should be next on the priority list – not pull. However, for purposes of this simulation, we focus on pull.

> **DEVELOP PULL BY THE CUSTOMER**

The fourth principle of lean thinking is to **Develop Pull from the Customer's perspective**. So the downstream operation, just like a river trickling down a mountain, in our example of the cylinder value stream, the tube has the first operation of cutting, then tube drilling.

Tube drilling is the downstream operation to cutting. It is the next step. So as we look at this, we are talking about the next downstream customer getting what they want by having it available to them in the supermarket, pulling that inventory and signaling the supplier to replenish. So that's the system of developing pull from the customer.

A key ingredient that is almost always missing in pull systems is the understanding that as you decrease the number of signals (inventory) between each customer and supplier, the velocity increases. The inventory moves quicker, and problems become exposed. Developing a pull-system should be more about exposing problems than the technique of signaling your supplier for replenishment. For now, we learn about what it means to signal (pull from) your supplier.

> **Lean's got some pull!**

An example of a pull system for most people is the pull system for bread. The customers realize that their household is running low on bread. And that they must replenish the bread box.

They must go to a super market and buy some bread. There is more than one supermarket to choose from.

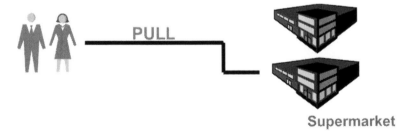

Supermarket

The customer chooses a supermarket and they go into it. They go to the bread aisle, take a loaf of bread off the shelf, pay for it, and take it home for consumption.

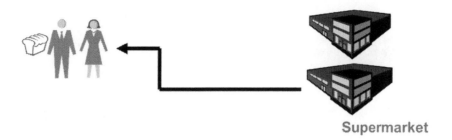

As more customers come into the supermarket and buy bread, the racks become empty. The empty racks signal the store staff to take them into the back of the store. Full racks are then taken from the back and moved to the empty homes(places) in the bread aisle. The bread inventory is filled again. When the supermarket's inventory of bread runs low, it is time to order more bread from the bakery.

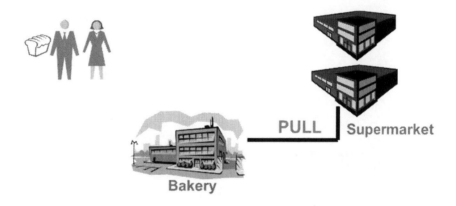

The bakery delivers daily.

The bakery fills up their trucks and delivers a shipment to the supermarket. The supermarket staff fills up the racks in the back. The supermarket is once again able to replenish the empty homes in the bread aisle.

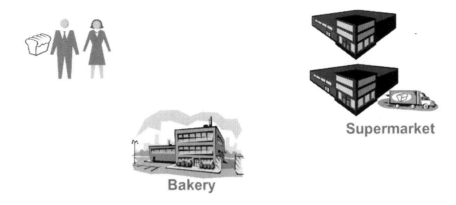

The bakery uses a variety of ingredients for its bread recipe. For example, flour. Sooner or later, its flour inventory runs low. And the bakery must pull from the flour mill.

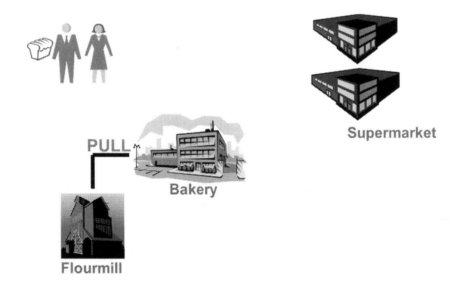

Flour is then shipped to the bakery to replenish the flour inventory. The flourmill uses wheat to make the flour. When the flour mill runs low on wheat it pulls from the farm.

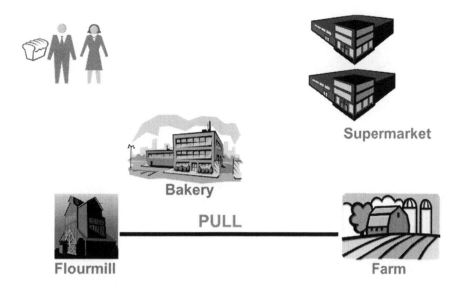

Wheat is then shipped to the flourmill to replenish the wheat inventory.

This pull system for bread demonstrates a simple pull system.

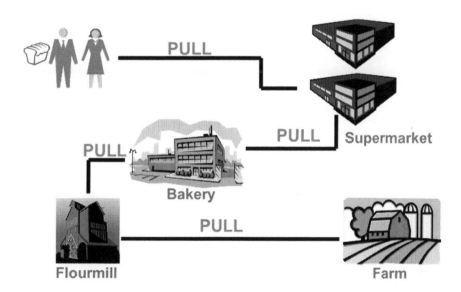

The customer pulls what they need from the supermarket that was designed to have what they want and when they want it. This pulling will and generate a chain reaction, as the spots become empty, the upstream supplier gets the signal to transport from the supplier to the supermarket. Then as the supplier uses inventory, their supplier does the same. Finally, it becomes obvious to everyone in the value stream that there is only one trigger, and a chain reaction that will supply as the customer physically takes inventory.

Section Key Points

- In order to get to this stage in the process we have to thoroughly understand the principles of lean thinking. We need to think about our future state but know also that we cannot get to this point until we understand our current state.

- You should strive to create flow first (single-piece), and pull where flow cannot be created.

- The third principle of Lean Thinking is to make the process flow. In order to improve flow, we must try to get our system to produce as close to the lead time of our theoretical minimum as possible. This way the percentage of time that we are adding value is greater over the total.

- Pull System – Any system that signals the upstream operation to deliver materials, or do work.

- Pull is developed from the Customer's perspective. It is always the downstream operation pulling the inventory and causing the supplier (upstream operation) to replenish.

- Supermarkets are a controlled inventory of items that are used to schedule production at an upstream process. A certain number of pieces must be maintained at all times. Within a pull system, a downstream operation (or customer process) withdraws the items it needs from a supermarket. The supplying process then produces to replenish what was withdrawn.

Section 02 - The Mock Company VSM – Future State

A main objective of the entire Lean Production effort is the concept of *flow*.

Ideally, production should flow continuously, all the way from raw materials to the customer. Envision realizing this ideal through a production system that acts as one long conveyor.

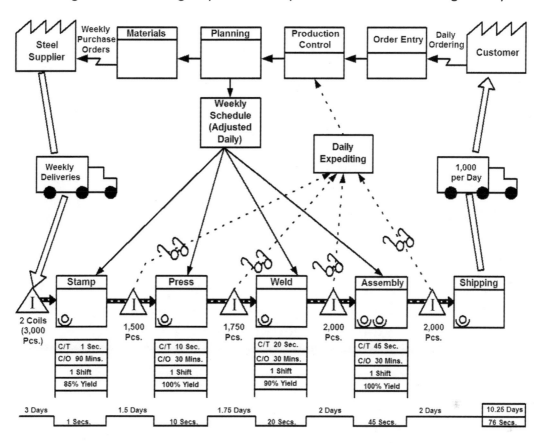

In our case study, that would mean making our process flow from our supplier of raw materials to stamp, to press, to weld, to assembly, to shipping and then to the customer.

Presently our production lead time is 10.25 days. The goal is to reduce this lead time. Perfection represents reducing it to the theoretical minimum of 76 Seconds. Improvements to the present value stream will have to be made. A future state map will be drawn that takes into account the whole system and makes improvements where they are most needed.

After brainstorming for improvements, the Mock Company produces the following Future State Map.

Future State Map

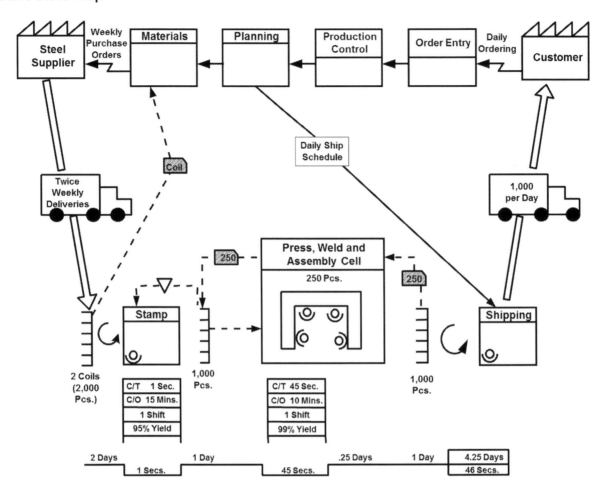

A decision is made to bring some of the machines together in order to create a Press, Weld, and Assembly Cell.

The machines are still in their natural order of processing and form the shape of a U. Cell operators may handle multiple processes and the number of operators is changed when the customer demand changes. The U shaped equipment layout is used to allow more alternatives for distributing work elements among operators and to permit the lead off and final operations to be performed by the same operator. Another benefit is that inventory goes directly to the machine rather than constantly moving inventory on and off a rack.

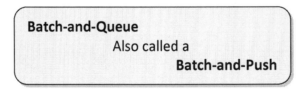

Batch-and-Queue
Also called a
Batch-and-Push

Our original Value Stream Map identified what is called a batch and queue production system. This means that we are producing more than one piece of an item and then moving those items forward to the next operation before they are actually needed there. Thus, items need to be waiting in a queue. This is also called a batch and push system.

Withdrawal

In contrast to this, is the concept of a Pull System. This icon represents a pull of materials usually from a supermarket. This is an alternative to scheduling individual processes.

Note how weekly schedules that were adjusted daily on the previous map, for each of the Stamp, Weld, Press and Assembly operations, have now been replaced with just one daily ship schedule.

1000 Pcs.

Supermarket

This icon represents a supermarket. Supermarkets are a controlled inventory of items that are used to schedule production an upstream process. The number below the icon represents the number of pieces that must be maintained at all times. With a pull system a downstream operation or customer process withdraws the items it needs from a supermarket and the supplying process produces to replenish what was withdrawn.

There are two types of kanban, production and withdrawal. Production kanbans (signals) authorize the upstream operation to produce, and withdrawal kanbans (signals) authorize the material handler to replenish what was taken.

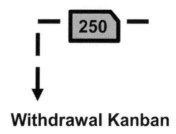

Withdrawal Kanban

This information icon represents a withdrawal Kanban.

This is a card or device that instructs a material handler to get parts from a supplying source and deliver it to the supermarket that triggered the material handler to replenish.

In our case study, as shipping pulls inventory as it needs it, it (the inventory) gets to a level where a batch of 250 units is sent upstream triggering either production or material replenishment.

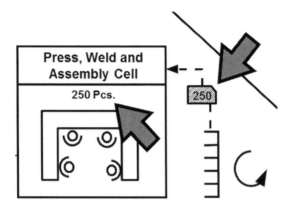

The cell is signaled to produce 250 more and then to replenish the supermarket.

In order for the cell to achieve this, it must pull its parts from another supermarket set up to supply their needs. If the withdrawal is 250 from the upstream supermarket, then it is shown as below. A withdrawal kanban of 250 goes to the Stamping supermarket and inventory is withdrawn.

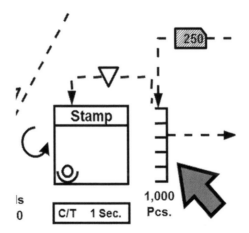

This next information icon is a signal kanban. A signal kanban is used when the amount of the kanban is right sized. In other words, the amount of this signal kanban is much greater than 250. The reason for this is obvious when you do the math. The change over time of this machine is 15 minutes. If we were to ask to replenish only 250 pieces, then it would take us 15 minutes to set up (change over) the machine, and a little over 4 minutes to run all of the 250 parts. For this reason, we use a kanban that represents overproduction, this is known as a signal kanban.

Signal Kanban

As a general convention, if it takes 15 minutes to set up (change over) the machine then you should run the machine for at least 15 minutes. A signal kanban lets everyone know that this type of inefficiency exists because of the economics of running the stamping machine for less time than it takes to change over. This signal would authorize the stamping process to produce and economic amount of inventory (say 1000 pieces) versus the 250 that was just withdrawn. Once produced, the supermarket is brought up to its quota of 1000 pieces once again.

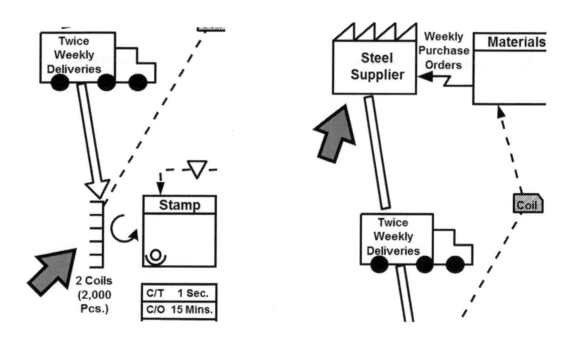

Stamp pulls from the raw materials (coils) supermarket and causes another chain reaction. The coil kanban card goes to the materials department. Then the materials department places another coil order on the weekly purchase order that goes to the steel supplier. The supplier delivers twice weekly. The number of coils ordered is the number that is replenished.

In every "real" lean system, there is only one trigger that starts everything in motion. It is very important to understand and build in this trigger so that priorities are not confused, and everyone has a chance to work within their loop of responsibility. You see everything is a closed-loop. The information flow and the material flow.

The information works its way from the customer, upstream. The material flows from the supplier, downstream.

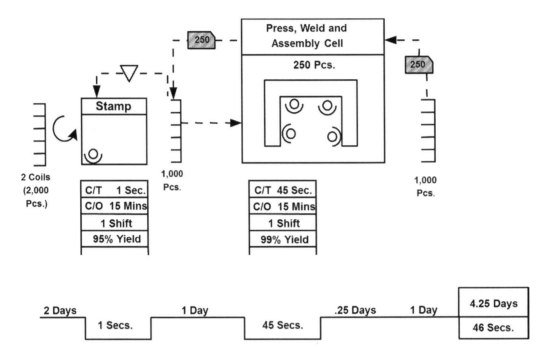

The information in our data boxes tells us that there is an increase in the yield. This results in a significant reduction in scrap. The way to achieve these improved results is by having the group most impacted by scrap focused on reducing the scrap. Getting to the root cause of the problem and eliminating it. The cycle time is really 45 seconds. The changeover times have been reduced as well. Deliveries from our supplier have been increased to twice weekly and coil sizes are smaller.

When we look at our lead time graph, we can see that the lead time can be reduced from 10.25 to 4.25 days. This is on paper. This is how the future state design begins, on paper.

> ## Brainstorm Improvements

These positive changes are due to the overall efforts by the Mock Company to improve their system. Once all of these improvements have been made, the value stream will be studied again in an effort to brainstorm more improvements. The future state becomes the current state, and the process of continuous improvement starts. This is done over and over until we have driven out as much waste as possible, and eliminated as much variability in our process as possible.

> **Continuous Flow Production**

> **1-Piece Flow**

One good example of next generation improvements is to create Continuous Flow Production. This means the items are produced and removed from one processing step to the next, one piece at a time. Each process makes only the one piece that the next process needs and the transfer batch size is a batch of one. This is also called a single-piece or one-piece flow. The benefits of such an improvement will be revealed in the next few sections of this course.

Value Stream Management is a process of continuous improvement, it is designed to try and reach the ideal. Although the theoretical minimum will never be reached, companies should continue to try and reduce overall production lead time. This translates into higher potential sales simply because customers will always want it done faster. Value stream management is the process of mapping over, and over again, until you reach the ideal state (you never reach this state). Value stream management represents the journey you take towards the ideal.

Section Key Points

- Ideally, production should flow continuously to satisfy demand all the way from customer upstream to the supplier. Envision realizing this ideal through a production system that acts as one long conveyor; all the activities along this conveyor qualify as value added from the customer's perspective. This is the theoretical minimum and represents perfection.

- The third principle of Lean Thinking is to make the process flow. In order to improve flow, we must try to get our system to produce as close to the lead time of our theoretical minimum as possible. One piece flow represents the "holy grail" of this type of initiative.

- The fourth principle of Lean Thinking is to develop pull from the customer. This means that the downstream operation (or customer) gets what they want by having it available to them in a supermarket. The customer pulls inventory as they need it. The supermarket is then replenished by a *move* kanban, or a *make* kanban. All upstream operations are replenishing as they are signaled to. This is referred to as a pull system.

- A pull system utilizes Kanbans (or signals) in order to provide instructions for the production or conveyance of items from one workstation/supermarket to the next.

- A Batch-and-Queue (or Batch-and-Push) system is driven by the idea of pushing pieces to the next downstream operation. More than one piece of an item is produced; then, moved forward to the next operation before actually being needed there. Thus items are forced to wait in a queue. This system is flawed. It does not allow for problem solving to thrive as well as a kanban system can. As the inventory is lowered in a kanban (pull) system, problems become exposed, and the team gets practice at solving problems.

- Continuous flow production (or 1-piece flow) refers to items being produced and moved from one processing step to the next. It starts with the customer, and the information on when and what to replenish works its way upstream. Each process only makes the one piece that the next process needs and the transfer batch size is one. Watch for the benefits to this type of system in the sections that follow.

Section 03 – The Runner, Walking the Process

CTD Company produces Hydraulic Cylinders. Part of the value stream is the shaft fabrication loop. This is a subassembly of a cylinder.

> Change must occur gradually over time

CTD decided to video record the path that a materials handler would have to take to travel with the materials as they were being processed up to the point of assembly. The results of their improvements are obvious.

In this example, the CTD operators have achieved the first step of their future state condition. One of the CTD Managers will walk the process with us. You will see systems of pull and flow put into action. At this point, the batch size has been set at 40 pieces.

Tote boxes such as this one are used to transfer parts between operations. Originally the operators moved their own raw materials and subassemblies between the workstations.

> Materials Handler

CTD decided that there would be a less waste if a newly appointed materials handler did the movement. If you view the video in the course, you will get a feel for the distances that needed to be travelled prior to the positive changes. Another excellent reason to appoint a material handler, and give them a specific route with timing, is that this person could report on whether production is meeting the pace that was set. If every 3 hours a bin of parts needed to be ready, then the material handler should be there every three hours.

George Trachilis, P.Eng.CPIM

Make the process flow - Results
2 Machines were moved and dedicated to the shaft loop.

☑ **HOW MANY FEET DID WE SAVE ?**   613 ft.

☑ **There are an average of 38 work orders per week.**

☑ **613 ft./work order x 38 work orders/ week = 23,294 ft per week.**

☑ **23,294 ft/wk   x   50 wk/yr. = 1,164,700   ft./yr.**

☑ **There are 5,280 feet in a mile.**

☑ **Therefore, the savings from moving 2 machines is …. 220 miles/yr.**

GEM Consultants Inc.

Section Key Points

- Too much change at once will not help the organization. It will cause confusion. Change must be gradual and take place over a reasonable period of time.

- The material handler moves inventory throughout the plant. This function should eliminate unnecessary transportation by individual operators. This not only reduces the waste of Transportation, but also unnecessary motion and increases the safety level to some degree.

- One common method of transporting material is via a Tote. The method of transportation is dependent upon the product produced.

- All organization should ultimately try to eliminate all handling of materials, and all movement. This is very challenging, but breakthroughs will only happen if they are a target.

158

Section 04 – Walking the Process, Kanban Example

Waste of Transportation

Cellular Layout

KANBAN

You will have noted that the route taken by the runner is a Waste of Transportation. In a later stage, we will create another future state generation in which we will reorganize the work area to a cellular layout. For now, the company is using squares painted on the shop floor and near their workstations as their Kanban Device.

Inventory

Production

Pay close attention to the kanbans or signals, used to control the Inventory and the rate of production. As we said earlier, a kanban is any signaling device that gives instruction for production or conveyance of items in a pull system.

This is a **QUEUE** square. Simply put, when the Queue is empty, the runner provides a batch of 40 to that spot on the floor. These are pulled from the workstation upstream from this one.

This is the **IN** Square. When the operator is ready to work or produce, he or she moves the batch from the Queue to the IN Square and begins.

This is the **OUT** Square. If the floor space marked OUT is empty, it signals the operator to produce 40 more pieces and fill that spot on the floor. When all the OUT spots on that workstation are full, this is the signal to the operator to stop producing. It is the runner's job to move items out of the OUT boxes and into the next downstream operation at the appropriate moment. In this way, overproduction is being eliminated.

Section Key Points

- Having a material handler move product, rather than many individuals moving product, is a positive move towards to the reduction of transportation waste. However, a material handler's route must be carefully planned to ensure the maximum benefit is realized.

- Material flow identifies the movement of physical product through the value stream. Information flow shows sources of data that tell a process what to do or produce. As items flow through the system we observe the material transformation process; in which, raw materials are transformed into sub-assemblies and eventually into the final product.

- Data boxes are used below each of the operations to record information concerning a manufacturing process, department, customer, etc. This data helps determine what changes will be made in order to improve the value stream.

- Cycle Time (C/T) specifies how frequently an item or product is completed by a process as timed by direct observation. It also means, the time it takes an operator to go through all of his/her work elements before repeating them.

- Change Over (C/O) is when a piece of equipment has to stop producing in order to be fitted for producing a different item (e.g. installation of a different processing tool in a metal working machine). Change over time specifies how long this takes.

- The Yield refers to the percentage of material that is being produced into usable product. This implies that whatever is left over is discarded. Generally, we refer to the discarded material as scrap.

- Lead Time (L/T) is the time required for one piece to move all the way through a process or value stream - from start to finish. Envision timing a marked item as it moves from beginning to end. By looking at a Lead Time graph, one can determine time spent on VA and NVA activities.

Section 05 – Brainstorming Improvements

Sky-View Airplane Company

Achieving a Future State

Upon reflecting on Day 1 of our airplane simulation, it becomes evident that the team knows what to do. We ask the group for feedback, and start brainstorming what improvements we can make, here they are:

> - Move materials to Point of Use
> - Rearrange the layout
> - Rebalance the workload
> - Open up communication
> - Reduce the lot size from 5 to 1
> - Reduce the Set Up time
> - PULL from the customer

Can we do all of the changes in one day? No, change must be gradual. For no other reason that I am the owner and I would like a controlled chaos for my first experience with Lean manufacturing.

Too much change all at once would result in much frustration for the workers in our plant, and this frustration can lead to an unstable manufacturing line. This may result in the stopping of the flow of product. For this reason, only 4 of the seven improvements are implemented during day 2:

> **DAY 2 IMPROVEMENTS**
> - **Move materials to Point of Use** ✓
> - **Rearrange the layout** ✓
> - **Open up communication** ✓
> - **Reduce the Set Up time** ✓

A key improvement we will consider first is *moving material to point of use*. Operators will no longer have to go to the stores to replenish their bins. All of the parts will be placed near the point of use. Rearrange the layout. Each workstation will now be situated right near the workstation that precedes it. Open up the communication.

The Airplane simulation was developed by Visionary Products, Inc. (www.visionaryproducts.biz)

All operators will be allowed to advise each other of defects and suggest improvements as they think of them. In a sense, everybody shares the duties of quality assurance.

Reduce the set up time. Both fixtures will become immediately available as the operator needs them. Either fixture can be used to measure the lengths of the white and the green planes. The need for a changeover has been eliminated.

It is expected that these improvements will bring the Sky-View Airplane Company closer to their goal of being able to guarantee their customer deliveries of 24 airplanes per day. Let's see the results of these selected improvements in the next lesson.

Section Key Points

- Brainstorming is a collaborative effort. All individuals that are active in the process being measured have something to contribute. Remember also, that a fresh set of eyes can be one of your best tools in finding alternate methods of performing the task at hand.

- In the brainstorming session, many ideas will be presented. All ideas are to be considered. Do not criticize anyone's input.

- Weigh all of the ideas and consider which ideas will be easy to implement in order to make immediate improvements. Depending upon the complexity of the process, perhaps only a few changes should be made for the first run through.

- Some ideas may include the rearrangement of the workstations in order that product flows smoothly and moving the materials to the point of use to avoid unnecessary waste of transportation. Just do it!

- Opening up communication can be very beneficial as quality issues can be identified early in the process and many good ideas come about by discussing current activities.

- Set up time or Change over times should always be targeted for reduction. This is a good area to focus in on, as it impedes flow.

The Airplane simulation was developed by Visionary Products, Inc. (www.visionaryproducts.biz)

Section 06 - Day 2 (Part A) - Scrap Cost Calculations

In this simulation, one minute is equal to one hour of real time.

Timer at 00:00 – Event – Start Production

Workstation 1 delivers into the queue of workstation 2. However, we are still producing in batches of 5. Workstation 2 delivers into the Queue of Workstation 3. Note how all workstations have been arranged in a Cellular Layout next to each other. This will reduce the transportation waste experienced in Day 1.

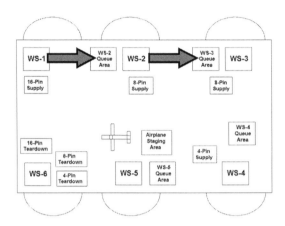

Timer at 01:04 – Event – WS-3 Start the White Airplane

Operator 3 makes the white plane first and decides to switch fixtures to measure the plane length. Inappropriate processing occurs as the fixture should have been right at the point of use (POU) and not on the other side of the room. The effort to reduce set up time has been compromised.

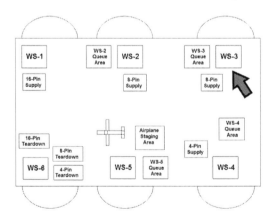

Timer 02:33 – Event – Changeover Occurs Again

Operator 3 is allowed to skip the 2nd Change Over in order to preserve the integrity of the simulation. She is also allowed to correct defects. The batch is finally delivered into the Queue of WS-4 in good order. Watch for Unnecessary Inventory between stations beginning to accumulate. Note how it becomes the source of some confusion.

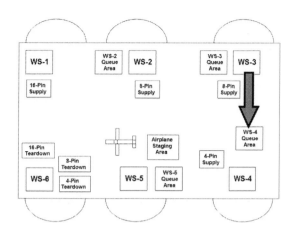

Timer 04:22 – Event – Batch of 5 Received in Queue of WS-5

Open communication has allowed operators to alert each other to Defects and make on the spot improvements. Operator 4 delivers into the Queue of Workstation 5. We have experienced an enhancement in Cycle Times from all of the workstations.

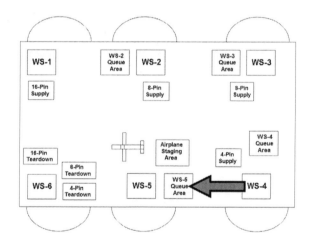

Timer 05:06 – Event – Batch of 5 Airplanes are Passed to Inspection

The first batch of 5 airplanes passes inspection. They are briskly moved into Workstation 6; ready to be shipped to the customer. Operator 6 is glad to be able to record a better Lead Time than was experienced in Day 1. We reach the 6-minute mark before the next batch arrives.

The Airplane simulation was developed by Visionary Products, Inc. (www.visionaryproducts.biz)

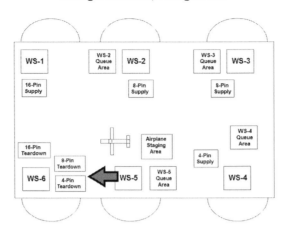

Timer 06:00 – Event – Whistle blows – What if we had a bad batch of steel?

> Scrap Exposure Costs

On Day 2 of our simulation, we stop once again at the 6th hour of production to collect data and calculate our *exposure* to scrap costs.

Sky-View Ariplane Company

Scrap Costs Calculation

16 Pin Cost: $10,000.00			8 Pin Costs: $5,000.00			4 Pin Cost: $3,000.00		

Day 2				Scrap							
		16 Pin				8 Pin			4 Pin		
	Sub Assy's	Parts per Assembly	Total Parts	Cost	Parts per Assembly	Total Parts	Cost	Parts per Assembly	Total Parts	Cost
Workstation 1											
	43	2	86	$ 860,000	0			0		
Workstation 2											
	14	2	28	$ 280,000	5	70	$350,000	0		
Workstation 3											
	5	2	10	$ 100,000	8	40	$200,000	0		
Workstation 4											
	5	2	10	$ 100,000	8	40	$200,000	6	30	$ 90,000
Total Sub Assy'	67									
				$ 1,340,000			$750,000			$ 90,000

Total Scrap Cost $ 2,180,000

It is important to note that, although we have improved our production, we now have even more subassemblies between work stations.

The total number of subassemblies is 67. This works out to $1,340,000 for the 16 pin parts used, $750,000 for the 8 pin parts, and $90,000 for the 4 pin parts used. The grand total of our company's exposure to the scrap cost problem is $2,180,000. It has become apparent that we have become more efficient at producing airplanes, but also more efficient at producing scrap. This is a problem that SVAC does not wish to have.

Section 07 - Day 2 (Part B) – Inventory Carrying Cost Calculations – Cycle Times

We have 2 minutes left in our Day 2 production.

Timer at 06:33 – Event – Another batch of 5 Airplanes completed.

During the last two minutes 3 batches of 5 are completed for a total of 15 airplanes. Operators are experiencing some success towards reaching their goal of 24 airplanes per day. They are still far from achieving this goal though.

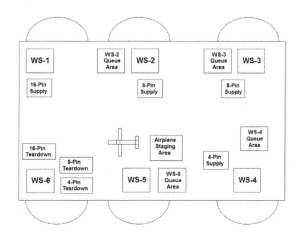

At the end of day 2, we stop and calculate what our carrying costs are.

Sky-View Ariplane Company

Inventory Carrying Costs Calculation (WIP)

| 16 Pin Cost: $10,000.00 | | 8 Pin Costs $5,000.00 | | 4 Pin Cost: $3,000.00 | |

Day 2		Inventory									
		16 Pin			8 Pin			4 Pin			
	Sub Assy's	Parts per Assembly	Total Parts	Cost	Parts per Assembly	Total Parts	Cost	Parts per Assembly	Total Parts	Cost	
Workstation 1											
	52	2	104	$ 1,040,000	0			0			
Workstation 2											
	11	2	22	$ 220,000	5	55	$275,000	0			
Workstation 3											
	6	2	12	$ 120,000	8	48	$240,000	0			
Workstation 4											
	4	2	8	$ 80,000	8	32	$160,000	6	24	$ 72,000	
Workstation 5											
	0	2	0	$ -	8	0	$ -	6	0	$ -	
Workstation 6											
Total Sub Assy'	73										
				$ 1,460,000			$675,000			$ 72,000	

Total Inventories $ 2,207,000

Carrying Cost per Month (2%) $ 44,140

The number of subassemblies in Day 2 is greater than in Day 1. The total # of subassemblies is now 73. This works out to a cost of $1,460,000 for the 16 pin parts used, $675,000 for the 8 pin parts used, and $72,000 for the 4 pin parts used.

This gives us a total of $2,207,000. We get charged 2% monthly for the carrying costs of having this inventory. This works out to $44,140 per month. It is a substantial amount to be paying out and SVAC realizes that they still have challenges that need resolving.

> Cycle Times

Let's take a look now at our cycle times between workstations.

Improved Airplane Production

Workstation Number	Cycle Time	TAKT Time	C/T (sec) for 5 Planes...
1	4.2	17.9	21
2	15.2	17.9	76
3	22.4	17.9	112
4	15.8	17.9	79
5	5.2	17.9	26

$$\text{TAKT Time} = \frac{\text{Available Time}}{\text{Customer Demand}}$$

$$= \frac{430}{24}$$

$$= 17.9$$

We mentioned earlier that our TAKT time is 17.9 seconds. This means that all of our cycle times should be less than 17.9 seconds. We observe that SVAC has achieved this goal in four out of the five work stations. Work Station 3 is still producing at a cycle time that is higher than the TAKT time. This is enough to hinder the company from producing the 24 airplanes that need to be guaranteed before they can accept their new contract.

Let's compare the graphs of Day 1 versus Day 2.

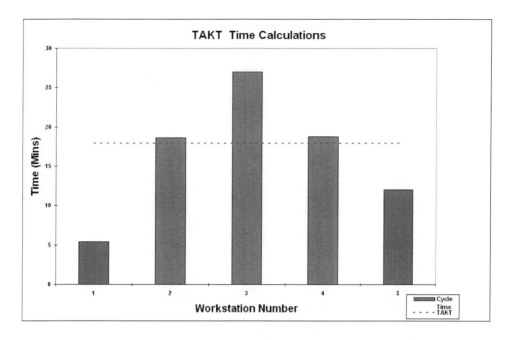

Day 1

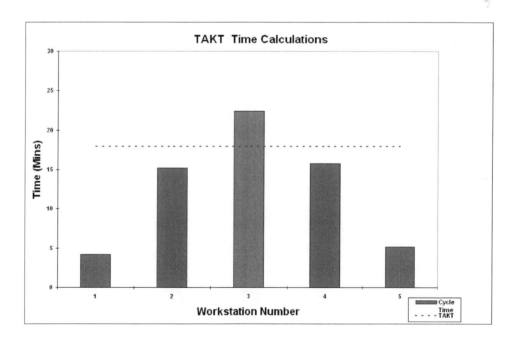

Day 2

Day one has 3 work stations not producing to the required TAKT time. Day 2 has only 1 Work Station producing to the required TAKT Time. A conventional, non-lean solution to Day 2 is that an extra operator could be placed at Work Station 3 in order to bring down the cycle time and meet production goals. Unfortunately, this would not eliminate the large amount of inventory scattered throughout the plant.

The Airplane simulation was developed by Visionary Products, Inc. (www.visionaryproducts.biz)

This still poses problems in the areas of scrap cost and inventory carrying costs. Another issue is that the entire inventory lying around gives rise to the presence of the seven wastes. This would jeopardize SVAC's ability to guarantee their customer 24 airplanes per day. It becomes obvious then, a better system is needed.

> **DAY 3 – REST OF THE IMPROVEMENTS**
> * **Rebalance the workload ✓**
> * **Reduce the lot size from 5 to 1 ✓**
> * **PULL from the customer ✓**

Four of the seven improvements were implemented during Day 2. This has not yet yielded the desired results.

During Day 3, we will add the rest of our desired improvements thus achieving a much-improved lean system. We will rebalance the workload. Operators are given new instructions to follow at their workstations. As the workload is rebalanced, the changes that occur at two given workstations are as follows:

Workstation # 1

Days 1 & 2   Day 3

For Workstation #2 and Workstation #3 the concept was similar, we distributed workload to balance between operators. Workstation #4 looks like the picture below;

Workstation # 4

Days 1 & 2   ## Day 3

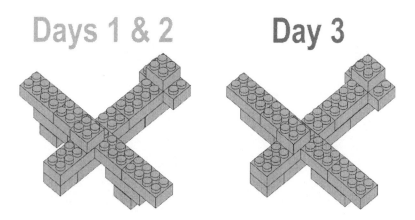

Obviously we are missing the landing gear, and in this case Workstation #5 has that additional duty along with inspection. I might point out that there needs to be a buy-in by the team for these types of changes to occur. It is always easier to get buy in when everyone knows "Why?" they need to change.

Why – in order to take on more work.

What – we need to implement "Lean Thinking" principles

How – through brainstorming, and good facilitation by George, we identified the initiatives that will get us to the future state.

We further reduce the lot size from 5 to 1. We do this by creating a simple rule. All operators must adhere to this rule. There must never be more than one plane in any given work station, also there must not be more than one plane in the queue of any workstation downstream from the operator. Once the queue has been emptied, the operator can place his or her completed subassembly into it and begin working on the next one.

Pull from the customer. By using this signal created by an empty queue we have created PULL. This in turn triggers a chain reaction wherein each of the workstation is signaled to build one more in order to replenish the supermarket.

In the next section, we return to our interlocking-plastic blocks simulation for the 3rd day of work. Management is excited about the prospect that this time their goal should most definitely be reached. The task of successfully building 24 airplanes is now in sight.

The Airplane simulation was developed by Visionary Products, Inc. (www.visionaryproducts.biz)

Section 08 – Day 3 (Part A) - Scrap Cost Calculations

As previously, one minute is equal to one hour of real time.

Timer at 00:00 – Event – Start of Production

Cycle Times improve dramatically this round:

- Between WS-1 and WS-2 = 4 seconds

- Between WS-2 and WS-3 = 3 seconds

- Between WS-3 and WS-4 = 6 seconds

- Between WS-4 and WS-5 = 5 seconds

- Between WS-5 and WS-6 = 14 seconds

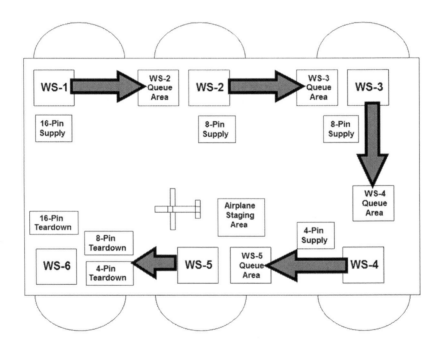

Timer at 00:32 – Event – First Airplane is shipped

The first batch arrives at Workstation 6 in 32 seconds. Lead Time has been cut down considerably. At this point, operators have **PUSHED** the first batch of 1 all the way through the system. From here on, all workstations are operating on the principle of **PULL**.

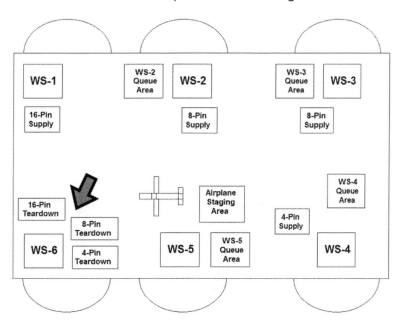

Timer at 01:58 – Event – The Team is shocked at the Improvement

Production has become efficient to the point where operators experience moments of down time. This is used to prep raw materials so they are ready each time a new plane comes through the system. Down time is short lived due to a re-balancing of the workloads at all workstation.

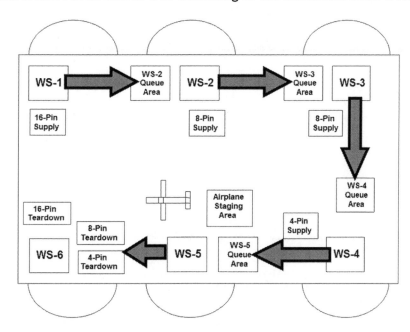

Timer at 3:52 – Event – Synchronization of Production Achieved

There is never more than 1 airplane in any of the Queues and/or in any of the work areas.

At the 3-minute mark operators have already assembled 15 airplanes.

At this point, operators are producing airplanes faster than Sales can sell them.

The Airplane simulation was developed by Visionary Products, Inc. (www.visionaryproducts.biz)

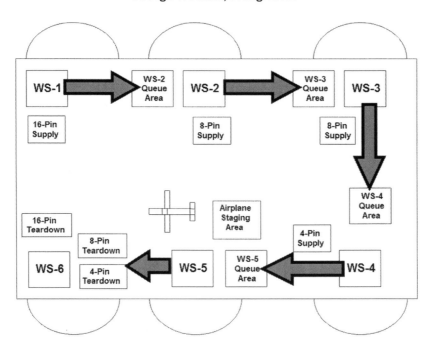

Timer 06:00 – Event – Whistle blows – What if we had a bad batch of steel?

On Day 3, our sixth hour of production, we stop to collect our data and calculate our *exposure* to scrap costs. It is important to note that we have dramatically improved our production as well as reduced the number of subassemblies between workstations.

Sky-View Ariplane Company

Scrap Costs Calculation

16 Pin Cost: $10,000.00		8 Pin Costs $5,000.00		4 Pin Cost: $3,000.00

Day 3	Scrap									
		16 Pin			8 Pin			4 Pin		
	Sub Assy's	Parts per Assembly	Total Parts	Cost	Parts per Assembly	Total Parts	Cost	Parts per Assembly	Total Parts	Cost
Workstation 1										
	2	2	4	$ 40,000	0			0		
Workstation 2										
	1	2	2	$ 20,000	5	5	$ 25,000	0		
Workstation 3										
	2	2	4	$ 40,000	8	16	$ 80,000	0		
Workstation 4										
	0	2	0	$ -	8	0	$ -	6	0	$ -
Total Sub Assy'	5									
				$ 100,000			$105,000			$ -

Total Scrap Cost $ 205,000

The total number of subassemblies is 5. This works out at a cost of $100,000 for the 16 pin parts used, $105,000 for the 8 pin parts used and $0 dollars for the 4 pin parts used. It is apparent that there is a lot less inventory sitting on the plant floor, waiting to be assembled.

The grand total for our company's exposure to scrap cost is $205,000. These are much better results than experienced in both Day 1 and Day 2. We are now overly effective at producing airplanes. This is a good problem to have. Our scrap problem has been minimized. SVAC will have to slow down their production or else sell more airplanes. Everyone votes for selling more airplanes!

The Airplane simulation was developed by Visionary Products, Inc. (www.visionaryproducts.biz)

Section 09 – Day 3 (Part B) – Inventory Carrying Cost Calculations – Cycle Times

Timer 08:00 – Event – Whistle blows – End of Production for Day 3

During the last two minutes operators have completed enough airplanes to bring the total to 39 airplanes shipped.

They have become a well-oiled, efficient, super-airplane-producing machine. Their superiors are very pleased with performance and will be providing sizeable wage increases for all operators in the plant.

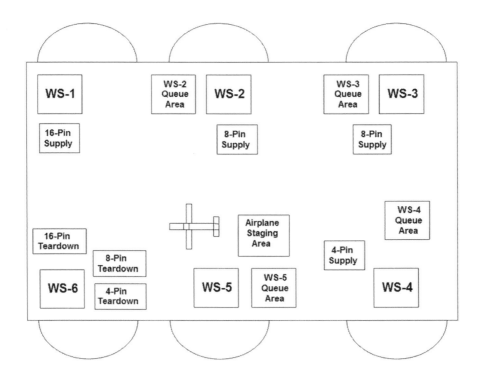

We now stop and calculate what our inventory carrying costs are. The number of subassemblies in workstations is dramatically less in Day 3 than it was in Days 1 & 2. Total number of subassemblies is now 5. This works out to $100,000 for the 16 pin parts, $90,000 for the 8 pin parts, and $0 dollars for the 4 pin parts used. The total worth of the SVAC's inventories is $190,000. We get charged 2% monthly for the carrying cost of having this inventory. This works out to $3800 per month. This is a much lower amount to be paying than that of Day 1 or Day 2. SVAC realizes that they have been able to exceed their goal to be able to produce 24 airplanes per day.

Sky-View Ariplane Company

Inventory Carrying Costs Calculation (WIP)

	16 Pin Cost: $10,000.00			8 Pin Costs $5,000.00			4 Pin Cost: $3,000.00		

Day 3				Inventory						
		16 Pin			8 Pin			4 Pin		
	Sub Assy's	Parts per Assembly	Total Parts	Cost	Parts per Assembly	Total Parts	Cost	Parts per Assembly	Total Parts	Cost
Workstation 1										
	2	2	4	$ 40,000	0			0		
Workstation 2										
	2	2	4	$ 40,000	5	10	$ 50,000	0		
Workstation 3										
	1	2	2	$ 20,000	8	8	$ 40,000	0		
Workstation 4										
	0	2	0	$ -	8	0	$ -	6	0	$ -
Workstation 5										
	0	2	0	$ -	8	0	$ -	6	0	$ -
Workstation 6										
Total Sub Assy'	5									
				$ 100,000			$ 90,000			$ -

Total Inventories $ 190,000

Carrying Cost per Month (2%) $ 3,800

Let's take a look again at our cycle times between the work stations. Our TAKT time is 17.9 seconds and our cycle times should be less than 17.9 seconds. We observe that SVAC has achieved this goal in all five workstations on Day 3. There is nothing to hinder the company from producing the 24 airplanes that they need to guarantee before they can accept their new contract.

Improved Airplane Production

Workstation Number	Cycle Time	TAKT Time
1	4	17.9
2	3	17.9
3	6	17.9
4	5	17.9
5	14	17.9

$$\text{TAKT Time} = \frac{\text{Available Time}}{\text{Customer Demand}}$$

$$= \frac{430}{24}$$

$$= 17.9$$

Here is a graph (workload balance chart) comparison of Day 1 & 2 versus Day 3. Our best scenario is to make all the changes we have brainstormed. Day 3 improvements are the logical choice. A new bottleneck has emerged in the area of sales. SVAC will now look at improving their marketing and sales departments in order to meet the new demand created by their increased ability to produce their product. They need more customers.

The Airplane simulation was developed by Visionary Products, Inc. (www.visionaryproducts.biz)

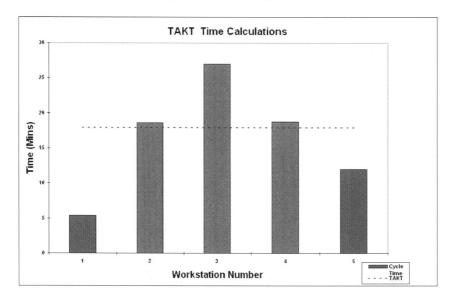

Day 1 – Cycle time calculations show that WS-2, WS-3, and WS-4, does not meet Takt time.

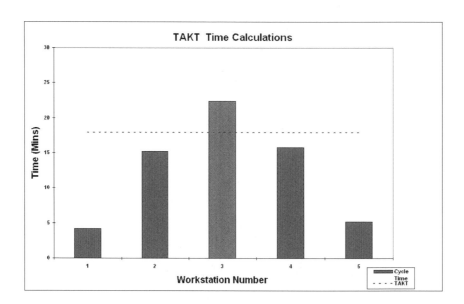

Day 2 – Cycle time calculations show that WS-3 does not meet Takt time.

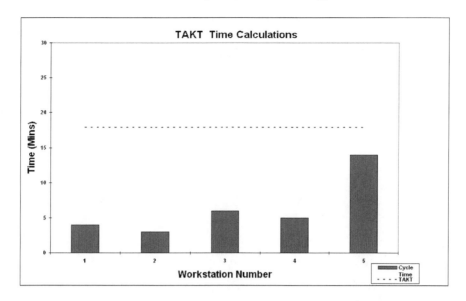

Day 3 – Cycle time calculations show that we are below Takt time, and can easily meet demand.

Section 10 – Evaluating the Final Data (Part A)

The production went from 4 planes the first day to 15 on the second, to finally 39 planes per day.

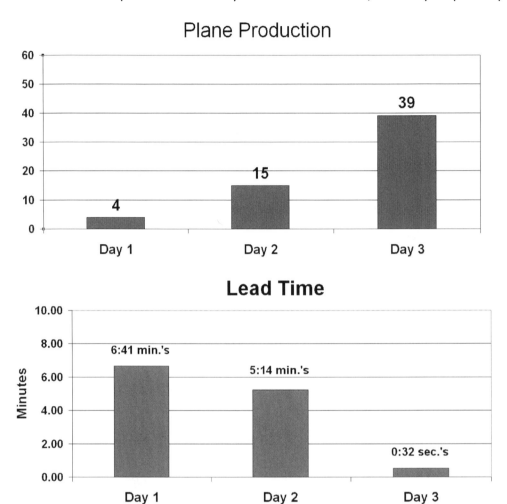

Lead time came down dramatically to get that first plane through. Now why did that lead time come down?

Lean results in a better system

What about scrap?

DAY 2 – produces more SCRAP

The system is such that we got more efficient at creating scrap during Day 2.

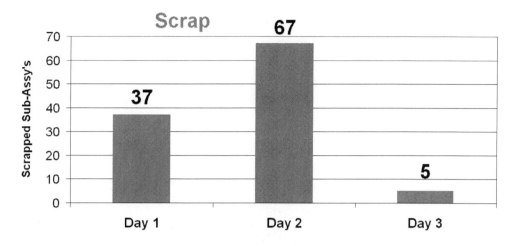

Then in Day 3, we went down to very little scrap again. As we forced the system to control the amount of inventory, the result was predictable.

DAY 3 – better inventory control

We placed the limit to no more than one in the queue and no more than one in each area. As we counted the scrap there should have been only one in queue and one in building – the system didn't allow us to have more scrap

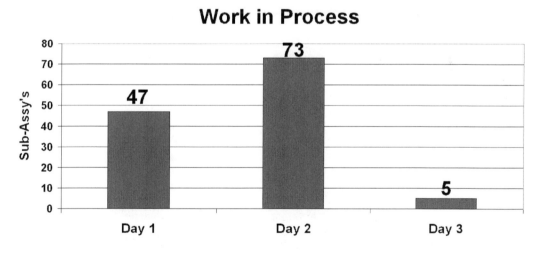

We had a lot of inventory in Work in Process. Same thing, Work in process went down.

All C/T must be less than 17.9 minutes

We wanted it to be under 17.9 minutes per plane in order to commit to the 24 planes we needed to get our contract.

The Airplane simulation was developed by Visionary Products, Inc. (www.visionaryproducts.biz)

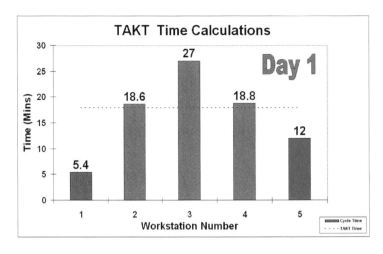

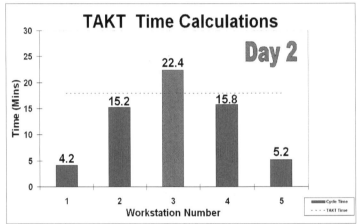

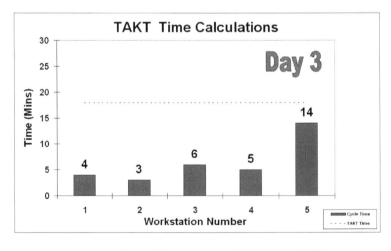

DAY 3 – able to make 24 planes

Can we guarantee 24 planes for our customer? We sure can, now!. But we still have waste in the system. Where is the waste?

The Airplane simulation was developed by Visionary Products, Inc. (www.visionaryproducts.biz)

DAY 3 – we are overproducing

Let's look at Day 3, Where is the bottleneck? We will talk about a bottleneck rather than waste. Workstation 5 appears to be the bottleneck, but is it really? How many planes do we need to produce? How many did we produce here? We actually produced 15 more planes than we needed. We do not have an internal bottleneck. So where is it coming from? Sales and marketing!

TAKT Time must be adjusted

So if sales went out and sold more, they could increase the demand. The TAKT time would come down. We found we could produce more so we should be pushing sales to sell more. This should be easy considering our new production lead time. They could take orders away from our competitors. That is exactly what they should do. And how can they do this? Not only have we increased the number of planes per day that we can deliver, but we have reduced the per-plane cost, which means we can sell at a lower cost than our competitors, and maybe even make more profit!

If you look at all these changes at the end of Day 2, you will note that we only did half of them and we did not do a very good job because scrap was high. Things were still chaotic; we got more efficient at making scrap. But after implementing all of the changes, we're doing way better.

So overall, if we implement the complete system we are doing great. If we implement half a system, the results are skewed. We know we are doing well, and on the right track, but the results won't show us how well we are doing. They are skewed.

Efficiency, now what do you think the efficiency was? Day 1, Day 2, & Day 3. From an efficiency standpoint, does everybody know what efficiency means in manufacturing? Efficiency is like doing it to a standard, and do we do it to that standard, yes or no?

How close are we to standard?

An engineer went to workstation 1, timed how long it takes to perform the work. When the operator is not hitting that time and taking longer, then they are less efficient. 100% efficient, is if they did it 100% to the standard in the standard amount of time. So in looking at these numbers, which do you think has the highest standard, Day 1, 2, or 3? Based on how many we are supposed to make.

The Airplane simulation was developed by Visionary Products, Inc. (www.visionaryproducts.biz)

In order to calculate efficiency levels, we need to prorate the time being wasted between workstations. In an exercise outside of this one, the standards were calculated. The task for us was to compare the actual to the standard to get efficiency. On Day 1, you could say that the efficiency rate was at 85%, while Day 2 was at 94%. Does that make any sense? We were working a lot harder during Day 2. We produced a lot more scrap as well, making us a lot more efficient at producing scrap as well as assemblies. Finally, during Day 3, this might come as a surprise: 76% efficient. We got a lot more product out the door, but our efficiency was lower. Any ideas as to why. Why on the day that we get the most planes out, would our efficiency be the lowest?

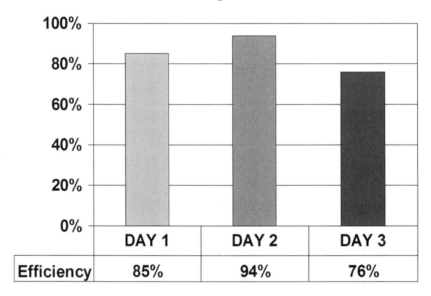

A lot of manufacturing companies use efficiency as the number one metric but they don't look at the whole operation. They don't try to optimize both, efficiency and reduce lead time at the same time.

> Efficiency does not look at the whole.

As a matter of fact, when we looked at this with PAL Manufacturing, everybody said "that's crazy, let's not do that again." Although a company wants to get stuff out the door as quickly as possible, it's best that we look at the entire system, not just how well one operation is doing.

However it was pretty shocking to see how bad our efficiency was on Day 3, which was our best day. Efficiency is therefore not a good indicator by itself. In this case, the best gauge would be the number of defect-free planes shipped.

The Airplane simulation was developed by Visionary Products, Inc. (www.visionaryproducts.biz)

Section 11 – Evaluating the Final Data (Part B)

Sky-View Airplane Company

Achieving a Future State

Let's now talk about the operator balance Chart.

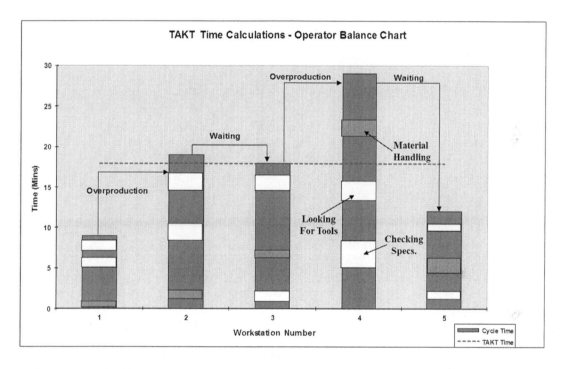

When we first started off, we're asked to take a look at this chart. WS-1 was producing way better than the TAKT time. The cycle time was below the TAKT time. So what happened between WS-1 & WS-2? We had overproduction, which results in inventory piling up.

What happened between WS-2 & WS-3? We had waiting, because one operator was going faster than the other one. That means that somebody's waiting, right?

What about between WS-3 & WS-4? We had overproduction; as you are waiting, inventory builds up, and this is even slower so you've got inventory building up.

And between WS-4 & WS-5? Waiting, yet again.

Now that we know how each situation looks, we have to go from one WS to another and look for the wastes. It all makes sense when you look at the graph. - This is how it would look for SVAC.

The Airplane simulation was developed by Visionary Products, Inc. (www.visionaryproducts.biz)

The wastes we have identified at are overproduction and waiting, then overproduction and waiting again.

Sky-View Airplane Company

So the future state of this company went to 13.3 days lead time and 87 minutes Value added time. We implemented changeover reduction, implemented pull and point of use inventory.

Sky-View Airplane Company

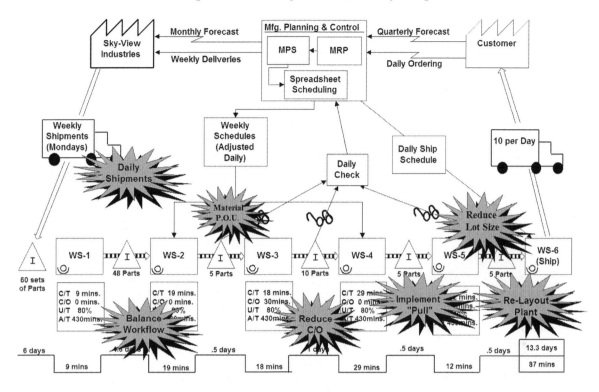

FUTURE STATE QUESTIONS

1. What is the TAKT Time?
2. Will we build to shipping or to a supermarket?
3. Where can we use continuous flow?
4. Where do we have to use supermarket pull system?
5. At what single point in the production chain do we trigger production?

We have to ask ourselves: how are we going to produce to a TAKT time. Remember TAKT time production is the heartbeat of the customer. How do we make sure that we internally are producing to the customer's needs? How do we pull the inventory through to create a continuous flow? At what point in the production chain did we trigger something to be produced? We had a system at the end of Day 3.

Let's assume that we are coming into work at SVAC at Day 4. What needs to be done before any plane can move out of the system? There is only one point at which we have to do something and then everything else is triggered and happens automatically. We just need to ship one plane.

The Airplane simulation was developed by Visionary Products, Inc. (www.visionaryproducts.biz)

This creates an empty queue, which is the start of the day's production. If we develop a system like that, no matter where it is, whether in retail, production, office, we've got little waiting and little overproduction because everyone knows what to do and when to do it. This is how the whole production chain works.

> **FUTURE STATE QUESTIONS**
>
> 6. How do we level the production mix at the pacemaker process?
> 7. What increment of work will we release and take away at the pacemaker process?
> 8. What process improvements will be necessary to achieve your future state?

We do not want one person working harder than another person. However, we should make problems visible. So having someone standing around while everyone else is working is a sign that a problem exists. This is good. We need signs like this so that we can focus on the problem.

The title of this graph should read "Cycle Time Calculations". Takt time is consistent at 17.9 min.

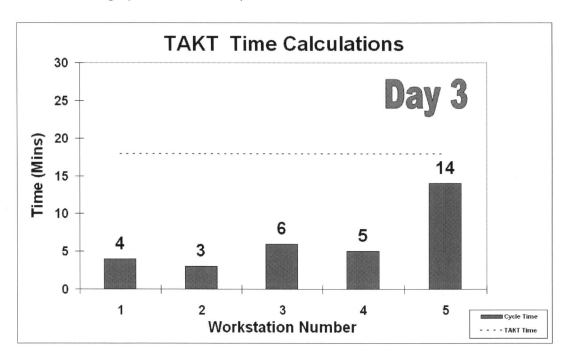

Problem: Our assembly operation is "over-producing" to the customer demand.

Solution: Ensure everyone is cross-trained, identify the total FULL-TIME people needed in the area. Finally, resource the area properly (allow 15% of their time to go to continuous improvement)

Recognize that in a Lean implementation we respect the people and their families, by reducing the workforce in this assembly area, we need to find other, more meaningful work for those that are re-assigned.

By adding up the C/T you get 32 minutes. Three operators would be able to produce to the takt time and have extra time for continuous improvement activities. The other two operators are freed up to work with the engineers in new product development. The company should be working on securing their future in the marketplace.

Here's how we are going to get the job done so let's go do it! Let's test it. If it doesn't work and we are at Day 2 instead of saying it doesn't work, we are going to make changes and do it the right way so that it works on Day 3. Then, we will implement slowly and make sure that as we are going through we don't introduce too much change as we are in it for the long run.

If you look at this value stream map, you will see a supermarket at the end of WS-5. The internal customer, WS-6 - shipping, pulls and ships to the customer. This triggers WS-5 and signals it to produce more work.

Sky-View Airplane Company

WS-5 takes it from the queue which triggers WS-4 to produce more work. WS-4 does the same which triggers WS-3, WS-2, and WS-1 to do the same.

Why does this daily schedule show information going to WS-1? What are they producing? Two models which come in two colors: green and white. The schedule tells them what color needs to be produced. If the customer calls and wants a white plane, we have to tell WS-1 to start making one. Otherwise no other WS is affected by this change. This is why the sequence or Final Assembly Schedule has to go to WS-1.

> **Lean does not change;**
> **We change.**

The Airplane simulation was developed by Visionary Products, Inc. (www.visionaryproducts.biz)

Section 12 – Day 3 (Part C) - Review & Conclusion

> **REVIEW**
> **SEVEN FORMS OF WASTE**
> - Overproduction
> - Waiting
> - Transportation
> - Inappropriate Processing
> - Unnecessary Inventory
> - Unnecessary Motion
> - Defects

Let's do a quick review of the 7 wastes, we covered all of them.

Here is a quick way to remember them. For the 7 Wastes, you might want to remember them as "Tim Wood".

> **SEVEN FORMS OF WASTE**
> **"TIM WOOD" ACRONYM**
>
> | | |
> |---|---|
> | T | Transportation |
> | I | Inventory |
> | M | Motion |
> | W | Waiting |
> | O | Overproduction |
> | O | Over processing |
> | D | Defects |

That's one way to remember all the wastes. But don't forget the other two wastes. They are the waste of human potential, and the waste of complexity. Typically organizations do not use the thinking power of their employee, and everyone gets stuck on situations that are more complex than they need to be.

> **REVIEW**
> **THE 5 PRINCIPLES OF LEAN THINKING**
> - Define value from the customer perspective
> - Identify the value stream
> - Make the process flow
> - Pull from the customer
> - Strive for Perfection

These are the five principles of Lean thinking. This is where we started.

As soon as you are doing the first 4 principles right, the fifth one is in sight. You can see things getting way better and you are starting to move into that direction. Keep on exposing problems, and solving them, and ensure you have a system to do that.

Skill Testing Question:

We want to go from 10 pieces per hour to 20 pieces per hour in Operation #3. All we have to do is invest $100. Should we do it?

Production Line

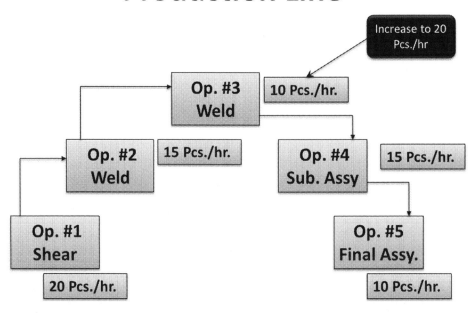

This is a system. You should not spend a single dime on any area other than the bottleneck. If you look at the above, there are different quantities of production at each station.

Even if you spent money at Operation 3, can the current system produce more? No. So you would be wasting your money. The system has to be the entire process we are looking at. And by the way, what if sales could only sell 8 Pcs. /hr. then there is no point looking to increase production.

In 1926 Henry Ford turned Iron ore to a finished car in 41 hours. That is pretty lean isn't it? Why were cars only available in black? It was the fastest drying color. So even in those days, they were thinking lean since the black paint contributes to shrinking the lead time.

In 1943, B-17 bombers were being built by farmer's wives. They actually built 17 B-17 bombers every day.

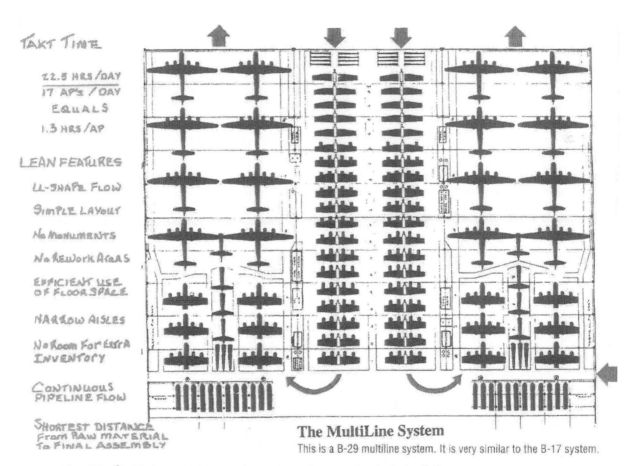

TAKT TIME

$$\frac{22.5 \text{ HRS/DAY}}{17 \text{ AP's/DAY}}$$
EQUALS
1.3 HRS/AP

LEAN FEATURES

LL-SHAPE FLOW

SIMPLE LAYOUT

No MONUMENTS

No REWORK AREAS

EFFICIENT USE OF FLOOR SPACE

NARROW AISLES

No ROOM FOR EXTRA INVENTORY

CONTINUOUS PIPELINE FLOW

SHORTEST DISTANCE FROM RAW MATERIAL TO FINAL ASSEMBLY

The MultiLine System
This is a B-29 multiline system. It is very similar to the B-17 system.

ACHIEVED 60% REDUCTION IN MANHOURS REQUIRED PER AP.

Here is the actual plant floor layout. When you look at this, you can kind of see the flow. Every 1.3 hours the line would move. What is that called? It's the TAKT Time. They balanced the cycle time of every operation to 1.3 hours. In those days, they were already implementing lean. The concept is very simple. The problem is that we think we need to be engineers to understand it. As an engineer, let me tell you that most engineers do not know this because many of our institutions do not teach them the history and these lean principles.

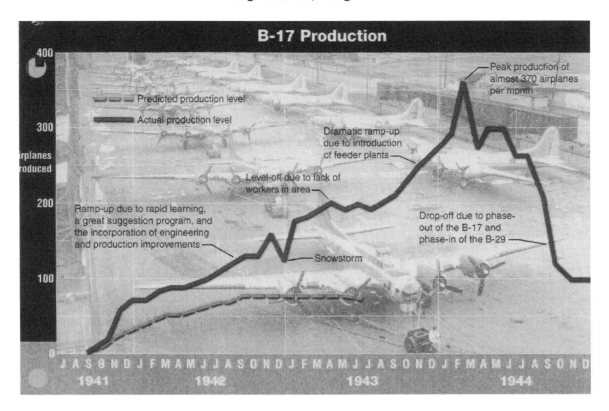

Production skyrocketed from 1941 to a peak of 370 airplanes per month in March 1943. This translated to 17 planes per day. The war forced manufacturers to have to do things differently. The workers they hired had little or no knowledge of how to build planes. Neither did the managers. So they got together and decided collaboratively (in a Lean way) how to build planes. They used sketches on the front lines to describe the build process, and every day they thought about how to do it better - they had to - their husbands and sons were depending on it. What do you think happened after that? The experts came home and they started companies. They were doing it right in those days and that is what a lot of manufacturing companies are going back to today.

CONFUSIUS SAYS:

What I Hear - I Forget…
What I see - I Remember
What I Do - I Understand

What I hear – I Forget   90% of what is heard is forgotten.

What I See – Remember   Approximately 50% of what you see you remember.

What I Do – I understand   the airplane simulation that we did was an exercise that should stay with you because you participated in the activity.

Cash Flow Example

Lean is all about Cash flow. It is about reducing the time from order to cash. Cash is what pays the bills. Effectively lowering your Cycle Times (C/T), increasing your throughput, and reducing cash-to-cash lead-time is what it is about. Regardless of what other books say the following diagram shows a typical manufacturing environment headed for disaster – this is how most companies go broke.

Current State

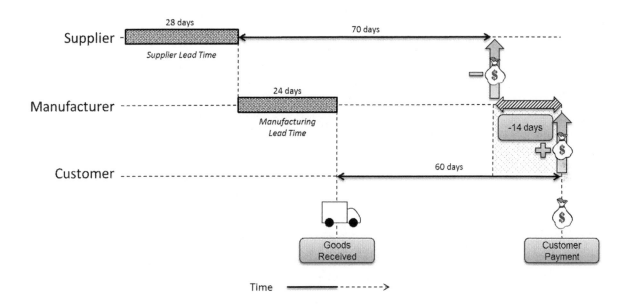

In the current state, we notice that:

- The Supplier Lead Time is 28 days and that the manufacturer has 70 days payment terms.
- The Manufacturing Lead Time is 24 days, which encompasses everything from the manufacturing process to the delivery of the goods to the customer.
- The Customer has payment terms of 60 days, effective from the time the goods are received.

Many companies have this kind of situation for doing business. These same companies experience cash flow problems sooner or later. This becomes a bigger problem when the customer orders increase or grow. With more customer orders come more requirements, with more requirements comes a greater need for raw materials.

With more raw materials more money is owed to the suppliers. This is the situation that companies fall into. This business will not survive in the long run.

This visual represented by the current state shows a cash flow deficit of 14 days, which means that the company is out money 14 days (for that order) before it receives money from the customer.

After Lean principles are applied to the manufacturer, we see that the manufacturing cycle has been reduced from 24 to 4 days; this reduction completely changes the cash flow situation from a deficit to a surplus of 6 days.

After Lean Application

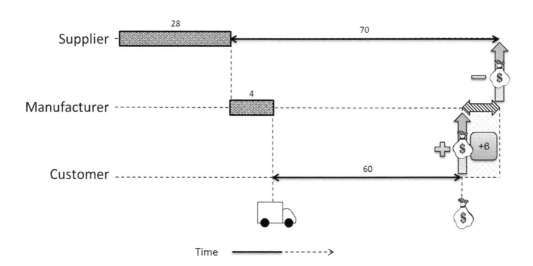

While this has significantly improved the manufacturer's cash position, it can be improved even more by sharing these strategies with your suppliers. This means that your business is taking ownership of its entire value stream. The subsequent diagram shows how the cash flow surplus can be further enhanced. By working with the supplier to improve their lead time, we expect a drastic drop in the supplier lead-time from 28 days to 7 days. With overall improvements in supplier and manufacturing lead times, customer payment terms can then be negotiated, in this case down to 30 days.

Future State
Applying to Entire Value Stream

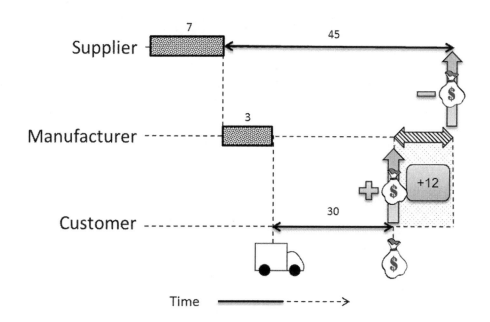

The bottom line is that everyone is happy. The supplier gets its materials out faster and gets paid much quicker. The customer gets its order delivered sooner. The manufacturer gets the benefit of having established a more efficient fulfillment stream. This always results in attracting more customers, and by removing much of the waste out of the process the manufacturer can also become more competitive in their pricing. But don't forget, the gains don't stop there. By repeating this process over and over, we continue to work on the right stuff, and instill the principles within our organizations.

We suggest your next steps be:

1. Purchase the Airplane Game and have your people "play" it.

   (www.visionaryproducts.biz - ask for a discount)

2. Hire a lean coach to help you through your lean transformation.

You might say "Why do I need to hire a lean coach? I'll just apply what I've learned here."
Good answer. You have all the knowledge to get the job done yourself. But, if time is a factor, or you are in a crisis mode and you need help, then ask for it.

And while we are talking about lean coaching, keep in mind that OEM Consultants has a GLOBAL network of coaches who have experience in many different industries and many different cultures and countries. OEM guarantees results. 'OEM Lean 101' implies that the concepts are very simple. And they are.

In fact, the concepts are so simple that anyone can go design a future lean system if they understand them. You need some experience to go through and make things happen and like all journeys, going down the lean journey, starts with a first step.

I really hope that this chapter inspired you to take that first step. Make the mistakes, fall flat on your face, pick yourself back up, and continue, because that's what this is all about.

If you get in trouble, and need a coach, you now know to Skype me at george.trachilis

"Without constant attention, the principles will fade. The principles have to be ingrained; it must be the way one thinks"

Taiichi Ohno, creator of the Toyota Production System (TPS)

CHAPTER 3 – The OEM Way – Principles of Lean Thinking - Redefined

Every business can apply Lean Thinking to dramatically change the way it does business, and the way it executes in delivering value to its customers. OEM Lean Thinking represents the best of Lean Thinking and adds strategy and long-term thinking to the mix. As an example, my consultants are scattered throughout the world, and I offer every one of them my OEM Lean101-Principles course as FREE training. In this way they are able apply these principles into any industry that they consult with. Every one of them is an independent consultant and therefore works for themselves. When they use OEM's name, and OEM methodologies, they gladly pay me 15% of their revenues related to that work. I am able to secure the right people for the right job at the right time, every time I need the additional help. My cash outlay is zero. My customers all pay me in advance of doing work for them, and I guarantee my clients results when I am done consulting with them. My problem is as follows;

How can I duplicate my processes?

I teach my consultants the basics through my OEM Lean101 series of courses, and further develop them and their thinking in the field in which they are aspiring to be an expert.

This book represents for my consultants, a starting point of the basics that must exist in their thinking. We call these mental models. We can also call them rules to live by. It is the "Know How" that we get from our experiences. Unfortunately everything about Lean Thinking is not obvious. And quite frankly it is counter intuitive if anything.

This book is the ticket to becoming an OEM Consultant. By implementing these principles in your business, industry, country, or even in your home life, you are able to guide others in the process of continuous improvement. There is a reason that these principles have guided Toyota to be recognized as the best company in the world. Use these principles, and together with our other OEM Consultants, let's work on Striving for Perfection as a team.

The 1st Principle of Lean Thinking:

know.

There is a pitfall immediately evident in **Defining value from your Customer's Perspective**. It is that you may not have specified who your customers are in the future, not just today. By working solely in your current marketplace, you are not creating new ones. History has shown us that this is a big mistake. Very few businesses can operate with product life cycles as long lasting as "cars".

Are you talking about creating future value with your current customers?

What about your future customer's needs and requirements?

Are you investing in your future - creating markets where there were none?

I considered the answers to these questions to be addressing the **Silent Voice of the Customer.**

I am currently creating another on-line course called the OEM Lean101 – Product Development. I am putting it together with Ronald Mascitelli. I learned a very interesting technique from his training years ago. It is the "dollar-more" technique. Simply put, would your customer pay "one dollar more" for a feature that you are designing for them?

There is only one of two possible answers to this question, yes or no. If the answer is no, then don't do it. Think about it.

Why? Why should you not add more value than the customer is willing to pay for?

In design they named this attribute *over-shoot.* Not adding more value than the customer is willing to pay for is a philosophy that everyone should be aware of. As an example, say you own a company that does design work for other companies. If your employees are working at adding more value (based on their perception) into the product or service, then they are wasting time. Let me explain it in this way. If the customer is not willing to pay for the EXTRA work you are doing, then who is?

Today organizations such as design companies are getting smarter about how they do business. They don't always deliver a finished design; they may be in the business of delivering a service. They identify with a profit model that allows them to grow in a less risk way. This model may be a "cost-plus" business model. This implies that if they take 100 hours to do a job, then they get paid for 100 hours. These hours should contain a profit margin that allows them to be competitive.

know.

Companies that compete for the same market share are in a scenario where:

PROFIT = SELLING PRICE – COST. The only factor that they have control over is COST.

know.

It is a difficult job to acquire the end user's needs when even they cannot articulate them. You have to PULL it out of them.

The entire organization must understand that saving 1 minute per person per day will result in the organizations productivity doubling in 3 years. The enemy of this kind of thinking is their current profitability. If there is no case for change, then people say, "We are making a lot of money, why are we changing anything?" The more profitable a company is the less the urgency there is to change. It is management's responsibility to ensure that the company remains that profitable in the future. Just like it would be government's responsibility to ensure that their country remains viable, and does not go broke. It is usually evident after the fact.

This is a meter-maid car used by New York City; it has many advantages over a large vehicle.

This is the gas, hybrid-electric, and electric version of the vehicle designed specifically for NYPD.

The inevitable is that if a company/organization does not allow its leadership to be 85% busy looking working on the future, it will be in trouble. We can call this continuous improvement, or strategy. Regardless of the name the leadership must look for new markets, identify new opportunities, define new customer requirements-not yet satisfied and ensure their company's future existence. An organization chooses to remove itself from the future landscape that they call their market by losing focus on the future.

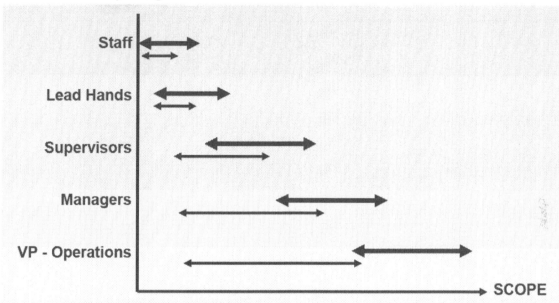

Companies should identify the time frame (scope) in which the organization operates, and adjust accordingly – from the current to the future. Each organization may look different depending on their business, product or service. Understanding the ideal is important.

A good way to adjust the scope of responsibility is to recognize the difference between strategic initiatives versus tactical initiatives. One area most companies have a problem with is that they do not clearly communicate and separate strategy from tactics. Regardless of your position in the company, you should understand why you are working on an initiative. You should be able to trace every initiative to the top of the organization's directives.

Making use of an X-Chart is excellent for making this connection between strategy and tactics.

X Matrix			Program Level	Employee Engagement to 80% by December	Increase Inventory turns to 12	On-time Delivery to 99% by December	Gross Margin to 30 % by Dec.31, 2010	Vehicles in sales pipeline to ..... By	George Trachilis	Production Manager	Purchasing Manager	Manufacturing Engineer	Design Engineer
⊙			Implement "Quick and Easy Kaizen"	⊙	△	△	O		⊙	O	O		△
⊙			Develop Value Stream Management Process								⊙		
O			Define True North Broad Brush Goals						⊙				
⊙			Develop A3 Problem Solving in all organizations							⊙			

Strategies (left side): Implement Lean Thinking Principles · Zero Production Defects by Dec.31, 2010 · Reduce Cost of Goods Sold by 35% by Dec.31, 2010

TACTICS / STRATEGIES / METRICS / RESULTS

Accountability
Respect
Root-cause

	Results		Employee Engagement
	Revenue	110 M	
	Gross Inventory	$38 M	O
	Inventory Turns	12	
	Gross Margin (%)	20	⊙

LEGEND

⊙	Direct / Team Leader
O	Strong / Team Member
△	Weak / Rotating TM

Correlation / Contribution

An X-Chart looks complicated but it is not. On the left hand side you would place your strategies. This would be the direction that the senior leadership is giving the organization. If you do this right, you pass on the responsibility to the remainder of the organization to fill in the tactics. As in the example above, **Implement Lean Thinking Principles** is a Strategy. The management team may have defined 4 TACTICS required to implement this strategy. One of them is **Implementing "Quick and Easy Kaizen"**. The area to the left of this tactic represents the correlation to the tactic. If you look at the bottom right of the chart the LEGEND identifies this as a **Direct** correlation. This means that the team feels that the successful execution of this tactic will have a direct impact on the strategy. All of the way to the right side of the tactics are the team members. As you can see from the legend again, George Trachilis is the Team Leader in charge of implementing this tactic. In between the team members and the tactics are the METRICS. The correlation (contribution) of the tactic towards the metrics are shown. As an example, implementing "Quick and Easy Kaizen" has a weak correlation to the inventory turns metric. Finally, you can also see at the bottom of the chart that we expect Employee Engagement to contribute directly to the Gross Margin and have a strong correlation to decreasing inventory to $38 M.

For large organizations the tactics at the top level become the strategies for the lower level. It is interesting to describe an organization as having a top level since my view of an organization is as follows;

2 Way approach

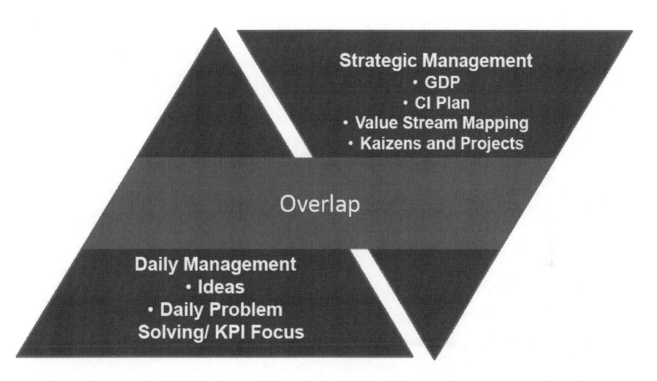

Support from the top of the left pyramid is given to the management team to work with every employee on developing problem solving skills, and encouraging ideas that are implemented. Support from the tip of the pyramid on the right goes towards the strategic plans of the company and projects that will make the company more competitive in the future. The Overlap is a challenge.

The "Value Test" should be performed where initiatives are identified that are not in the current plans of the organization.

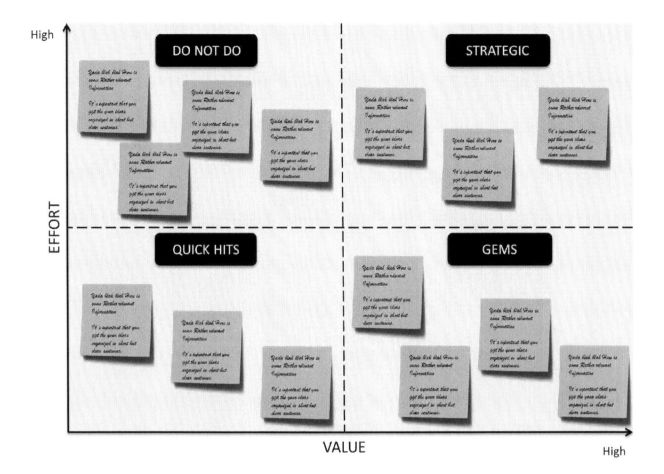

The value test is a simple sticky exercise with the team. On a sticky they identify the initiative that they want to do that is currently outside of their responsibility. As a team they identify whether the initiative requires **More Effort** or **Less Effort**. Then they identify whether the initiative is of **High Value** or **Lower Value** to the team. Finally, they place the sticky in the quadrant and take a step back and look at their results. The team should elevate the STRATEGIC initiatives to upper management, they should do the QUICK HITS, but place them in a later priority than the GEMS. From this exercise, performed monthly, they should have an excellent engine for change.

The time that you spend on tactics versus strategy depends on your position in the organization. A good ratio to use is 85% strategy and 15% tactics for the most senior levels in the organization, and the ration should reverse to 15% strategy (continuous improvement), and 85% tactics (standardized work) at the most junior level.

Our goal at OEM is to attain the knowledge that exists in this world that gives our clients the competitive advantage over their competitors. This is the main reason for writing this book. The airplane simulation is the most efficient way to describe Lean Thinking. There are techniques that give every business an advantage over their competitors. Lean Thinking is a philosophy that deploys a lot of techniques that work at delivering value sooner with less effort.

The flaw in using the customer's perspective.

To get the customer's perspective you need the eyes and the voice of the customer. Most organizations don't have the luxury of having their customer come in every day and observe what is happening. They don't produce a to-do-list every day so that the manager can call the team together and work on improvement.

There are a couple of problems with the customer's perspective, one is that we don't have the customer present every day in our business to clarify what they would pay extra for. The other is that we need to help our customers define what they really want. At times, the customer does no know what they want until we give it to them.

Regardless of these problems, the first principle of Lean Thinking has absolutely no value unless our organizations can execute as a valued partner in their supply chain. Engaging our entire work force to define customer value is an excellent daily exercise. We help everyone become problem solvers and provide opportunities to celebrate daily.

The 1st Principle – the OEM Way:

Engage everyone in delivering value to your customer's future requirements.

Use everyone in your organization to achieve the ideal state for your customers. In order to understand your ideal state, you need to understand where your customer's ideal state is. Draw an ideal state map – and post it for everyone to see. Make sure your company is directly tied to your customer's company. In this way your customer knows that you are committed, not just involved.

The basic fable runs:

> A Pig and a Chicken are walking down the road. The Chicken says, "Hey Pig, I was thinking we should open a restaurant!". Pig replies, "Hmm, maybe, what would we call it?". The Chicken responds, "How about 'ham-n-eggs'?".
> The Pig thinks for a moment and says, "No thanks. I'd be committed, but you'd only be involved!"

Sometimes, this story is presented as a riddle:

In a bacon-and-egg breakfast, what's the difference between the Chicken and the Pig?

The Chicken is involved, but the Pig is committed!

OEM uses a simple kaizen form to get everyone committed to this change in behavior, on in which problem solving is a requirement, not a nice to have.

Kaizen is a Japanese word that is becoming popular throughout the world. This is because there is deep meaning behind the word. In order to apply this type of process you must engage every worker in your company to do the same thing the customer would want. Saving money is really the outcome of improving processes, which result in saving time.

Most organizations have FEAR smack in the middle of them when it comes to implementing change. This fear is devastating. Initiatives from the top are deflected because of it, and middle managers never make the expected changes. Also, initiatives from the bottom are deflected and middle management again do not take these initiatives up to the senior levels. Driving fear out does not work either. The fact that you have to drive it out means that you are using fear to get rid of fear. Instead, introduce safety and respect to everyone in the workplace. I implemented Quick and Easy Kaizen in 2006. It's the easiest system with the highest value that respects people. But you as the leader need to have trust in your employees.

 How does the Quick and Easy Kaizen work?

- ✓ Employee gets an idea
- ✓ Employee talks to the supervisor – gets approval.
- ✓ Employee makes the change (with help if needed)
- ✓ The change is inspected by the supervisor and receives a thank you!
- ✓ The **My GEM** form is filled out by employee
- ✓ The **My GEM** form is posted on wall.

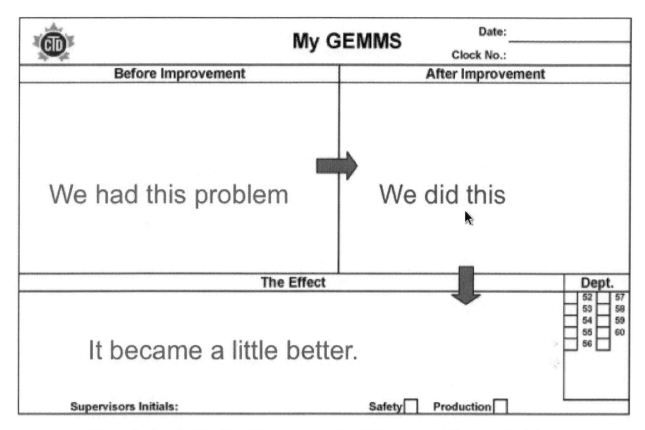

From the book, *The Idea Generator* by Bunji Tozawa and Norman Bodek.

At the time, the "production system" that I introduced was called GEMMS, Growth-Enabling Manufacturing and Management System. Whatever you call your system of doing business it is important to engage everyone in the company in making sustainable change happen.

There are a few rules in introducing this kind of dramatic change in your business. The most important is to educate the group on what this is. Then don't let them leave the room until everyone has filled out a form. In this way, the fear of doing it is gone.

- ✓ Keep it Simple
- ✓ To the point
- ✓ 3 minutes or less
- ✓ less than 75 words

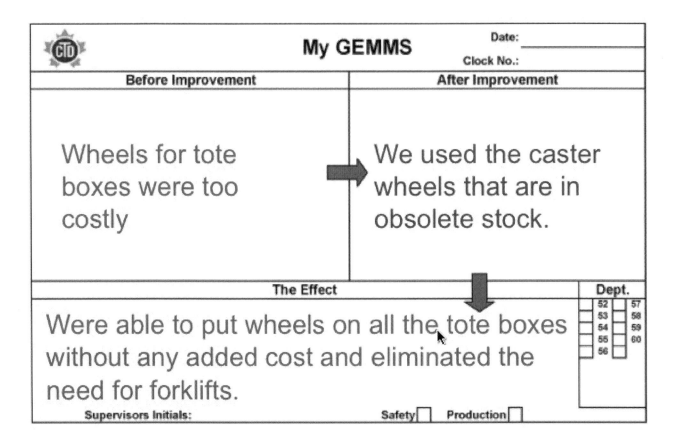

Each month we celebrated our team success with the improvements and each month we put the best of them on the wall. We considered people treasures, and celebrated their minds and what they can do with it if given a chance by management.

Celebrate the wins on a daily basis. As a manager, ensure that you compliment someone four times before you give them one piece of constructive criticism.

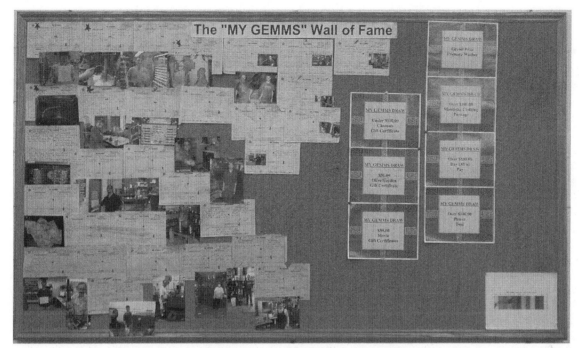

By engaging everyone in the company to THINK we were able to minimize the Waste of Human Potential almost immediately. This required going to the place where the action was daily, the *Gemba*. Making sure that people were encouraged rather than criticized was the key to launching respectful processes that required engagement. If criticism starts, and is allowed to continue, consider your lean initiative over.

Make all things visible. The flow of information and product should be easily understood by everyone entering the organization.

Making the customer's needs visible goes a long way towards everyone satisfying those needs.

The 2nd Principle of Lean

Define the Value Stream

A value stream is represented by all of the activities, value-added and non-value added that deliver a product or service to the customer. In manufacturing, the value streams are relatively easy to identify. A more advanced course than this is needed to explain it in depth, but there is a lot of literature out there on manufacturing.

Let's look at an industry that you are all familiar with, health care. This industry confuses the hell out of me. I continue to be surprised at how mismanaged this industry is. I lost my grandfather 30 years ago and my father 10 years ago, due to mistakes made by the same hospital, in the same city, in Canada. And Canada is known for its excellent health care system. Although it was not the same mistake, it doesn't make me feel any better.

Toyota produces a car that is close to "defect-free". However, we cannot produce procedures in a hospital that are defect free. What is the world coming to?

 What value do we put on a patient? Based on reality, it is less than a car.

Imagine if you will that we are going to apply Lean Thinking to a hospital setting. First, we identify the customer. Then identify the stakeholders. Then follow this process;

1. Consider the hospital a machine and form a perimeter around it.
2. Identify all of the patients over a period of one year that have entered the perimeter.
3. Identify all of the reasons that they are there and group them into value streams.
   a. Emergency
   b. Cancer Care, etc.
4. Identify each value stream and identify the future demand on each value stream.
5. Pick a value stream to improve.
6. Identify the current state of that value stream, draw a current state map.
7. Identify a future state of that value stream. Draw a future state map.
8. Identify the actions that get your current state to become the future state and assign teams and owners
9. Do the actions.
10. Review every week for 3 months and perform a formal check of the entire process.
11. Repeat the entire process over and over again, until the customer is happy.

What do you consider non-value added at a hospital? What you will find, is that the same wastes that apply to a manufacturing facility apply to a hospital setting. In this case, the raw material is you, and each time you go into the hospital, value should be added. But is it?

The wastes in a manufacturing facility as they may apply to healthcare are;

1. Transportation (the patient being transported more than they need to be)
2. Inventory (the excess routine paperwork)
3. Motion (the nurse leaving the room to get materials that should be present)
4. Waiting (the patient waiting in queues with others)
5. Over-production (the patient moved too quickly from one area just to wait in another)
6. Over-processing (the patient undergoing procedures that they don't need)
7. Defects (Error's made in any part of the process)

Do you think the waste of human potential applies in a hospital setting?

Do you think the waste of complexity applies in the healthcare industry?

These wastes are directly translated, and more can be found specific to each industry. When lean is applied to industries other than manufacturing there is a need to make accommodations regarding naming these wastes. Make it an exercise with your team.

What is clear is that you must identify what you are trying to optimize first. That is what you should call the value stream. If the value stream is the doctor's time, then you have just missed out on the first principle. Who is the customer?   THE PATIENT!!!

I cannot emphasis how important it is to do these steps in the right sequence.

know.

First identify with the customer, or the "voice of the customer". Then identify the value stream.

There are many value streams when it comes to health care. As an example, you can choose Patients that require emergency care. The value stream may also have many paths of complexity that require simplification.

The eighth, and ninth waste are; Waste of Human Potential, and Waste of Complexity apply as much as the first 7 wastes. Not surprisingly, by NOT using everyone's knowledge appropriately we have created a system in which little learning is happening. The Waste of Complexity is not visible to many in that industry until they allow the "fresh eyes" to come in and scrutinize processes and question everything as a child would. Why? Why do we do this? Why is it done that way? Do you think we can do it this way? Why?.

Today when I take an organization through a Lean Thinking implementation, I help them create an Ideal State Map before they create the Future State Map. I ask the team, "Imagine if there were no bottlenecks in your value stream, how would you go about delivering value?" The ideal state map allows everyone on the team to look at the world of tomorrow. To identify an ideal amount of time that it should take to deliver the value. After that future is created, I start asking the questions, "Why can't we do it this today?". Asked differently, "Be specific, and tell me what is preventing us from achieving this future state now?" Of all the answers, 50% are mental blocks and are not founded in reality.

The 2nd Principle - The OEM Way

Commit to Continuous Value Stream Management.

Create the organizational structure that will put the right attention on the value stream. Creating titles such as C.V.O or Chief Value Officer may go a long way in encouraging the right behaviors. It becomes very difficult for a manager with silo responsibility to become product focused as well as manage a large group of people. That is why value stream leaders are created. These individuals immediately focus on the product flow through the organization (or information/service flow), not the people flow. As the C.O.O. at the time, it was important to ensure that the change towards the new way of doing business was solidified.

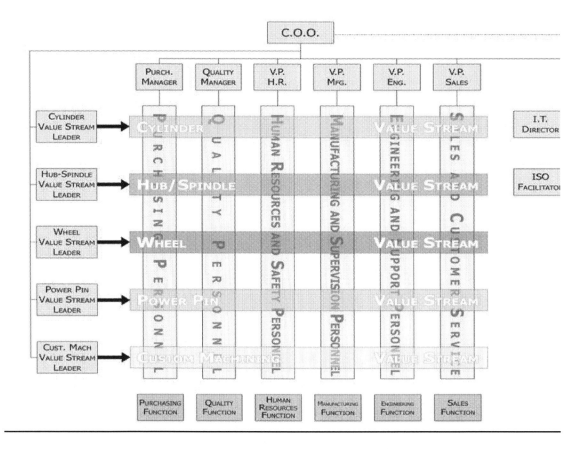

It was critical that each value stream leader understand what their job was. The primary function was to take the organization from **Current State** – to – **Future State**, and then repeat the process over again, and then again repeating this process we had market domination. This type of endless pursuit of improvement was the key to understanding what the journey was about, and what Value Stream Management is about.

The manufacturing industry in North America is well along the way of understand what Lean Thinking is, but what about other industries?

Value Stream Mapping –Dentist Office

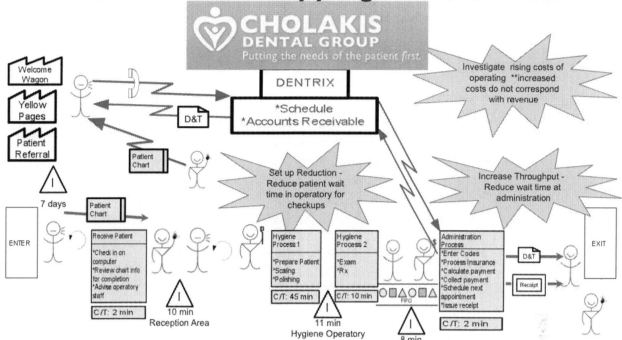

I was sitting in my dentist's office one day, with my mouth wide open. I don't know how I managed to get the words out, "You need to apply Lean Thinking to your practice". Well my dentist just happened to be one of the most forward thinking dentists in the country. Not only did he take me up on my offer but he also demanded that his suppliers get aligned with him so that he can deliver an experience for his customer's that exceeds their expectations.

When we started mapping out this process, it became very evident that the process was exactly the same as in a production environment. We needed to identify the current state with the team, and communicate it on a whiteboard or piece of paper. All that was missing were a few icons. The rest of the ingredients were there. We created an icon for every position in his organization, and used the other basic material and information flow icons to communicate the current state.

  Collections,   Hygienist,   Receptionist, etc.

By considering the patient as being the product, we mapped what the patient experiences as being the process. By mapping the entire value stream, it became evident to everyone else that in order to improve drastically certain suppliers needed to be considered as an extension of the business. So we included them as part of the whole. This extended value stream included the manufacturer of bridges and crowns. Success meant daily deliveries and this daily demand was made visible by the creation of a scheduling board.

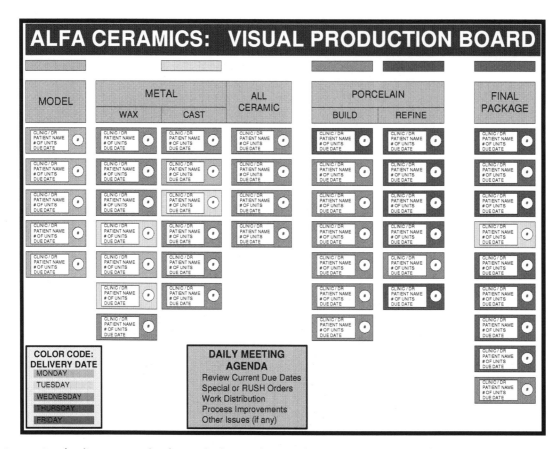

Alfa Ceramics (a direct supplier) needed a tool to understand the dentist's requirements, that tool was a visual board. I had the pleasure of working with Alfa recently, six years after the initial introduction of Lean and I can tell you that the visual tools are still there, and being used.

know.

When things make sense to use, people use them, when they don't, they don't.

Make the Value Stream Management Process Visible

Value Stream Mapping Process

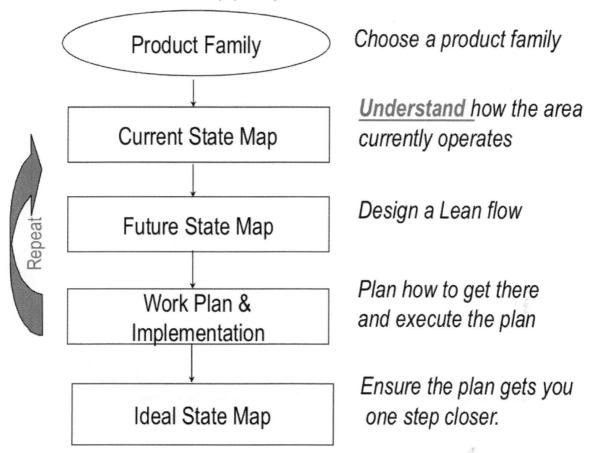

Product Family	*Choose a product family*
Current State Map	*<u>Understand</u> how the area currently operates*
Future State Map	*Design a Lean flow*
Work Plan & Implementation	*Plan how to get there and execute the plan*
Ideal State Map	*Ensure the plan gets you one step closer.*

During the Lean flow design, make sure to use lots of whiteboards, and stickies. Try to visualize how the future design will work, and predict problems in advance. Make sure that you identify areas of responsibility by placing a loop around it. In this way, someone is responsible for the entire from of the product or service from beginning to end in that loop.

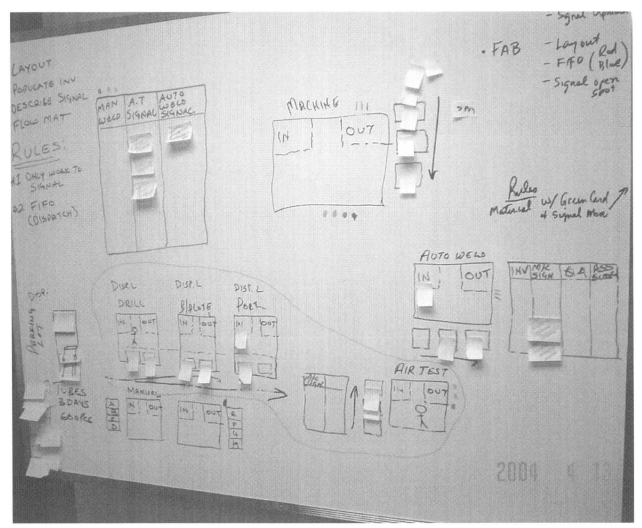

Try using a time phased approach to the simulation, pretend one hour goes by… then ask what happens? By releasing stickies into the flow that represent incremental work, the team gets a feel for the challenges that may arise. Then repeat this over and over to understand the problems in the design.

You will notice a line circling 4 operations. This is called an implementation loop. The reason for circling these operations is that they represent flow of the product within the value stream. One person should be responsible for the loop of activities. These natural loops usually start and finish at supermarkets.

The Value Stream Mapping Steps are;

Step 1. Gather information about the customer

Who is the main customer(s)? What is the customer demand? Packaging requirements? Draw customer icon on the sheet, and place all relevant information below the icon.

Step 2. Walk the process

Walk the process through at least once before you begin drawing. Then begin at the end closest to the customer (shipping) and move your way upstream. Draw the process boxes.

Step 3. Fill in data boxes and inventory levels

The data collected needs to be appropriate for the area, i.e. cycle time, machine capacity, shifts, people, etc. Document where inventory is held. (Remember, this will be a snapshot in time.)

Step 4. Document how goods are delivered to the customer.

How often? In what quantities? Mode of transportation?

Step 5. Gather information on your suppliers

Who are the main suppliers? How are materials delivered? Quantity? How often? If you have a large number of suppliers, focus on the largest ones first (possibly two or three).

Step 6. Add Information Flows

How does the customer communicate requirements to us? How are the requirements communicated to the floor? How do employees know what to build? How does the supplier know what to send and when to send it?

Step 7. Sketch how material moves between processes.

Is it pushed, pulled, FIFO, etc.?

Step 8. Draw production lead-time/value-added timeline

This is added at the bottom of the current state map. It is good practice to calculate the % VA time. Simply divide the value added time by the Total Lead Time and multiply by 100 to get Percent VA.

The Value Stream Map is a visual picture of how the business functions. The VSM is a tool used in the Value Stream Management Process.

The Value Stream Management Process also has 8 steps, and they are...

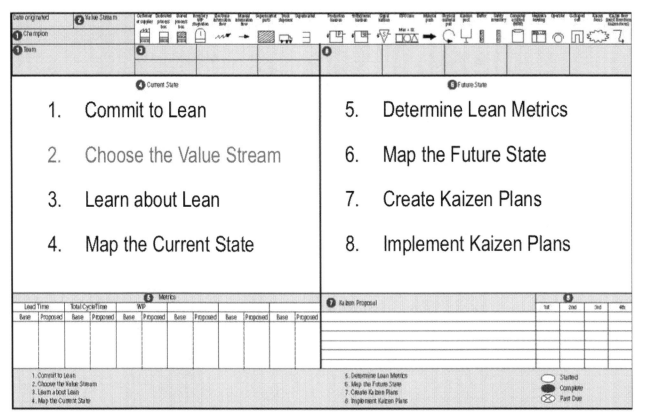

From *Value Stream Management* by Don Tapping, Tom Luyster, and Tom Shuker

Don't forget that repeating these steps over and over, and over again, will develop the habits and behaviors that make an organization "Lean". Until you achieve your ideal state you are not done. That is why this is called a journey. You never arrive so ensure the journey is exciting for everyone. Enjoy the problems that arise, and treat your people like treasures in the process.

The 3rd Principle of Lean:

Make the process Flow.

know.

Flow is achieved when the value you deliver takes the theoretical minimum time required to deliver it. This next example should shock you.

What if we were value stream mapping the healthcare system – say, a hospital. And what if the customer was considered to be the patient requiring assistance.

What would an ideal state map look like for healthcare service to the patient?

This Lean Healthcare system considered the patient the *thing going through the process*. And what if they measured the delays and defects that you experienced as being something to eliminate. Imagine, the hospital's success would be measured to be how long it takes to satisfy your needs. Here is how it would look.

Imagine that you (the patient) are working fine, then, all of a sudden something goes wrong, and you are dizzy. In the year 2020 (let's say) you are equipped, like most cars, with a GPS device (on a bracelet). The device knows something went wrong. It triggers your local ambulance. What is unique is that in the year 2020, a doctor must accompany every ambulance. The doctor slides down a pole (like a fireman would), and gets all of his/her equipment (which really should be in the ambulance), and is transported to your location.

On the way, he/she reviews your chart, knows your name, has a picture of you, and mentally stores it. Then the doctor arrives no later than 9 minutes and 59 seconds (Single-Minute Response Time – not double digit). Finally after all that time, you are looked at, diagnosed, and if done right the first time, we have a good system. This system needs to be further improved by reducing their response time to 9 minutes and 58 seconds on average. Then 9 minutes and 57 seconds on average. Then 9 minutes and 56 seconds on average. Until finally, they figure out what the root cause of why you got dizzy was, and share the findings so that no one in the world gets dizzy again.

I would be happy if someone in the healthcare industry thought of my time as being more important than the doctor's time. That would be a good start. I am the patient, and I have rights in this new world that I am creating for myself. Remember flow is about one thing and one thing only. Minimize the time it takes for the value to be delivered. This is why a defect-free production is a minimum requirement towards achieving the ideal state. Remember this is a dream, and not reality. The ideal state is just that, a dream. But how powerful would your organization become if you could deliver on that dream.

Making the process flow is the realization that each future state map tries to deliver on. It gets people believing that it might be possible, at a minimum, aligns the future state maps so that they are heading in that direction. This gets us one step closer to our ideal state. Create the ideal state with the people doing the work, not just with the managers. This way everyone understands what your vision is, and everyone can be enlisted to help your organization get there.

The problem with Flow is the reality of getting it to happen.

Three weeks after I wrote the above section in this book, I met a friend that I have not seen for 20 years. I was coming out of a small 10-person company that I took on as a client. They supplied the dental industry with crowns and bridges, and other dental components. My friend told me he worked in that industry as well. He has been working on setting up a mobile dental services industry. He explained that his business was quite unique. He told me that his staff was mobile. they go to where the demand is for their services. Many of his clients are located in nursing homes. They set up the entire dental office in the building wait for the patient and the dentist to arrive.

I was not surprised, as I am not surprised much with innovative ways to get the job done. What I would have been surprised with is if he had 20 vehicles travelling the city doing this type of activity. I asked him how long he has been in business, and the answer was 5 years. Then I asked "How many vehicles do you have doing this kind of work?", he said, "one". I then asked, "Why? Why only one?", it seems like a great idea, and it should catch on, why only one vehicle?

 What is the problem with his business model?

The answer was too obvious; the dentists that he talks to are not interested in getting out of their offices to help in this fashion. They are comfortable doing things the way they used to.

Today, I make quick work of assessing a company's ability to execute on the techniques related to Lean. If they are not willing to deal with the tough stuff, and the tough stuff is all related to people, then I don't work with them. The only way to get out of this mess - previously created in our companies/organizations - is to get people/employees excited about the good they are doing by helping their fellow human being. Education and enthusiasm go a long way in explaining the WIIFM, what's in it for me?

There is a theory that we are all 100% selfish. Everything we do, we do for ourselves. Why does this theory have so many followers?

Of course, after appealing to everyone's good side – if the results don't come, policies may just need to be written for the greater good. You see, there are two types of motivation, crisis, and leadership. My job is to help create leaders that will take the road less travelled, and if that is selfish, so be it.

The 3rd Principle - The OEM Way

Target the ideal state and remove barriers that keep you from achieving it.

One of the most powerful ways to solve a problem is eliminate incremental approach to getting to the future. The incremental approach was described earlier though achieving the future state, over and over again. In this case, try to achieve the ideal state as soon as possible. Do the stuff that get you the biggest return on your time spent. This means that you are measuring the gap from the ideal state backwards, not the current state forwards.

I was promoted by one of my customers to helping their customer. Their customer was Princess Auto. This is a chain of stores across Canada known for catering to "the man". They are proud to be known as "man" stores. They have everything come through their store at some point throughout the year. The way that they advertise is through a flyer that is sent to millions of customers throughout the country. In this way customers (a good portion are farmers) come to the store only when they know that their trip into the city will be worthwhile. Only when they know the store has what they want.

This happens to be a picture of the cover of their flyer used when we performed a test to see how far from the ideal state we were. The VP of Operations, at the time, asked me to help them get organized in the store. He knew what we did with their manufacturing division was excellent, and wanted some of the same benefits. Well, manufacturing and retail are different, but everyone is able to explain what the ideal should be for the customer. The customer should be able to find what they want in the store as soon as possible. Especially considering that they have a picture in their hand.

Devise an appropriate test to determine the gap from the ideal state.

The test that I devised was one of determining the customer's ability to find goods. We came up with what we called the 20-item test. We circled an item on every second page of the flyer and asked the store manager to find these items in the store. We also knew that a customer would have a much harder time, but it was irrelevant, we are measuring the ideal, not the current state.

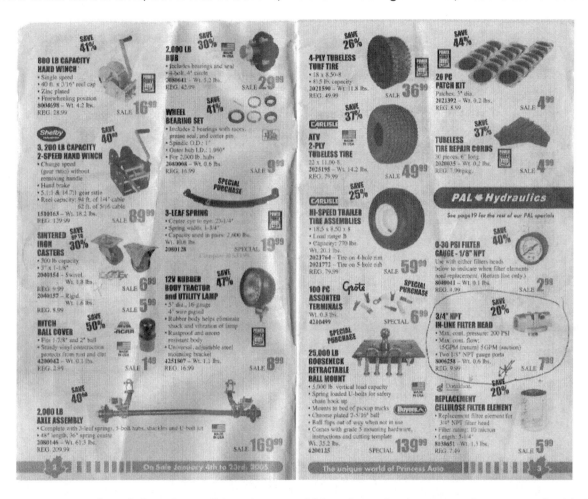

The manager predicted that the walking time would be about 6 minutes, and we agreed with his calculation. The test was performed early in the morning when the store was closed to the public to ensure that there were no distractions. We recorded this test on video to show every team member the results, and more importantly the waste that everyone misses each and every day. The test was very successful. It took 22 minutes, instead of 6 minutes as compared to the ideal state. The gap was huge.

The next step was to analyze where we went wrong. We needed to understand what happened and what did not happen. That is why taking a video recording is critical. There is no way to do this without the analysis. After creating a spaghetti diagram of the path the manager took to acquire the goods, it was obvious that there was no logic applied to his methods.

More importantly there were 5 errors that cost the company about $550 in revenue. It also became apparent that the manager required the use the computer system to look up where inventory was located in the store. We placed only one look in the warehouse, when there were actually about three. Regardless the path the manager took looked exactly as follows;

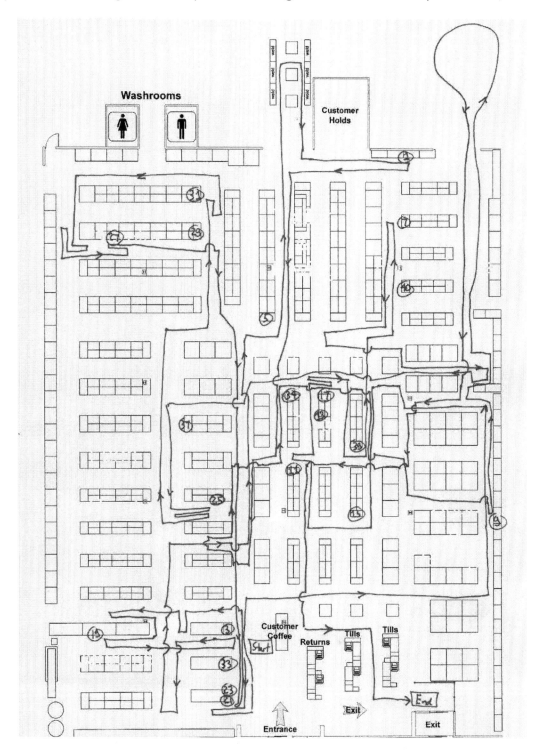

A spaghetti diagram shows the waste of transportation.

Everyone was so excited with the results that we decided to do it again with another two team leaders. The results were the same. When the comparison to the ideal state was done, the questions for the group became the starting point of the implementation.

 What would it take for us to achieve a 6 minute turnaround without any mistakes?

Now the creative juices start flowing. After everyone realized that the best manager/team leader was one of those that took part in the exercise, any criticism as to our approach was eliminated. We eliminate the tendency to blame the person when we use the best person to take part in the exercise. We had great ideas from the team. We ended up identifying certain kaizen events.

These kaizen events were;

- ✓ Develop visual systems to identify promo material.
- ✓ Develop home replenishment system.
- ✓ Develop warehouse management system.
- ✓ Develop system to identify and reduce excess inventory.

Everyone forgets the concept of PULL being a key to working towards an ideal system. Most companies forget how visual things must be in order to eliminate waste of complexity. But that is why I exist as a consultant. I am there to remind them that the pull system works. As a matter of fact, it was the Princess Auto retail team that took part in the airplane simulation in the OEM Lean101 – Principles course http://Lean101.ca.

By identifying the ideal state first, the team was able to get the flyer color coded for all of the stores in Canada. This, along with information centers that were created in each of the areas allowed customers to find things immediately. Eliminating the necessity of asking a team member for assistance.

The initial visual board contained the color-coded flyer and the rack locations for each item.

After running the 20-item test the second time, the results were drastically improved. It took 9 minutes to get all of the items in the cart, and this time, there were no mistakes.

The team should never stop at the first iteration of change, continuing the same journey gets the biggest results.

"Princess Auto has been thrilled with the work that OEM Consultants have done for us. The current project in our Panet Rd. Store has exceeded our expectations and we certainly plan on continuing to work with OEM to roll the project out to other stores across Canada."

Michael Leach, Sr. Vice President, Retail Operations

Princess Auto Ltd.

The 4th Principle of Lean:

Develop Pull from the Customer's Perspective.

Find your customer and develop a way for your customer to ask of you EXACTLY what they want, and when they want it. In this way the customer pulls from you. A Lean Organization calls this a Kanban system. Kanban simply means signal. It is a signal for you to do something. There are usually two types of kanban, one is to move material – or a **move kanban**, and the other is to produce – or a **make kanban**.

Most companies don't realize this but Kanban is a technique to make your process move faster. It is also a technique for the controller of the kanban quantities to force problem solving to happen. By understanding this, you will understand the real meaning of Kanban. Please go to http://lean101.ca/weboffice.htm, join the Global OEM Consortium and pull all sorts of presentations on kanban systems.

Flow where you can - exhaust all possibilities of flow first - then pull in an effort to get to flow.

One Kanban system that I noticed in the restaurant business is the "menu". When you go into a restaurant, and find yourself seated with your family, and each person has a menu. You are then expected to make your choice of food to eat.

The unwritten rule at some restaurants is that when you place your menu at the side of the table, overhanging a little, it means that you are ready to order. This signals the serving staff to come over, and take your order. A Kanban is nothing more than some signal that authorizes or communicates to your supplier that you would like service.

By applying this technique, and understanding the difference between Takt time and cycle-time, opportunities for improvement make themselves obvious. Kanban is a system that should be used for increasing the velocity of a process. Not just signaling some work to get done. By understanding the difference, you can make a consulting business happen from educating the world around you on this one concept.

know.

Norman Bodek, "The Godfather of Lean", was the first person to communicate the Toyota Production System to North Americans, he called it kanban in those days. It wasn't until years later when Jim Womack's team coined the term "Lean" that it took off as a thinking process.

The 4th Principle - The OEM Way

Continually increase flow by removing bottlenecks that impede flow.

My suggestion is to take no prisoners on this topic. Whenever I implement systems that are counterintuitive such as many of the lean concepts, the first thing I hear is "that won't work". I know it's just human nature, and I know I do it too – but it ends up getting under my skin when I am the one wanting the change to happen, and I feel I am consistently meeting resistance.

 Why is there a consistent resistance to change?

What I have it down to is that there must be a law in this world, something like Newton's third law – for every action, there is an equal and opposite reaction.

For that reason, I am showing you best example of Kanban that I have seen in my years implementing this kind of change. It came from one of my coaches in 1996, Bob Bailey, he developed and implemented the kanban systems for Hewlett Packard and later joined Oliver Wight (a consulting firm). I purchased the original slides back then so that I can use them to transition everyone's thinking in my company.

What was the first kanban system known to be?

Milk delivery. In the old days when you were done with the fresh milk, you placed the empty jar outside your door. When the milkman did his run, your jar was replaced with a full one.

know.

The first thing to understand is that kanbans (signals) establish the upper inventory level of your system.

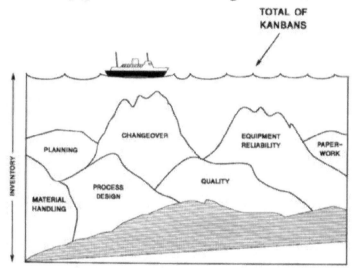

It is the inventory level on a shop floor or in an office that hides problems. Planning, material handling, process design, changeover, quality, equipment reliability, paperwork, and the list goes on. The number of problems are endless. Since we (management) control the number of kanbans, we also control the inventory levels. By controlling the inventory levels, we can choose to expose the next problem so that we, the team, can attack that problem and eliminate it. In this way we have prioritized the next project.

There are two simple rules to kanban production.
1) Never start working unless you have an open kanban
2) Never pass on any known defects

Here is how it works.

Say we have two work centers. Work Center A and Work Center B. In each work center we have enough inventories for 3 sets of customer requirements. We are calling the three floor locations that they are situated on, kanbans. There are thee kanbans per floor location, this makes a total of nine kanbans which represent the ceiling of our inventory.

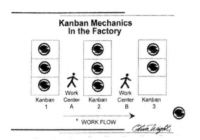

Step 1.

Work is complete. All kanbans are full .

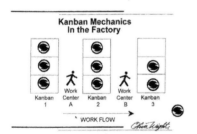

Step 2.

Internal customer takes one part from Kanban 3 location.

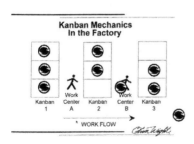

Step 3. Kanban 3 location works based on a FIFO system, first in, first out.

Step 4. Operator sees open kanban – takes material to work on.

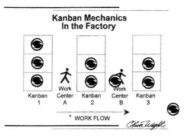

Step 5.

Operator in Work Center A is authorized to work.

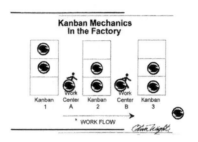

Step 6.

Material handler (warehouse) is authorized to replenish Kanban 1 material.

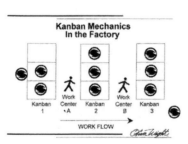

While this was done, work was completed at WC B, and WC A.

QUESTION:

How much time would it take for that material – just replenished - to make its way through the entire process? Use 1 hour cycle time, with customer pulling every one hour.

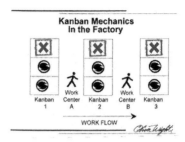

If you reduced the number of kanbans in each location from 3 to 2. What then?

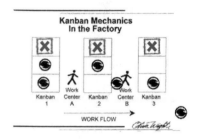

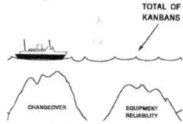

Not only does the water level come down, but the water starts flowing faster. Ah-ha!

Your process is capable if the interruptions to this process are minimized.

The final question. What would it take to achieve one-piece flow? This is what every production system should strive for. Achieving this state is evidence that you must have removed all of the obstacles. Surely, they must have been uncovered first, and then removed.

When all of the rocks from the river are nothing more than sand, you can celebrate the achievement of flow. Everyone should know that there is a strategic amount of inventory required in a company, just like there would be a certain amount of water needed to get a ship like ours down the river.

It is management's responsibility to systematically remove inventory, exposing problems that we would not otherwise see. If management does not do this, then, there is no continuous improvement. They – management - fail their people by not giving them the opportunities (problems) to work on, and this means that they don't help people develop themselves. Problems are treasures, now treating your people like treasures would be something. Give them problems to work on.

The 5th Principle of Lean:

Strive for Perfection

When I first heard about this principle in a Lean101 workshop, I thought to myself, "Now there is a great opportunity for me to expand on this". If I could define what "Strive for Perfection" means, I could make these Lean Principles become my principles. Well, fact is I have. Lean is a journey, not a destination. So the best I can do is describe where I am in my journey so that others may learn from my successes and usually more importantly, my failures. And, without surprise, I do learn from them.

I took some training in March, 2012, on the Harada Method, provided by Norman Bodek, known to many as the "Godfather of Lean", and he is onto something known as the Harada Method. This is the world's best system for developing people in an organization. I will endorse this, as a previous student, and it comes directly from Japan where it was identified as the best system for day-to-day standardized work.

Those who really "know" lean, such as Henry Ford, and Taiichi Ohno, know that it was about the people first. The thinking is first, because the thinking will change people, and people create systems and systems are made up of tools. Most organizations forgot this fact and try to get the numbers first. The "people" side of Lean has been missing from many implementations. The consultants that do this right make lots of money, and more importantly, get results for their clients. I am proud to say that I am looking for more of these consultants to call OEM their partner.

Striving for perfection, from the "people" side of the equation represents finding the passion within. What do you want to do in order to be the best in the world at? By just answering this one question, for you, the mountain of confusion disappears. The purpose of your existence is revealed to you, by you or a higher power, and from that point forward, there are coaches that will help you achieve what you have set forth to achieve. The coaches here at OEM are dedicated to assist your thinking, and assist you in achieving what you never thought was possible.

It requires a little discipline, but what good thing doesn't?

An organization needs to challenge its employees each day to "think". In North America there are many businesses that have been put out of their misery because they tried to compete with low labor rates and exchange rates for their dollar. We need thinkers, not doers. OK – we need both, but don't compete doing work that can easily be duplicated. Make your business system unique, and make sure you choose the right set of tools to satisfy your customer's needs better than any of your competitor. You can only do that through the proper use of your people. If your organization is striving for perfection, then you are doing business differently. You have set up an initiative for creating opportunities for continual learning and growth for your employees. You have addressed many of the human resource issues that plague a Lean implementation.

The 5th Principle - The OEM Way

Identify your deep purpose in life, and share with your company.

Imagine that on the first day of work your company handed you my book. This book identifies the principles of Lean Thinking, and the OEM Way of consulting and educating. You are asked to finish the OEM Lean101 online course, and this book. You are now scheduled for a meeting with your new boss. Exciting... right...   Well, you may be terrified, depending on whom you are. But, no worries. Imagine that your employer starts asking you questions on what your aspirations might be 3 years from now. Have you thought that far? Do you know what you would like to be doing 3 years from now? Do you have an idea of the skills that you would like to pick up along the way?

Your boss saves you a lot of anxiety by letting you know his intentions. His intentions are to get the most out of you at work. To engage you with tasks that you love, so that you deliver the most value for the organization. To encourage you to challenge yourself at work, and above all give you the respect that you deserve.

This is my world. I know it is a little unfair as I do work for myself, however the companies that I work for have this exact mindset, otherwise, you would not have been handed this book.

Enjoy the remaining chapters. You will get information from some of the most respected people in the lean community. As you see the following icons scattered throughout book, please note, they were placed within the articles by a variety of contributing authors. These authors, Jeff Liker, Mike Hoseus, Norman Bodek, et al, offer us a lot is insight and wisdom from their areas of expertise. I parallel the use of these icons interactively throughout the book to connect with you.

The 5 Principles of Lean Thinking - The OEM Way

1) Engage everyone in delivering value to your customer's future requirements.

2) Commit to Continuous Value Stream Management.

3) Target the ideal state and remove barriers keeping you from achieving it.

4) Continually increase flow by removing bottlenecks that impede flow.

5) Identify your deep purpose in life, and share with your company.

CHAPTER 4 – Implementing Lean- An Expert's Perspective

From Lean Processes to Lean Thinking – by Jeffrey K. Liker, author of the Toyota Way

When The Machine that Changed the World introduced the concept of lean it became clear that the model was Toyota. That book was quite prophetic and took a very broad view of the lean enterprise covering every major function of the company to become an agile, innovative, learning organization, a message I have continually reinforced in my books about the Toyota Way.

Unfortunately, the broader message too often gets lost as companies focus narrowly on tools and improvement of specific processes missing the "thinking" part.

  What do you think Jeff Liker means regarding the "thinking" part?

If we look back at the creation of the Toyota Production System, originally led by the great Taiichi Ohno, we see that challenging conventional thinking was always at the heart of the system. Like all great Toyota leaders Ohno's quest started with a challenge. Kiichiro Toyoda announced the concept of "just-in-time" as the backbone of Toyota's efforts to become a credible global automotive company. This was no trivial feat since at the time Ford with its huge volumes was estimated to be 9 times as productive as Toyota. Moreover, the concept of JIT was just that, a concept.

know.

It is challenges like this one that help an organization center around a purpose.

Ohno's task was to make JIT a reality and catch up to Ford's productivity in three years—a challenge that would make many lose a lot of sleep at night. Ohno already had a good deal of experience with creating flow lines in the original loom company of the Toyoda family. But automotive was an entirely new arena. At the time he was managing the machine shop making engine components. Machining still to this day is one of the more difficult places to apply lean as mostly they are organized into job shops with similar machines put into individual departments while parts go through routings from department to department, with a good deal of inventory sitting everywhere. There are changeovers in machining so the usual answer is building in batches to take advantage of economies of scale, which was Ford's approach to productivity. Ohno knew that with the scarce resources and tiny demand of Toyota he could not imitate Ford. He needed flexible processes with little inventory to adapt to the changing demand for small volumes of different types of vehicles in Japan.

When an organization can identify with a better way to do things than the current-industry leader deploys, this organization is carving its own path to success.

Ohno's solution was what we now call the one-piece flow cell. He bit the bullet and moved machines into a cell organized based on the operations that needed to be done to a family of parts. This reduced inventory as long as he could reduce set up times. But he also needed a great deal of human flexibility. This turned out to be more challenging. In Ohno's vision machinists were machinists and should be able to operate any type of machine. This would allow Ohno to flex the number of people working in the cell based on the demand for those products, the Takt. Twice the demand meant the Takt (time to produce each piece) should be cut in half and by doubling the number of workers the Takt could be achieved.

Demand is reduced in half and the Takt increases and you take half the people out of the cell. This is simple arithmetic, but not simple to put into practice.

know.

Having an excellent understanding of Takt time and cycle time relationship is extremely important, again, take advantage of the course http://Lean101.ca.

It turned out machinists did not consider themselves machinists. A lathe operator ran lathes—end of story. The driller wanted to keep drilling holes. Now Ohno was faced with the challenge of changing the thinking of people, far more complex then arithmetic. When asked how he did it he explained that he had to go to the gemba and be with the people every day. He had to learn patience—totally alien to him up to this point. He had to change his own thinking about his role. He was becoming a change agent, not simply a manager or technician.

To this day, I am surprised when a company finally learns that leadership happens in the trenches. I don't know how some companies can afford the time to do this, all I know is that they must to be successful.

Ohno continued to be harsh and aggressive though he had a soft side. For the professionals he trained in TPS he was unforgiving and never satisfied. He was pushing them to observe deeply and think about what the real problems were asking why over and over. They had to find the root cause, solve the right problems, and always achieve the challenging goal. One disciple of Ohno explained to me that Ohno revolutionized his way of thinking and life.

He explained that as an industrial engineer he had been taught that he should always try to balance the work among team members to 85% so that there was adequate rest breaks.

That is, if they worked at a normal pace they would complete each cycle of work in 85% of the time. Ohno insisted the only reasonable target was 100%, not by making people work themselves to death, but by eliminating waste. Ohno realized that if someone actually achieved 100% they would do further kaizen and the percent would go down naturally as they got better giving them more rest time. Start at 85% and it will soon be 75% actual work time.

know.

It is human nature to take advantage of time savings as Ohno realized above.

As he conducted his experiments in the machine shop, Ohno discovered what the greatest innovation in the Toyota Production System was. As he worked with the people to eliminate waste and move toward the ideal of one-piece flow the actual process became more challenging to keep running. Without inventory, and with everyone building to Takt, any disruption whatsoever would stop the cell—there was little room for error. Equipment problems, training issues, motivation issues, poorly designed parts that were hard to manufacture or any other problem would immediately surface and shut down production. This was a very immediate and dramatic consequence of disruptions. It forced an even higher level of kaizen and soon the team members were doing it, not just Ohno.

Thus, Just-In-Time, defined originally by Kiichiro Toyoda as a way to eliminate slack from all processes for the sake of cost and efficiency, really meant striving for perfection. Ohno used to talk about "the factory that god would build," as the ideal everyone should be striving for. It would not have extra inventory, equipment would work perfectly, people would perform their job to perfection, there would be no defects, all materials coming in would be to specification and just in time, and of course it was an impossible dream.

know.

The impossible dream is not as far-fetched as it used to be back then.

Ohno preached that in the real world there is always waste, but through intensive kaizen everyone should be striving to eliminate that waste to move closer to the ideal of perfection.

Another term for waste that causes lead time to be long is variation. Any variation in the way people perform the work, incoming materials, the way tools and equipment operate, of the availability of materials when they are needed will cause a lean process to stop. In fact for work that is not completely automated Ohno took a page out of the book of Sakichi Toyoda. Sakichi Toyoda established the andon system for automated looms so they stopped when a single thread broke and a signal went up for help. Ohno set up the andon system for manual work as well and the worker signaled when they were in an out-of-standard condition and help would come. This was necessary for heavily loaded jobs as a stress-relief valve, but also was another way to surface problems and drive continuous improvement.

Andon systems are very powerful for identifying an exception in the system that requires attention.

In short, when processes are tightly linked, problems cannot hide. They become immediately visible. This then drives problem solving. If the problem solving is mere containment—focused on the symptoms—the problems will come back and production will keep stopping. Only through finding the root cause, putting in effective countermeasures, and carefully monitoring the process will it stabilize. At that point management raises the standards, for example, by further reducing inventory. It is a brilliant system that integrates process improvement, people development, and problem solving leading toward highly stable processes that get closer and closer to perfection and people who become more and more skilled at problem solving.

So why isn't everyone doing it? Because they did not get the memo of what Ohno learned. They still think the key is to rearrange the processes into a cell and specify the standardized work and then step away and let the process improve itself. Guess what, the process self-implodes. It gets worse over time naturally. If leaders hear that they need to focus more resources on people development they usually agree in principle but do not have the deep commitment necessary to follow through. They want results fast and cheap, and patient investment in people and process improvement is simply too much working and too much thinking. It also requires a strong vision for what it takes to be excellent.

So there you have it. Weaknesses in the thinking of leaders who do not grasp or deeply believe in the power of a total lean system, will automatically resort to picking off pieces, the easy parts, and assume if they spread the tools fast and wide they will get fast results. To change the success of lean requires changing the thinking of management, which requires that they dig in and get their hands dirty to learn the hard work required and the incredible power of kaizen. The Toyota Way to Lean Leadership talks about the process necessary to really develop lean leaders from top to bottom. It is not a cookbook and there is no easy path that avoids patience and hard work.

Jeffrey K. Liker

Professor, University of Michigan and President of Liker Lean Advisors, LLC
Author of the Toyota Way and (with Gary Convis) the Toyota Way to Lean Leadership
http://jeffliker.com/

Dr.Jeffrey K. Liker was a keynote speaker in Winnipeg, Canada for the Lean 2012 conference.

CHAPTER 5 – Implementing Lean Culture –The reality

A long-term strategy must exist with short- term results

Mike Hoseus, co-author of Toyota Culture

Co-writing the book "Toyota Culture" has given me the opportunity to travel to many parts of the world and come into contact with many organizations working on improving through "Lean Management". I have observed many problems and misunderstandings of what it takes to be a Lean organization. This is why I'm so excited to introduce a book to you that seeks to and in my opinion, addresses these problems.

Most organizations view lean as a program to eliminate waste and cut costs. Operations are "leaned out" and the assumption is that if well-trained experts properly implement the tools the efficiency gains will be self-sustaining. Unfortunately these companies are missing the very essence of the Toyota Way.

 What do you think the essence of the Toyota Way is?

The Toyota Production System (TPS) aims to intentionally expose problems and engage all members in solving them. These two points are usually missed in the common "Lean Implementation" where Leadership delegates Lean to a set of champions or "belts" and then asks them to report results. Leadership goes about business as usual and the champions are out cutting costs through implementing some of the lean tools. The problem is that most times these tools are used to reduce the number of people, which results in losing a valuable resource in those that leave and the trust of those that stay. Meanwhile, the improvements that were made do not usually last because they didn't include the people doing the work and were not systematic.

Toyota's approach is much more broad and holistic. It starts with a philosophy that the strength of the company is based on continuous improvement and respect for people. Measurement of success is multidimensional and reflects the success of the enterprise, not specific projects. The leadership hierarchy is not there to delegate improvement to specialists but rather to be leaders at every level and play an integral role in daily improvement - leaders are teachers to develop team members. There is a broad set of methods available for improvement but the unit of improvement is primarily at the level of the work group led by a group leader. Hourly team leaders who facilitate kaizen events at the team-member level support group leaders. Improvement is not focused only on large lean projects. More members lead small incremental improvements so there is strong ownership of the process and predictable results. Over time, continuous improvement by identifying and solving problems strengthens the company, which can be regarded as a learning organization.

know.

A learning organization is the key to sustainable growth in your organization in the future.

Leadership is vital for a successful Lean Transformation. Another vital, yet commonly missed component is a strong Human Resources Department that is given the proper role in a Lean organization and then has the knowledge and experience to perform that role. Many times HR isn't even included in the lean implementation model. However, if the organization understands that Lean depends on Leadership who can build purpose, trust, and partnership in the organization, as well as the lean processes. Then this dramatically changes the role of HR. HR will need to be the coaches for this "army of problem solvers".

Human Resources then become the "keepers of the values" of the organization, owning the processes that will make "continuous improvement and respect for people" a reality. This includes hiring (and promoting) the right people who "fit" the lean organization. People, who share the same values, can solve problems, work in teams and in the case of leaders, and coach others to do so. After selection, these processes continue with training and development, daily engagement, evaluation, compensation and communication.

 Does your Human Resource department view itself as having these responsibilities?

I always emphasize that I was taught by my Japanese Sensei "to keep it simple" and I found that the more experienced a trainer was, the more simply he could explain and teach TPS concepts. To say Lean is simple is by no means to say the Lean Transformation is easy. It is anything but. For this reason it is wise to seek guidance from experienced coaches.

This experience and hands-on learning is so important because it helps to minimize the big mistakes made and to learn from the small ones that are made. Lean is more than a set of tools. It is a system that integrates methodology, management systems and cultural change. It's possible to get some "low hanging fruit" with implementing some of the lean tools. But, if you want to realize the full potential of lean, you'll need to address your entire system.

When talking about the "system" it's easy for leader's to "depersonalize" the process and delegate responsibility. Organizations and Systems are made up of people and it's easy to conclude that "they are not doing this". I want to challenge you to first ask "how does this apply to me, and what can I do personally to improve?"

The last challenge is to have patience. There are many pressures both outside and inside organizations to get results and to get them quickly. This is not going away. It's important for leaders of the lean transformation to connect "process along with getting results".

Too often, I see leaders focusing on the short-term results at the expense of "process". It is possible and recommended that you use the short term needs as the impetus to build your long-term processes.

know.

Sometimes sacrifices must be made to short term results for the purposes of showing your team how to respect the process.

The "Plan-Do-Check-Act" (PDCA) is the process that lean is built on. This is the process that leaders must model and coach their entire organization on. This will allow you to get the short term results needed to address the short term needs, but more importantly, allow you to build the long term systems and processes needed to sustain lean.

PDCA, and A3 Problem Solving are the best planning and execution tools to use in a lean implementation.

An effective Lean Transformation "taps" into the potential of your entire organization. Strong leaders and engineers are important, but more important, is their ability to build the systems that engage the entire organization. People want to be part of a larger vision and purpose and they want to be involved. Everyone wants to contribute their skills and abilities and be productive. We just have to lead and structure the organization in such a way that gives them the chance to do so. Nothing is more important to their success, your success and that of your organizations.

Mike Hoseus, co-author of Toyota Culture

CHAPTER 6 – Implementing Lean- A Leaders' Perspective

A leader's perspective on leading people through a Lean implementation by R.Jungkind

Imagine this situation... You toured a plant that has been utilizing lean for a number of years and you want the same positive results. You have made the decision to lead the lean implementation in your organization. Should be easy right? After all, there are unlimited resources on the internet and an endless number of books. Many organizations will tell you that they have already implemented lean and they are proud to tell you how they accomplished their results. I have been involved in lean implementations for 20 years, and during that time I have seen many variations of success. One common denominator in the most successful implementations has been the success of the leader in engaging his employees. This experience as a leader has taught me some basic guidelines that will help achieve the results you have set for your organization.

1   Expand your knowledge

As a leader you need to understand the lean culture you want to create for your organization. Lean 101 is a great way to start your knowledge. Utilize resources from many different sources and understand the how the lean tools can be utilized to create the culture that will ultimately help achieve your vision. What are you trying to achieve with 5S? Do you want shiny machines and lines on the floor or do you want a means to visualize waste and identify opportunities to resolve in the process of achieving continuous improvement? What benefit can you get from value stream mapping? Is lean something you do during the slow season or is it a culture that becomes part of your activities at all times?

2. It is your vision.

This is your vision to communicate and support. This is not something you can delegate and ask for updates as part of your monthly review. The energy, support and enthusiasm you demonstrate will directly correlate to the success of your implementation. Be prepared to allocate 40 to 50% of your time towards this implementation. That is a big number; however this is a big commitment. You will spend your time in meetings, kaizen events, communications training and spending time where the value added activities take place. You will be spending more time with your employees than ever before.

3. Engage your executive group

There will come a time in your implementation when you will expand beyond the boundaries of your operation. This may occur in a matrix organization or from a corporate office or another branch or division. An example of this can be material flow. You may be ready to expand the value stream to your suppliers.

If there is a lack of support from corporate purchasing you can find yourself in a situation where you won't achieve your goals. This can create friction and confusion and generally, a lack of cooperation. Even though other groups in your organization may not have the depth of your understanding or share in your enthusiasm, you will need their support. It is better to get this support as early as possible.

4. Chose a Consultant

Why chose a consultant? I have been challenged on this from all levels of the organization. "If you know so much about lean why don't you save the money and do it yourself?" The answer is simple. You already have a busy full-time job and all the distractions that come with that job. A consultant comes in with the single focus of providing guidance for your lean implementation. They bring a different set of eyes and a wide range of experience to help you overcome obstacles.

Choose your consultant wisely. They reflect your style in their communications and interactions with your employees. They are an extension of your vision. You know you have chosen the right consultant when he is no longer thought of as a consultant but has become part of your team. Never lose sight of the fact that you are still the leader and provide direction. Eventually you will have to become self-sufficient and phase out your consultant. Make sure your consultant tells you this up front. His/her job is to work themselves out of a job.

5. Select your lean team.

You can't do this alone. Who in your organization shares your enthusiasm for achieving this vision? Who will embrace the changes required? Look beyond your management team. Identify people from all levels of your organization. Form a steering committee that will help guide the direction and priorities of your lean implementation. Help this team expand their lean knowledge. Actively engage them in implementation leadership roles. These people will be the catalyst to engage more people at all levels of the organization.

6. Identify Key Performance Indicators

Don't confuse your organization with excess charts and metrics. What are the most important things to measure? The majority of your communications will take place where the work actually happens. Chose no more than six key measurements that indicate how your operation is performing. These indicators should be relevant, timely and easily understood at all levels of the organization.

Each department in your organization should be able to contribute to these indicators. When your people understand these indicators they will be able to identify with a tangible goal that will help direct and focus value-added activities.

Remember that it's the value of the information that will engage your associates. If it's all "dog and pony show" the novelty will wear off before any benefits are realized.

7. Look for sure fire wins

You are leading your organization through some strange tides. Even the most optimistic people in your organization will be unsure. Implement lean in stages. Pick an area with a team that you know will be successful. Start by removing doubt as early as possible and show your organization what the future can look like. These areas will be the catalyst for discussion and interest and will go a long ways towards getting people engaged early in the process.

8. Don't Stifle Engagement

At some point during your implementation you will not be able to keep up to the level of excitement generated in your organization. I will use 5S as an example. As stated in my earlier point, "look for sure fire wins", I was in a situation where we had generated that sure fire win that always exists with implementing the 5S system. Soon everyone wanted 5S. We didn't have the resources to train everyone and monitor the activities as per our master plan. I had a choice to make. I could hold everyone back and wait until they were trained properly. Or I could let them to do it "free style" and deal with it later. The negative was that they were not following the 5S standard as set by the implementation team. The positive was that we had areas in our organization that were previously very negative about lean, and were now actively engaged in changing their work area. In the end, we decided that misguided engagement was the better direction for us. As it turns out it, it was not very difficult to convert all areas to the same standard for 5S. That standard was different than we originally thought it would be, however far more effective than we expected. The engagement of our employees and the positive change generated was more important than the color of line on the floor or type of font on the signage.

9. Not everything is a success

As leaders we have an expectation to always be successful. Accept the fact that you will have failure during times in your implementation. How you lead during this time will affect your overall success. Lead your organization through these opportunities. Be actively engaged and be part of the analysis of what went wrong. Help demonstrate and guide your organization as you mentor them to become effective problem solvers.

Let your employees make mistakes. If you see a project or plan going wrong, you can make a few choices. As a leader you need to weigh your options. You can say "no that won't work. Here is how I want you to proceed".

You can guide them through the project as a mentor and co- worker. You can let them fail. In my experience I always measure the impact of the failure. If it's a big impact I will take on the role of a coach. I might let them fail if they are highly engaged and the impact won't be overly harmful to the business. It's a fine line that we walk as leaders between stifling creativity or engagement versus standards and compliance. Be clear about the guidelines and levels of authorization for projects. The wins will far outnumber the losses. The learning experience will provide positive results now and in the future.

10. Celebrate

Take the opportunity to celebrate all your events and positive results. Early on celebrate even the smallest of positive results. People like to know when they are doing well. Some of the most successful celebrations did not cost anything. Have a town hall meeting and acknowledge the team. Invite a member of the executive team to recognize the success of a project. Let members of the team lead new projects. When conducting plant tours actively engage team members. Let them meet customers and show your customers the improvements they have made.

11. Expand Your Knowledge again

If you're doing this right you will find that you never stop learning. You will always have to seek out new knowledge and expand beyond your current comfort zone. This will allow you to continue to challenge and engage your employees to heights that extend beyond your original vision. Learn with your employees. Take the same courses as they do. Send them to higher level training and let them teach you. Who doesn't like to know something that the boss doesn't?

Lean implementations and the direction and success will be as varied as the people that work for you. Your implementation should be a reflection of you as a leader. You can't do this alone. Utilize the strength of your employees to lead your implementation. As a leader there is nothing more rewarding than seeing your vision realized. Your development and growth during this process will make you a better leader in the future. Why do you think Richard's last step is a repeat of his first step? Create a team of future leaders and share the results of their success

Richard Jungkind

Richard Jungkind (left) is a long-term client of OEM Consultants Inc.

CHAPTER 7 – OEM Lean101 Applied to a Creative Industry

Applying the OEM Lean101 – Principles to a Brand-development Agency

My name is Kyle Romaniuk. I am a global partner of ClarkHuot/Cocoon, an integrated brand development agency with offices in Canada and New York City. I first met George Trachilis about seven years ago when we applied lean thinking to my service-based agency. At first, our agency seemed very different from a manufacturing business, but I soon realized just how many similarities they had.

know.

When you look to find similarities between your industry and the "Lean Thinking" knowledge, you know you are on the right track to improvement.

At the time, I was working closely with a client of ours, Dr. Hamza Musaphir. He was a process engineer and he was very familiar with lean. He was president of his organization; he had a real-time dashboard on his computer tracking all key performance metrics of his operation. Hamza had the entire business broken out by key activity and trending by the hour, day, week, month, and quarter at his fingertips. It enabled him see and forecast issues to best focus the time and attention of his resources.

One day, Hamza asked if we'd ever looked at our own business in the same way. Did we have our processes documented, and were we tracking where our time was spent? In his business, it was easy to see how key activities were all very repetitive and predictable, and how even an improvement of just a few seconds each day could result in increased profitability, capacity, or earned value. But for us, as a service provider and charging by the hour, it seemed ridiculous - if not even a little offensive - to compare our creative process to a manufacturing process. But I was open to the idea and very interested in the possibilities; I took his suggestion and gave George a call.

I Don't Know I don't know why but I have found it extremely satisfying trying, and applying Lean Thinking principles to all sorts of businesses. The Marketing and Branding business was no different.

This came at an opportune time for our agency, as we had recently doubled in size. This sudden growth introduced a few complications. We found some types of projects that used to get done with ease weren't going as smoothly as they once did. An increase in demand resulted in the need to scale up. In our business, increasing scale means adding more people - not faster machines.

Having more people allowed us to split projects up into tasks and have people in more specialized roles to perform different tasks. The problems occurred when projects fell into limbo and it was not clear what needed to be done or who was responsible. It became pretty obvious pretty quickly that we needed to document our processes.

I had an initial meeting with George to get a sense of how he could take what he did every day in product manufacturing, and apply it to a service industry. Something I believe had never been done before. We talked about lean principles, 5S, the benefits of eliminating waste, documenting the current and future states of our processes.

We also talked about Takt time, kaizen, FIFO, defining our key business metrics, documenting our procedures and policies, building a system for our scheduling boards, and the five whys to help us identify and eliminate the root cause of absolutely any problem that may arise.

To be honest, getting the creative team on board was a little bit terrifying. After all, we were supposed to be creative; it did not seem appropriate to prescribe where and when we should have an idea. But I knew the secret to get everyone on board.

We were lucky enough to be in an industry where we are expected to challenge the status quo every single day, but in an environment where most of our clients at the time were afraid of change. It seems contradictory, but that's just the way it was. People are afraid of the unknown - but not keeping up with changes around us has a much greater risk long-term than sticking with what may have worked in the past. One of George's first lessons in one of our first meetings was about embracing continuous improvement. Our creative team already believed in continuous improvement and embraced change every day on behalf of our clients. They just needed to view our business through the same lens.

Our secret to getting clients on board when they are not sure about the type and amount of change we are going to recommend is simple: we involve them. So we invited our creative team to help document their process - as it's been done. Then we had them document the ideal future state for the way it should be done. Guided by the lean consultants on George's team, we were able to self-assess what was working, what could be improved, and how to implement those changes immediately.

 Trust is always built by asking the team to describe their desired outcome.

It can be difficult - if not impossible - to estimate the time it's going to take to have the ideal concept for an advertising campaign, come up with the right brand name, or build a mobile application. The scale and scope of almost every project is so different, how could we possibly standardize anything compared to the time and tasks of producing a million widgets in a factory?

To make the concept work in a service-based company, we identified:

- All of the tasks we'd like to have ideally as a part of each process
- The minimum amount of time required to make the task even worth considering
- Which tasks could be optional if forced to scale back the budget
- The ideal amount of time to allow for every task

This resulted in a range of process scope that could be scaled to match project value, and a minimum that would prevent us from accepting a project that would not allow us the resources to hit the expectations we had for ourselves - and the expectation our clients had for us. This was based on the benchmarks set in our previous work or our demonstrated ability to do the work.

know.

When the behaviors change, the cultures change.

Once we had everything in place, it changed the culture of our business. The knowledge of what went into creating projects not only increased effectiveness and efficiency, but morale was improved because everyone understood their role in the bigger picture.

All of this took place about seven years ago, and we recently merged with two other agencies. The other agencies were not tracking any metrics and had not documented their processes. I can't imagine what the integration process would have been like if we didn't have the baseline of our 'lean thinking' metrics and processes to provide a platform on which to build from.

As we combine the best practices of all three agencies, we are evolving everything once again - always coming back to the 'lean thinking' first introduced to us by George. A new variable just recently introduced to our weekly metrics is earned value. This is nothing new to our company, as we are always looking for new ways to create value for our clients' brands. We just hadn't thought to measure the value we deliver to our clients before.

Our education in lean principles may have happened seven years ago, but it's a tool that continues to help us improve our business today.

Thanks again, George.

CHAPTER 8 – OEM Lean101 Applied to the Healthcare Industry

Applying Lean Thinking to Improve the Delivery of Healthcare by C.Jimmerson

Cindy Jimmerson, Lean Healthcare West, Missoula, Montana, USA

Healthcare costs are rising at a rate of 10-15% per year. Certain services are being outsourced, health care professionals imported and services reduced. The solution is to learn the lesson of Lean promoted by the Toyota Production System. Health care, like manufacturing is a system made from processes and procedures. There is tremendous opportunity to remove the wastes from the system. Focused efforts in patient in/patient out, paperwork flow, and supply-chain will result in bottom-line improvements. Health care professionals must spend their valuable time directly involved in patient care, not supporting functions.

What is **Ideal** for Healthcare?

- Exactly what the patient needs, defect free
- One-by-one, customized to each patient
- On demand, exactly as requested
- Physically, professionally, emotionally safe
- Zero Waste

In the past 10 years scholars and practitioners of Lean have observed and measured waste in healthcare delivery processes at a staggering 30-70%, or *somewhere between one and two trillion dollars per year* in the US alone! Globally, the numbers are unimaginable.

The Beginning:

This report evolved from research conducted by **Cindy Jimmerson** and **Durward Sobek** in a three year study based in a 135-bed hospital in Montana funded by **National Science Foundation** grant to Montana State University. The goal of the research was to investigate the possibility of using the principles from the Toyota Production System to healthcare to reduce errors, reduce waste and improve the workplace experience.

Why Toyota?

At the time of the study, Toyota produced the most *defect free* product in auto industry with the best record of employee satisfaction, the best record of introducing new technology and the best record of waste reduction with their relentless pursuit of perfection.

Why can we get to producing defect-free cars, and we don't stress the urgency for defect-free procedures in healthcare?

Why Healthcare?

A 1999 Institute of Medicine report revealed that over 99,000 deaths each year in the US were caused by errors in patient care. The cost continues to skyrocket, estimated at $3 trillion in 2012. Additionally, there exists a healthcare worker shortage and because of decreasing job satisfaction, a growing culture of apathy is rampant among current staff.

Why Now?

The "Baby Boomer Phenomenon" is like a locomotive coming down the track, increasing demand for services, decreasing the supply of healthcare workers, and glutting a top-heavy government-funded market.

Healthcare as an industry has traditionally responded to the cost crisis by cutting full time employees (FTEs), the most critical resource in this highly educated, labor-intensive sector of the economy. As we know from manufacturing models, labor is only a portion of total cost. As with manufacturing, *waste in healthcare* is a more cost-effective target for reduction. Nationally, waste in healthcare is reported to be between 30 and 35%, but our study found that figure to be closer to 60-65%.

Answer: Cut waste, not resources. Increase capacity for care with existing staff and successfully recruit new talent.

Two power tools that should be used in healthcare are Value Stream Mapping and A3 Problem Solving.

The Toyota Production System brings two main methods to problem identification and resolution that can be quickly and successfully introduced to healthcare. The engagement of staff and leaders in "Lean thinking" supported by these two methods ultimately results in fewer errors, more satisfied patients and workers and much lower operating costs.

While this approach may look simple at first, the execution requires strong and *participating* leadership, a realistic goal of time-to-maturity and widespread frontline involvement. More complex "Lean tools" can be applied when these two methods are mastered, but there is great power in the simplicity and agility of these two methods.

Value stream mapping (view of a problematic process from 10,000 ft.)
(Based on work of Womack, et al)

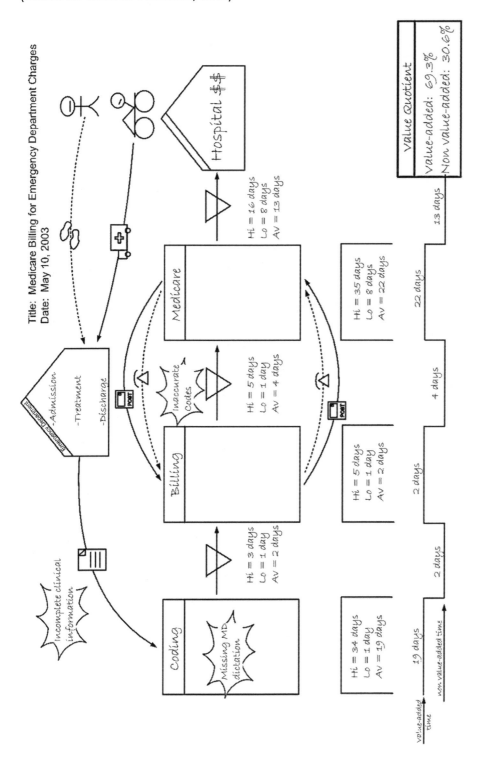

A3 Problem Solving (view with a microscope at a specific problem)
(Based on work of Bowen/Spear, modified slightly by Jimmerson/Sobek)

ISSUE   Pt. measurement of glucose delayed in Truama ICU

BACKGROUND
Intensive Glucose Testing research depends on regular and timely blood glucose analysis. In the 12 bed-ICU the average number of patients on the Intensive Glucometry protocol = 9
Observed nurses took average of 17 minutes to draw/measure/treat when glucometer not in room

CURRENT CONDITION

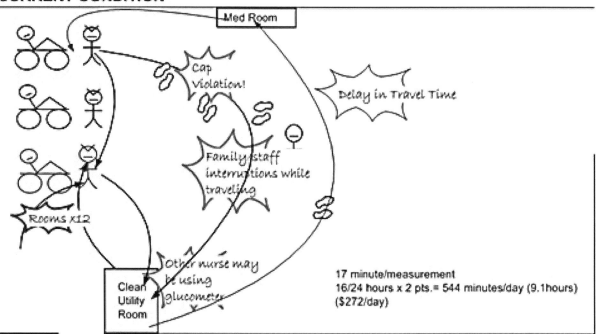

17 minute/measurement
16/24 hours x 2 pts.= 544 minutes/day (9.1hours)
($272/day)

PROBLEM ANALYSIS

1. CAP VIOLATION
    Why? unlabeled blood is out of the patient room
        Why? glucometer is housed in clean utility room
            Why? must be shared by 12 patient rooms

2. Delay in treatment
    Why? Travel time to use glucometer in clean utility room
        Why? one glucometer is shared and must be centrally stored
            Why? glucometers not at bedside
                Why? not enough glucometers
    Why? Distractions between drawing blood, checking value and treating patient
        Why? Often stopped by family/staff when traveling
            Why? glucometer not in room

3. Potential for error
    Why? Blood not labeled when taken from room
        Why? glucometer not in room

262

TARGET CONDITION   Title: Glucometer Availability

TO	Lorie
BY	Kathy
DATE	October 12, 2006

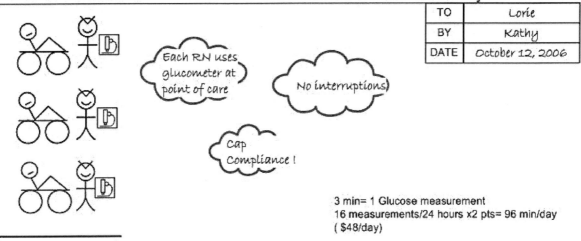

Each RN uses glucometer at point of care

No interruptions)

Cap Compliance !

3 min= 1 Glucose measurement
16 measurements/24 hours x2 pts= 96 min/day
($48/day)

COUNTERMEASURES

1. Place glucometers at bedside
2. Review glucose protocol and new glucometer use with staff

IMPLEMENTATION PLAN

What	Who	When	Outcome
Get approval for additional glucometer purchase	Lorie	10/13/06	Initiate purchase of 8 glucometers
Get funding	Dr. K	10/20/06	Purchase glucometers
Calibrate/install new glucometers	BioMed	10/20/06	All glucometers standardized
Orient staff to new machines/policy at staff meeting	Kathy	11/1/06	Staff prepared to use new process!

COST / BENEFIT

Cost	$$$
Staff time to travel/share glucometer	$99,280/year
Benefit	$$$
Staff time ($$) with glucometer in the room	$17,520
Consistent measurement and treatment of glycemic variance	Quality

TEST

Measure time it takes to do glucose testing at bedside vs. travel time and sharing one machine in

FOLLOW UP

November 12, 2006
Staff time measuring blood glucose at beside: 3 minutes

263

The most enlightening finding was that the Lean principles exemplified by the TPS were immediately applicable in every department of the healthcare organization and that specific gains could be realized within weeks. The staff embraced the concepts and enjoyed the real improvement achieved in their daily work, while learning.

Lessons Learned:

- Senior Leadership must participate, not just endorse the activities, to build staff confidence.
- When the conceptual education (the *why*) accompanies the improvement activity (learn by doing, the *how*), the "flavor of the month", syndrome can be avoided. The improvement activities must be done by the people who do the work, and the improvement work must be meaningful to the workers. *This is essential for sustainability.*
- Each Improvement Activity must be treated as a project using project management techniques to ensure completion and adherence to schedule, budget and performance objectives. This is made practical using the A3 Problem Solving format of thinking.

Findings:

Lean absolutely suits the challenges of healthcare! It should be applied with a method that is easy –to-learn and easy-to-teach and each facility should plan from the outset to become internally capable of spreading Lean thinking to improve care and develop a culture of problem solving.

Example #1

- Intensive Care Unit reported 7 medication errors related to wrong IV drip rate in 3 month period
    - Observations:
        - not all nurses calculated same way
        - not all medication delivery machines were calibrated the same
        - no standard way to report IV status from shift to shift
    - Improvements made:
        - One way to calculate and report activity designed and accepted by all nursing staff
        - All machines calibrated the same; Biomed department included in process to assure they were consistently maintained

Result: no medication errors related to wrong IV rate in subsequent 3 months

Conclusion:

The challenges in healthcare are that, the number of issues is overwhelming, and the issues are very complex. Borrowing techniques from the Toyota Production System (Lean) will allow healthcare to recognize the non-value added activities that complicate the delivery of patient care and reduce the observed waste by instituting more value-adding and cost-effective processes.

Cindy Jimmerson.

know.

Lean Thinking is the solution to many of the world's problems.

Lean Healthcare West (LHW), under the direction of Cindy Jimmerson, has been conducting research, offering Lean education and certification and implementing Lean in healthcare organizations since 1999. I have partnered with Cindy as part of the Global OEM Consortium to share their experience world-wide, join us at http://lean101.ca/weboffice.htm

What everyone needs to understand is that Lean will solve many of the world's economic problems by the application of its principles in the right areas; healthcare is one of those areas. When I speak to experts in almost every industry, they continue to re-enforce for me that the learning provided by OEM Lean101–Principles course is fundamental to becoming profitable, stable, and avoid going bankrupt as a business, or a country.

In another Healthcare study that Cindy Jimmerson was involved in, the study identified that over 63% of what the hospital was doing was considered waste. This waste **could be** completely eliminated, freeing up time for doctors and nurses to do more. The wastes comprising of 63% of the hospitals time were:

⇒ Looking for things that they could not find
⇒ Clarifying things that were not clear
⇒ Doing redundant paperwork

These results are exciting! (Remember to celebrate – not judge) It means that we have a lot of opportunity to make a great impact immediately. It is time to learn about the most basic of Principles – Lean Thinking, so that we can create the time to get out of the crisis that we have put ourselves into.

CHAPTER 9 – OEM Lean101 in the Construction Industry

Applying Lean Thinking is desperately needed in Construction

Ted Garrison, Global OEM Solutions, Senior Leader, Construction, U.S.A.

Ed Anderson, Global OEM Solutions, Senior Leader, Project Management, U.S.A.

Many people believe that lean doesn't apply to the construction industry because they think lean applies to manufacturing only. Nothing could be further from the truth, because lean isn't about specific sets of tools or activities. It's a way of thinking that can be applied to any situation. Lean thinking is focused on eliminating waste in every effort regardless of the industry. Of course, lean is applied differently in the construction industry than in manufacturing, but that is to be expected.

The construction industry is the only significant industry that hasn't increased productivity in over 50 years. There are probably many reasons for this but a fundamental issue is that the construction industry focuses too much on sub-optimization instead of looking at the whole. Most of the waste in the construction industry occurs between the tasks, not during the task. Studies reveal that individual tasks are completed over 90 percent of the time within the estimated duration. However, on non-lean projects this number goes down to 50 percent. The number one reason for this low success rate is that the task was disrupted or delayed by another task. In essence, the task was negatively impacted by another task or multiple tasks that constrained its start or scheduled activities.

 Many construction projects are allowed to go over budget, why?

In contrast to conventional project management that focuses on the individual tasks, lean project management focuses on improving and measuring the improvement of the reliability of people to make and keep promises related to the flow of the project. We often hear from project people who were on unsuccessful projects statements such as, "We just couldn't get a rhythm going." What they mean is that keeping their promises was neither measured nor re-acted upon. This also means that the work flow was continuously interrupted. When contractors use a pull-planning process they observe that the percentage of completed tasks assigned on a weekly each week basis, soars to over 80 percent. This means that the hand-offs are occurring and a rhythm is established between the trade's people instead of everyone working only towards their own ends.

A lack of reliability of contractors working on a project is a major source of construction delays and cost overruns. The typical construction industry approach is to apply increasingly greater pressure to the non-performer, but this doesn't necessarily solve the problem because often that contractor's delays are caused by factors outside their immediate control. What are needed are strategies for greater and more meaningful collaboration and accountability, which drastically improve reliability. What's different about the lean approach is it forces the responsibility and accountability down to those performing the work. Instead of managing by pushing the work, the trade foremen pull each other into action by making and keeping commitments and they are taught to do this through collaborative sticky-note planning sessions. This concept is consistent with the teachings of people like Edwards Deming, Jim Collins, Henry Ford, Taiichi Ohno, and Marcus Buckingham. When this approach is applied, amazing results occur. Lean works because it provides tried-and-true methods to make things happen.

know.

Amazing things happen when the right people come together to solve problems.

Pull planning impacts the project's day-to-day operations by highly motivating the workforce. Through effective pre-planning of the project an environment that minimizes these challenges can be created. Effective pre-planning is the key to eliminating issues that arise by not planning.

For example, one of Ted's clients called him one day and said, "This is crazy. We have less work than normal because there is less work available due to the recession. The work we take is at a lower than normal fee, because of the intense competition. However, we are making more money than before."

Ted asked him to explain, and the client's response was, "Because we have less work we have taken our extra office people and assigned them to our current projects. Their specific responsibility is to pre-plan them as much as possible. The result has been a sharp decline in problems, delays and mistakes. This resulted in our costs having dropped all of a sudden."

Pre-planning is what every project needs, but too often it is merely skimmed over or ignored despite the fact that studies demonstrate that contractors that pre-plan are more profitable. Pre-planning is not a mystery. It is merely a process that looks ahead to anticipate potential problems, establishes procedures to insure collaboration, and insure the right people are assigned the tasks.

Again, lean construction doesn't just say do these things, it provides the processes and techniques to make pre-planning highly effective. Many think that pre-planning is best when done in isolation, meaning each subcontracting organization pre-plans on their own. This is just another form of sub-optimization. The best results occur when ALL stakeholders are involved in the project from conception through to startup, especially in the design phase when construction subcontractors should be asked to give input weekly as the detail design progresses. Front-end costs will exceed past standards but can result in back-end costs and schedules being greatly reduced. This is not empty theory. Ask those who have done it, and if, by choice, they would not do it any other way.

In summary, lean construction provides the techniques to significantly improve productivity by eliminating the waste associated with poor coordination & collaboration. Contractors that perform these lean processes have seen their profitability soar. In fact, one lean contractor told Ted, "We can get any job we want because our costs have dropped so much."

Both Ed and Ted, having taken the OEM Lean101-Principles course, http://Lean101.ca and agree, that even though the course is based upon manufacturing, the Lean principles apply to anything, especially design, construction, and project management.

To learn more about how to implement lean thinking on your construction projects, whether you are a project owner, general contractor or a subcontractor, contact us.

Ed Anderson, Lean Project Management   Ed@OEMsolutions.ca

Ted Garrison, Lean Construction   Ted@OEMsolutions.ca

CHAPTER 10 – The OEM Way of Problem Solving

Step 1. Understanding the Goal - Get Educated first

If the goal is to create an organization of problem solvers, then what is your best approach? The cheapest way to educate your entire work force on Lean is to have them educated for you. Allow OEM the privilege of educating each one of your employees on the basics, and in the process you will get some insight on the deep learning that must be adopted in order to make this paradigm shift occur in your organization or country.

know.

You need to live it, in order to be Lean.

Out of the first 8000 students of OEM Lean101-Principles in 2012, we asked each one of them during the last quiz, "Would you like to represent OEM in your country?" Over 50% said yes. Let your employees take this training, and I can guarantee that 50% of them will get it. Use them a s change agents in your company instead of looking for the same challenge in another organization. Give them the head start that you would like to have. Make them your own internal consultant.

I had Norman Bodek speak at the Global OEM Consortium twice in the past two months, April and May, 2012. He challenged all of the attendees in the webinar. Show me a company out there that is "Lean". Can you imagine? The "Godfather of Lean", who published hundreds of book on Lean. This man who brought over learning from the greatest minds in the Japanese manufacturing industries, not to mention republishing Henry Ford's books and exposing current generations to our own lean heritage that is over 100 years old. He was coached by one of the greatest problem solvers of our time, Shigeo Shingo. Shingo was also the co-creator of the Toyota Production System.

Trust me; we should have many more companies doing it the right way than we currently do. Especially in manufacturing where the Toyota Production System flourishes with these concepts created by Ford and developed by Deming and others. We have the knowledge, but we do not have the process for learning? If you think you are doing it right, this could be a problem.

know.

If you don't think there is a problem, then in your mind there is not.

For your own benefit, consider that you may be mistaken. Consider that you may be able to learn from this material. And the FIRST thing you must learn from this book is that you can and must learn from your own people. Simply asking them what is wrong and taking their advice is the FIRST lesson of going lean. This is not singing Kumbayah and sitting around a circle. This is asking, "what can we do differently?" then DOING IT.

Come up with a test for your company, or your own personal life. Then perform that test, see what the results are, and adjust something if you are not happy with the results. Perform, and do the test again.

It is easy to communicate a physical standard, not so easy to communicate a philosophy.

When I started my business in 2002, my first long-term contract was with a company called Gerdau Ameristeel. This is a steel mill in Manitoba, Canada. The General Manager at the time was looking for a consultant to assist over 550 people in implementing Lean. It started with the 5S System. They did not want to implement Lean. They wanted to implement the Gerdau Ameristeel Business System. Every company and organization should create a name for their management system and place at its foundation, the principles of those in the OEM Lean101-Principles course.

I immediately formed a steering team (committee) with the Steelworkers union and management being team members. This was difficult to start with, as all of the comments I received from the union were related to their experiences with past consultants, and how their experiences resulted in failure. They also had bad experiences where their management failed them. Understanding the past is the best way to understand how to make progress into the future.

know.

It is difficult to start a new initiative especially if the previous one failed.

As a consultant, my job was not to get them to focus on the future. My job was to get everyone to understand where they failed each other in the past. List these failures, and develop countermeasures to ensure that we do not fail again in the same areas. The only thing the steering team needs to know is that it is their job to give approval for the proposed activities over the next week/month.

The Education Process – Commit to Lean.

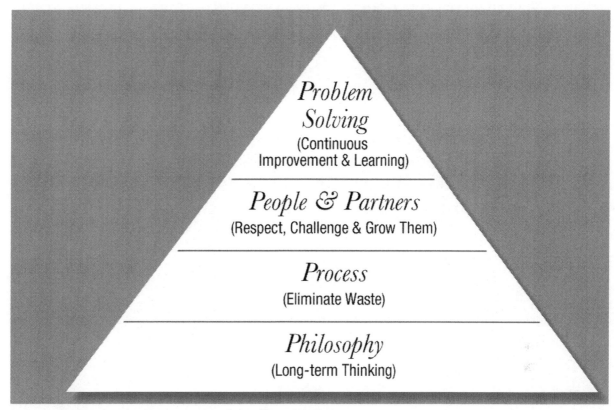

From the book, *The Toyota Way*, by Jeffrey K. Liker

The above visual is known as the 4P's of the Toyota way of doing business. By adopting long-term thinking in your organization, you know that if you had to make a sacrifice, you sacrifice the short term gain so that you can achieve your long-term goals. Most companies today operate in the *Process* area, and they never really become lean because of their myopic view of what Lean is.

The OEM way is a strategy in which Global OEM Solutions, and OEM Consultants globally operate initially in the *People & Partners* area of the 4P's. This is because I believe that the key to solving this mystery of why are there very few companies that implement Lean (in manufacturing) lies with the leadership because they don't foster learning opportunities for themselves and their people.

Everyone that receives this book from their company, is being told, that they should *do some homework*. Here it is.

As a student of Lean Thinking:

Ask these questions of the person/organization that purchased this book for you, or answer these questions for your own organization.

Ask these questions of the person/organization that purchased this book for you.

1. What is our long-term philosophy? (Or, are we supposed to create it together?)
2. Where do I fit in? (Or where do you want me to fit in?)
3. How do we serve our community? (Or, how do we define community?)
4. How do you apply the 5 Principles of Lean Thinking in this business/environment?
5. How are the wastes identified in our environment? (Do we call them by different names?)
6. How do we safeguard again the Waste of Human Potential? (Or,How are we using fresh eyes?)
7. How are you going to help me develop myself in the organization? (Or, how can I help you?)
8. Where is a Future State Map located so I know the direction we are going?
9. How do we measure our partners? (How do our partners measure us?) How are they doing?
10. How do our partners measure us? (How are we doing?)
11. What are problem-solving tools and are they approved for use? (What tool kit do I have?)
12. Who do I use to create a future state plan with (What is my area of responsibility?)
13. When (within 6 months) can we schedule time for the same questions to be asked and answered?

I know that I am a systems thinker. And if every new person in your company asks you – The Boss – these questions, you may not like it, but you need it. You need to be able to identify answers to these questions, and it cannot be a task for you to do. It must be a task for your employee to do. So give them this book, and they only have two tasks.

 Ask twelve questions and schedule one activity.

This will force some consistency in your answers, and force you as the boss to get answers to these questions. Engage your people by having open and honest discussions regarding their future and the company's future.

Back to my story, Gerdau had a long-term philosophy that related to engaging people to participate in creating their own future state. The start of this project – implementing 5S - needed to be very strategic and calculated. You see for me it was a project, for them it was a philosophy. But we both had an idea of what we called success.

We created a plan in order to ensure that everyone knew what to expect. This plan contained key decision points for the steering team members to voice any concerns. Education was the first priority, always. We started in a small area, engaged each employee to create a vision of what they wanted their future area to look like. It is a simple exercise.

Call the meeting with the group, and then say, "Ladies and gentlemen, we are going to be making some changes in the near future. Here's why... Today, all I'm going to do is ask you to answer one question." Then add paper to the wall, use stickies, or write on a whiteboard - create a heading called **current condition** and to the right of that **desired condition**. Then ask each person to describe one thing that they would like to fix.

The strategy in the previous paragraph is simple. We ask them to describe a problem, or a goal, and enlisted everyone around the room to share in that vision of the area.

We picked a 5S target area to start creating the excitement in people. The target area needed to;

- ✓ Deliver a good return on the investment related to training, and consulting time spent.
- ✓ Be very visible to all of the workers in the area. Visible enough for everyone to ask "What is going on here?"
- ✓ Be small enough where success can be guaranteed.

Make the standard visual, show it to everyone.

Completing one small area to the approved-company standard is critical. In this way everyone knows WHAT the end result will look like. It took over 4 years to implement a companywide standard that everyone followed. Keep in mind that this was over 100 acres of real estate, and the improvements were sustained all the way.

The steel mill had a long-term philosophy and I was part of it. They viewed the company as a whole, and we broke down their real estate into areas of responsibility.

Letting everyone know what is expected is critical to success. Showing everyone what a standard area looks like makes it real easy to have owners take control of their area.

The change you see in these photos happened with little to no support after the initial training. It was clear that the area owner just got it he knew what 5S was. He knew what to do and how to get it done. He also knew why he needed to do it. The steel industry is one of the most competitive industries in the world. And costs must continually be reduced. By organizing his area properly, he saved time and saved the company money each day after he got organized. It allowed the people to be more engaged, productive, and the companies promised and kept good on their promise and kept everyone employed.

Step 2. Encouraging the Right Behavior.

Only 3% of people's behavior is conducted consciously. 97% is conducted subconsciously.

I would like you think about events in your life, and specifically think about the changes that have happened recently to you. Was this change planned, or did it just happen? Did you get pressured to change? I know the answer. After all, I am like you, a person who likes to live in their comfort zone. All I can say to this is STOP IT.

 know. Only through routine can you replace bad behaviors with good ones.

Everyone should have Long-term Thinking as part of their DNA. I am shocked at how long it took me to develop myself as a Lean Thinker, and I am still working on it. I failed in some key areas in my life and I am putting counter-measures in place so that I do not repeat this process of failing.

What this means is that we operate like zombies, doing the same thing, at least 97% of the same things over and over again. Failing, over-and-over again. The good news is that we can be succeeding over and over again as well.

What makes the difference between failing and succeeding?

Our organizations' philosophy.

Our organization either challenges us as employees, or it allows us to do work that is not challenging. And just like a parent, who spoils their child, our organizations spoil us. And how bad is that? They not only lose out on the unlimited potential that we possess as human beings, the fall organization falls behind the times and eventually gets consumed by their competition, or confused about their priorities.

What about a small country like Greece, what are they confused about?

I can't imagine what the people in a small country like Greece are going through. Actually, I can. I go there every year. I am fortunate enough to have a home in Santorini Island in the Aegean Sea. Not only can I imagine, I hear about it first hand and how it impacts my family in Athens, and on the island.

On one hand I say, "It's about time that the economic environment has forced change to happen", and on the other hand, I say, "The people of Greece need some time to embrace this type of required change". Regardless of whether you are living in Greece, or the United States, the time is now to do business differently. I don't just mean implementing "Lean Thinking", I mean implementing the people-side of "Lean Thinking". An organization or company that thinks they can do business as usual is in self-denial about the chances it has of being in business in the future.

Picking the right people, systems, tools, and generally the right thinking early enough, may be the difference between making a profit and going out of business.

Routine is the answer to breaking out of the old paradigm and into the new paradigm.

A coach is a critical component to a Lean implementation. The reason for this is that the coach's main purpose is to create a different way of behaving for people in the environment that they have been invited into. You can measure routine, and you can force yourself into a routine that is good for you as a person or a business. Think about it. 97% of peoples' behavior is conducted sub-consciously. The things you do and say are the most obvious giveaways of who you are and what you believe in. If you have a problem in how you are perceived by others, change the way you behave, in this way, you have just changed your thought pattern as well as solving your invisible problem.

The #1 Company Goal – Create a system that forces problem solving at an increasing rate.

When I use the term *problem solving,* I am really saying goal setting and executing to those goals. You see, problem solving is best interpreted as a state of being that you find less than ideal. If you want to change something – then you have a problem. If you want to be in a different state – then you have a problem. And generally, when a problem comes up – of course, you have a problem.

Continuous improvement starts from within, and works its way out. The term continuous improvement is so over used, and the meaning of the word is becoming lost to most people. Regardless of the term, before you ask your organization how they are continually improving, make sure that you know how you are. If you don't know what continual improvement means, you cannot help them. More importantly, you won't understand it well enough to explain it to them. It comes from within. If they try to convince you otherwise they do not understand the concept.

Can you force continuous improvement to happen? I used the word "force" problem solving as if you need to force it. However, this is completely the opposite of what needs to happen. You need to find a way to get passionate about it. This way, you don't force anything; the energy that is derived by you becomes contagious. Force is not the way to go. Encourage is, and most definitely finding people with the passion it takes to make your business successful is. Force is not. Encourage is.

The good news is that when a company focuses on improvements as a team, it can expect at minimum 50% reduction in the wasteful activities. Said differently, it can expect a minimum of 50% improvement in their processes. What you may be asking yourself now is, "What industry is George talking about?" The answer is simply, every industry, and yes, in every country of the world. We especially include government, healthcare, and charitable organizations.

This book is not about Lean Manufacturing or the Toyota way of doing business. So please continue to read on. Enough books have been written about Toyota. What I want to make clear is that this book is about a new way of thinking and a process for getting started. Applying this process will create a way of thinking within the organization and business that you work in.

One of my favorite authors is Dr. Jeffrey K. Liker. His contribution to the manufacturing industry with his book, *The Toyota Way* is very much appreciated. In his book he talks about one of the best manufacturing companies in North America, let's call it Lean Company X. The Toyota Supplier Support Center (TSSC) picked this company to work with so that they can learn, and teach them the Toyota Production System (interchangeable with "Lean Thinking"). They took one product line, and applied nine months of teaching/learning. Now remember, this company is the best in North America and it received the Shingo Prize to prove it. The production line where this change took place leapfrogged the rest of the plant on all key performance indicators, including;

- 93% reduction in lead-time to produce the product (from 12 days to 6.5 days)
- 83% reduction in work-in-process inventory (from 9 to 1.5 hours)
- 91% reduction in finished goods inventory (from 30,500 units to 2,890 units)
- 50% reduction in overtime (from 10 hours to 5 hours/person-week)
- 83% improvement in productivity (from 2.4 to 4.5 pieces/labor hour)

Remember these achievements came after this company had received the prize for being the best in its industry - manufacturing. Interesting enough that the best in North America does not come close to being the best elsewhere in the world. We compete on a world scale not a North American scale. Improvements like this are not easy especially if in manufacturing. However, no matter what the industry, you should expect a 50% reduction in waste or 50% improvement in productivity and in a period of time no more than 3 months. These results can happen much quicker than that, and more importantly – over and over again.

Businesses/Organizations fail to;
- Plan for the long run (25 years+, should I venture to say 100 years)
- Engage and Respect their employees (ask them where they see themselves and support them)
- Implement Lean Thinking throughout their divisions and suppliers (educate and collaborate)
- Help their managers become leaders (first the owner must make it personal)
- Help their employees become self-reliant (awaken each employee to the possibilities)

What was really missing in Lean Company X?

It is back to the basics for most "Lean" organizations. The reason for this is that they are not "Lean". They just say they are. It is good marketing by a supplier to say that they are Lean to their customer. This façade will not last for long. I specifically am excited to get my first publications to market so that everyone, who knows anything about Lean, specifically this book and OEM Lean101 course can differentiate between organizations that talk a good story versus those that are a good story.

I have had many experts who have taken my online course over the past few years, and they have encouraged me to communicate my thoughts in this book. Before I talk about a solution, we should all understand problem solving. Part of the process of problem solving includes agreeing on the problem. The company system that you create needs to have many components to it, but there is an engine. That engine is people.

If the engine is people, then respect, trust and truthfulness is the oil.

It is commonly mistaken that a company is lean because there is white paint on the walls, and lines, labels, and signboards exist. However, this is not "Lean". Lean is about the bond that each employee shares with one another, and the use of this bond to create systems that force each employee to strive for continually improving their processes. When that bond is healthy, and the outcome is continuous improvement, then the company is Lean.

It all starts with the relationship that is leveraged between two people to challenge each other to get better. TIME is the measure. Delivering more value in an increasingly shorter time is the endless target. Measure productivity and remember it all starts with the creating the bond, and the way we do this is we share a problem together, and we solve it together.

James Bond (an actual person) is a senior partner with Global OEM Solutions; he has worked with Toyota for 25 years. Below are a few examples that illustrate the benefits of creating an environment of Trust and Respect for people within an organization.

James Bond, Senior Leader, Global OEM Solutions Inc.

My Lean journey began some 25 years ago at Toyota and I'm still on the journey. As Lean Thinking principles are applied to any organization, it becomes a Learning Organization.

People within all organizations learn and drive innovation by applying the same basic Lean principles contained in the Lean101 course.

To ensure innovation organizations must create an environment in which there is Respect for People including respect for all stakeholders, mutual trust and accountability with open communication as well as teamwork that provide personal and professional growth opportunities. This approach allows employees to work toward their goals and contribute to the organization. An organization must make this commitment to its employees. These actions will create an environment of trust and respect that promotes continuous learning and as a result create a growing knowledge base within the organization.

Is it easy to create this environment of Trust and Respect? No, but when it happens it is very rewarding. It requires dedication and follow-up but the results are very gratifying on many levels from organizational perspective. This approach creates an environment of openness and honesty and transparency in which problems are identified immediately so that they may be eliminated.

Like all things people need to be shown.

3 Short Stories by James.

1) One day at a well-known company there was extensive damage on a door in my area. When asked what had happened and the response was, "I'm not sure", by the employee. However, he did offer a potential cause, it was that he may not have properly latched the door together (employees were very open about volunteering this kind of information). This information was offered freely as an environment of trust and respect had been developed within my teams. I then asked, "What can we do in the process to prevent this?". The team member thought for a few moments and said, "well I could check by just pulling on the door before it left my station". "Are you able to complete this extra task during Takt time?", I asked. The team members said "Yes". In an effort to build consensus, I discussed this with all the other members of the team who agreed. Then we proceeded quickly to make changes to the standardized work we retrained everyone and then this became the new standard.

 What can we do to prevent this from happening again? (Mind Kung-Fu)

2) I arrived at a client's facility to create a model area (target area) by applying Lean principles. After my initial discussions with the Senior Leadership team I went to the floor to observe the current condition. Neither my presence nor my responsibility had been communicated to the people on the floor. As a result there was some initial resistance (an opportunity). I immediately took all the time required to talk to every employee on all shifts in the model area and explained to each of them that I was there to help them make their jobs easier and I wanted to understand the opportunities that existed in their areas. This took several days and long hours to complete. An environment of respect and trust began to develop. With this trust

came open and honest communication, which resulted in not only the surfacing of problems but potential solutions as well. Observations included lack of timely leadership support, lack of process understanding, lack of daily management interaction, and lack of follow-up with floor operators. It became evident that the floor operators had some possible solutions to some concerns they had raised. These were discussed with the Senior Leadership Team, and as part of my discussion with this team we developed a go forward plan. We developed systems and processes, including involvement by the leadership team, and we further developed a Management Accountability System to ensure the systems sustainability. Then through a Visual Management System we reinforced the rules in the area that made this a success.

As I left, the Director of this organization said to me "James, I finally got it" and he did truly understand the Lean principles. He realized it's all about the people that provide the innovation and knowledge in the future that will make his organization successful.

Why does it take outside eyes to make gaps evident so that they can be closed?

3) Some people in an organization become disillusioned for a variety of reasons. One must understand first that there is a concern and then an opportunity to turn that negative into a positive. My goal has always been to create an atmosphere of Trust and Respect with everyone in my group and beyond...

With this comes transparency and openness. I remember when there was a person with a bad attitude in my group and that attitude translated to a negative impact on the team's' morale. I spoke with this individual in private to try to understand what had caused this attitude to manifest itself. He told me his story in great detail because of that Trust and Respect that I had been developing with him. "Can't change the past", was my response. "However, you can change your own future". With empathy and support and some additional training that person became very positive, got promoted and became the best programmer/trouble-shooter for a specific piece of equipment in the area. This individual worked with Maintenance to collaboratively solve problems.

know.

Everyone tries to do a good job get to the root cause if you think they are not.

This focus on people is evident as it is contained in the first principle of 14 principles of the Toyota Way (Jeffrey K. Liker). It encourages employees "to be responsible, decide their own fate by acting with self-reliance and trust their abilities". This self-reliance is exemplified in the Harada Method.

James Bond, Senior Leader, Canada, Global OEM Solutions, Inc.
James@OEMsolutions.ca

Step 3. Understand the Two Problem Solving Rules

Let's start with the assumption that everyone in this world agrees that Lean thinking is the solution to many of the world's problems. There is an issue with this. You see, human beings have a short attention span. And remembering that they are doing Lean because it is a solution to their problems is not good enough. It should be about the problem. Without stating the problem first, people, lose sight of why there needs to be a solution. Not only that, but one of the questions often asked is, "What's in it for me?" Well, this is a completely irrelevant question if we start by trying to fix a problem that we have. If we have a problem, then we know what's in it for us. It's obvious, you get to solve the problem you have.

More and more, organizations have come up with tools to solve problems, but they forget to state the problem correctly. More importantly they don't get consensus on what the problem is.

RULE #1 – Agree on the problem (if you don't think there is a problem then, there is no problem)

When I coach executives through a process of getting organized, I make absolutely no distinction between personal tasks, and business tasks. The reason for this is because it is not the tasks that I am interested in optimizing, it is their time. In the process of identifying tasks that are necessary versus unnecessary the executive quickly realizes that they can drop 75% of their perceived activities from their to-do list. This is not done by me telling them to do this, this is done by them thinking about their time and making a choice.

The first rule in problem solving is to agree and correctly identify the problem. There are many problem solving techniques. Some are used with teams of people, such as brainstorming. Some are individual, statistical in nature such as collecting data and converting it to information using a Pareto chart. What is unclear is that before you go out and solve a problem, understand the problem. This is one of the most important lessons in this book. DO NOTHING until you have a full grasp of the problem. It is important to give out problem assignments that are increasingly harder. However, you may want to start off small, so they have created a success with the first one. You need to hold your problem solver to the understating that they will do nothing until they are able to communicate this problem and proposed solution with you.

Later in this book I make an attempt to problem solve WHY 95% of the organizations in this world fail you as an employee of theirs.

Applying the OEM Lean101 – Principles to the Home Building Industry – Please!

In 2005, I had my new home built for me by a very large and successful builder. This builder received quality awards, and was regarding as the best builder in their category.

I recognized them as the best, and as such, I trusted them to make my experience a good one. I freely give out trust to everyone I meet, but when they are recognized as the best, I try to learn from them.

This organization had nothing to offer, I was considered a piece of the equation for them, and the equation ended up where they made money, regardless of my experience. I did learn from them. I learned that when I ask a company for their vision, and mission statement, and it all sounds good and I should not trust that their entire organization believes it or follows it. I should assume in the year, 2012 anyway, that organizations would rather grow then deal with their defects. Their defects in this case are related to individuals in their organization that do not exhibit the behavior indicative of their mission statement (why they exist).

The incident happened when my family was about to move into our new home. I decided to make a final inspection the day before to ensure that everything was ready. The carpet in the basement was not yet in installed. I noticed that the edge along one wall had water stretched over a 2 foot length. I asked the builder what that water was, and they basically lied to me. They said that it was moisture, and they will dry it off, lay the carpet down, and put a dehumidifier there and eliminate any re-occurrence. I trusted him.

The next day all of my worldly possessions were moved into the house, and a lot of them were placed in the basement. We finished moving, and then the excitement started. The boxes were soaked along that same wall where I had found "moisture" the day before. The moisture was now water. I called the builder and explained the problem.

The builder asked me to pull the carpet back, and remove the underlay. Then drain the water from the carpet by any means necessary, and finally, place a fan on the area where the water was coming from. I must say, this is where my trust completely disappeared.

A problem well stated is a problem half-solved.
Charles Kettering

I can tell you what the problem was not. It was not the wet boxes, and it was not the water in the basement. You see those were the symptoms of the problem. I was lucky enough to be called upon by my clients to do problem solving training for them. So I thought, this is a great example to show them. I ended up forcing the builder to get to the root cause. However, the builder did not have any root cause training, or capability related to my problem.

So I ended up doing their work for them. First, I called in an expert with a moisture meter. This meter identifies how much moisture is contained in wood.

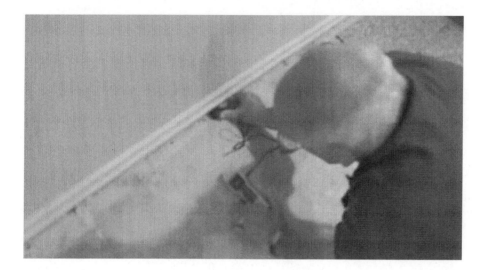

We tested the area which had a length of over 4 feet now. We discovered where the moisture in the wood should have been 15%, and now was 24.7% which fell into the "red" category on the meter. I knew it was not good. We localized the problem. We knew where the water was coming from.

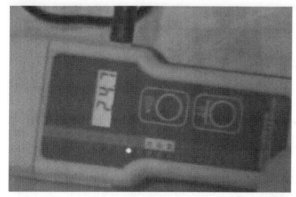

Next I cut out the drywall, in that section of the wall, removed the plastic and the insulation, and saw where there were watermarks coming from the wall itself. I looked at where the watermarks finished (this was really the start – remember I am going upstream). Since the water was coming from the wall, and now I know from where, I am now able to formulate the problem statement.

Everything done to this point was simply, Understanding the Problem. This is the most critical component to problem solving, and if you remember nothing else, remember this. Understand the problem before you agree on a solution to it. After becoming an expert on the possible causes, it was determined that this was a "honeycomb". I found out that a honeycomb occurs in basement walls when they pour the concrete, and then go on a break for a while. They are supposed to continue to agitate the concrete between the pouring processes. If this agitation is not done properly, or not done at all, a honeycomb forms. Under the right circumstances, when the water level in the ground is high, it allows water to seep through my basement walls, and onto my carpet on the floor.

Needless to say, the builder did not want to pay for the entire list of costs. They wanted me to consider that I was lucky to have found this before the new home warranty expired. I hate finding someone else's errors and then root cause of their errors, and finally not being appreciated. I was thoroughly upset that I had to do their work for them, especially for free, and at the cost of a few arguments within my family.

Well, all you need to know about root-cause analysis is this. Don't do anything, until you understand what the root cause is.

Remember, unless you get to the root cause you are looking at an effect of the problem. Fixing the symptom will not make the problem go away. You see the water on the carpet identified where we needed to lift up the carpet and look for the origin. When we placed a moisture meter on the wood, we were able to localize the problem. When I cut into the drywall of this new basement, was able to remove the vapor barrier, then the insulation, and then I found it. The evidence was the watermarks, coming through the exterior walls and winding down the wall to the place that the carpet was soaked.

 RULE #2 - Find the root cause and eliminate it.

The two rules of problem solving are all you need to know about problem solving. First, agree upon a problem. And, second, identify the root cause of that problem and eliminate it. When implementing change in any organization, it is good practice to describe the problem first. Agree upon a problem with your team.

There are 3 words to remember in the business of implementing the Lean Thinking in organizations. These words also have a sequence, first the WHY, then the WHAT, then the HOW. Everyone should know the WHEN, the WHEN is now. This basically implies that people going through change, especially drastic change, should know the Why they are going through it? Why must they endure this pain? Why is it necessary?

If you give them the answer, they may not agree with your assessment. But at least they have your perspective. Are they with you? Do they agree with your assessment? The best way to ensure that they agree is to involve them by getting them to identify the problem with you. There are too many tools that help you with problem solving. I say this because everyone seems to focus on the tools again and not the thinking process.

Step 4. Develop Countermeasures to Stop the Bleeding

know.

The biggest waste of all is the invisible waste, the waste we don't see.

The best low-cost way to educate your entire work force on Lean is to have them educate you. Let OEM educate each one of your employees. You will also learn the process that gets you back in control of your business. Not your business having control of you.

Our OEM consultants have shared many lessons-learned in the previous chapters, and here is another one about the interaction with people in an organization. There are obvious ways to measure if an organization is to be considered Lean. Measures like customer service level, and first-time quality are obvious ones. The interesting part is that an organization of Lean would behave differently by nature of their thought process. The conventional business has the business owner behaving in a certain manner. The behavior is one of a boss, saying things like, "Do this, this way", or "I want you to make sure you do it my way". In the Lean approach, the boss who is now a leader asks questions like "What do you think?"

 George's secret:

Ask questions to learn, and ask questions to teach.

If you can go through just one-day by asking questions in your organization, something miraculous will happen to you, and in the process others that are in contact with you will notice this. You will realize that people will perceive you as very knowledgeable when you may know very little about a process or your topic of discussion. You will learn more than you have ever learned before about your surroundings, including learning more about yourself. Try it for one day. That is my challenge to you.

know.

One of the best quality systems in the world today is Six Sigma.

know.

One of the best systems to help eliminate waste in the world today is Lean Thinking.

These improvement systems placed together are very powerful because there is a criterion that is set by both of them that is very difficult to achieve. Especially considering that at the base of all people-based business systems is a human process.

The criteria for a process to be "Six Sigma" are for it to have only 3.4 Defects per Million Opportunities (DPMO). Imagine that you put yourself through this process. Imagine that your task is to eliminate any misunderstanding that you make with interactions your peers. Imagine that you must communicate clearly with your verbal words, and your written words. Imagine that your communication to others must be perfect. In this way, you may be able to call your communication process a Lean Six Sigma (LSS) certified. You say exactly what you mean, and you mean exactly what you say. In this way, you have completely eliminated any miscommunication.

This is why my secret is to, **Ask questions to learn, and ask questions to teach.** I am still working on understanding my internal communication process so that when I say something, I say it in an efficient way so that others cannot misunderstand me. I am striving for perfection in my communication process. Since, I realize that this is next to impossible, I have resorted to working on the process that will allow me to get better. That is why my primary focus as a leader in Lean has me guiding others to be leaders. Encouraging the questioning process to monopolize their communication style and interaction with others.

"A problem is a state of difficulty that needs to be resolved" (WordNet)

know.

Most organizations think that the goal is to get to zero problems. With this type of thinking, problems are associated with a bad situation.

You see if a problem comes up, it becomes an indicator that you failed, and that you are not achieving your "zero defects" initiative. However, with the Lean way of thinking, problems are treasures. Problems are used so that understanding can be formed about how to improve the process again, and continual improvement is the ultimate goal for either people or process in a company that wants to be a global competitor.

know.

By being stable, with no problems, your company is moving backwards. This is simply because every company that you call a competitor is getting better by exposing and solving problems.

Assuming your problem is not about a process it is with people. After the learning about a people-type problem is the question, "What are you going to do about it?"

know.

This is not as easy.

For human beings it is completely about behaviors. I heard something very interesting once. It goes something like this… You are just as likely to get someone to work harder by paying them more, as you are likely to get a hard-working person to slow down. The programming we have in our minds causes us to behave in certain ways that we may not be aware of. After you understand your programming, it is extremely hard work to change it. The secret is in creating new routines.

In order for you to change the behavior of a person in your organization, one or both of these things must occur. One, describe what they get out of a change in the process. Educate them on what is in it for them, this way they may be able to see the benefit, and potentially do the right things on their own. Two, force new routines to occur in this way they change their thinking simply because they are engaging in new activities.

PROBLEM: My focus in my organization is on too many projects, and I am not focused on ensuring everyone understands what "Lean Thinking" is, and how to apply this thinking.

If the above statement is a problem that you own as of today, then I feel for you. You need only commit to talking with one of my coaches, there will be over 300 coaches available. More will arrive on an as needed basis. OEM is prepared and ready to help educate your employees on Lean Thinking.

First of all allow me to thank you for the online training course on lean thinking. I imagine that it took you a while to put together such an interactive and explanatory environment to show Lean. For me it was an eye-opener training course since I am a software developer. I wanted to learn more about the concepts and the basics of Lean before I introduce myself in the Lean Software Development world. So, this training course was just what I was looking for. Thank you! And keep up your good work.

Rui Gonçalves, student of OEM Lean101 – Principles, Portugal

I have had a long-enough experience in the consulting business to realize that companies (especially in North America) do not think on a long-term basis. This is one of their main failures.

After a company goes through an exciting, and enlightening change called Lean, they forget to do some of the obvious things. One of them is to train their *new* employees in the process of Lean. These employees need to be trained on the basics prior to entering the workplace.

PROBLEM: Training of new employees has not been adequate in the past.

 COUNTERMEASURE: Purchase this book for all new employees.

STANDARDIZE: Call Human Resources, ask them to ensure a book is purchased for all new hires.

By doing this above task, you will have saved yourself tens of thousands of dollars. Hiring the right people is not usually possible, however, finding people who are passionate about solving problems, and acquiring knowledge in the process, is very possible. In this way, you will have ensured that everyone in your company knows that saving time and money is not an option. It is mandatory.

 How do we get everyone working together to adopt this long-term philosophy?

A countermeasure tries to ensure that your problem does not get worse as you try to solve it. It gives you some time to deal with the root cause (after you find it) and gives assurances that the problem is not growing.

In essence, you are "stopping the bleeding". Every one of your employees should be able to communicate the 5 principles of Lean Thinking. It just stands to reason, without a certificate from the OEM Lean101 – Principles course, they should not be allowed in the door.

PROBLEM: My focus is not on the customer. I don't even know who my customer is.

Michael L. Chan - OEM Senior Leader, U.S.A.

There are many examples in my past experiences related to converting "naysayers" to Lean Thinkers. People (management and workers) that block the Lean initiatives have a hidden agenda, which is usually that they must control and retain power.

They do not want to relinquish that power, if they did it would enable workers to be more self-reliant and responsible for Safety, Quality, Delivery, Costs and ensure on-time delivery of product and services to their Valued Customers.

*The best approach is to be patient and to work with these people. You need to see if they can be converted into supporting the Lean Culture change. By showing those individuals that their responsibilities will not be taken away, and power become a different kind of power, the cultural change process has a great chance of succeeding. In fact, they will become **Team Members** or **Management Coaches** and they will have more responsibilities towards their fellow workers and subordinates. Again, the OEM Lean 101 course highlights this people development process and through the Harada Method and the OEM way these people can make the Lean culture change with the rest of the folks on the **TEAM**!*

A word of caution however, there is a 10% leaders, 80% followers, and 10% draggers distribution in every company. The draggers impede and circumvent the change process. Do not spend too much time with the 10% draggers. If you spend too much time on the draggers, the followers will migrate downwards and the leaders will leave your organization for greener pastures. Every one of the draggers will be converted or weeded out. Concentrate on the helping the 10% leaders drive the process and support the 80% that will follow the Lean culture change philosophy.

Michael Chan, Senior Leader, U.S.A., Global OEM Solutions, Inc.

Michael@OEMsolutions.ca

Step 5. Solve Problems with Teams

The best approach to take regarding involving your team in problem solving is to give them a problem, and ask them to solve it. Listen, it works. Regardless of if your business is large or small. You should try it. If you run any small business, say of 10 people, call your employees together, and then state the obvious. But state it in a certain way.

Say something like, "Everyone! I have a problem". The key word in this sentence is "I". Not "You". You can continue by describing the problem that you want them to resolve. You need to appoint a Leader who will report daily or weekly regarding progress, and give them a deadline.

"I would like you to solve this problem for me". No one should feel any pressure. They should feel excitement that you are asking them to solve the problem for you. You see, you said it was your problem, not theirs. You have the problem, and now your employees are enlisted to solve the problem for you. Or better yet, solve the problem with you. You should be answering questions that they have that surround the problem. Only answering questions. Let them develop the skill of asking questions.

Trust should be freely given, but ensure that you minimize risk by giving the group or leader increasingly larger projects to complete.

Many companies around you are getting better every day that goes by. If your pace of becoming a better organization is not faster than your competition, then you are falling behind.

What are you going to do?

The best problem-solving tool in the industry today – any industry – is called the A3 Problem Solving tool. It's the simplest form of problem solving. It contains certain categories that take the team through a problem-solving process.

The "A3" name is given to the size of paper that the problem-solving story is written on. It should be on one piece of paper. The piece of paper represents what you are to be held accountable to achieve. However, it's more of a coaching tool, rather than an accountability tool. The owner should be able to coach you on what to do next by asking you questions.

Most of the questions should be related to how you got information, how you engaged your team members, and what you learned from going through the exercise.

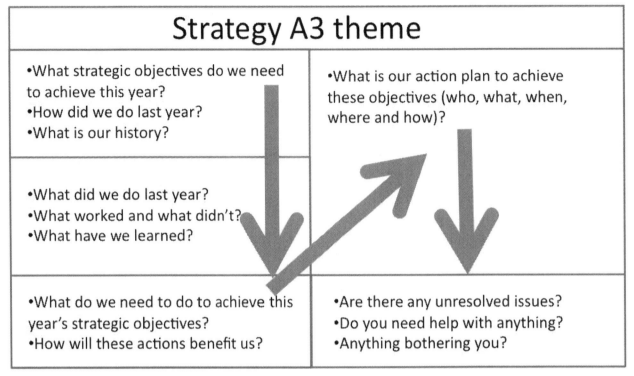

Strategy A3 theme

- What strategic objectives do we need to achieve this year?
- How did we do last year?
- What is our history?

- What is our action plan to achieve these objectives (who, what, when, where and how)?

- What did we do last year?
- What worked and what didn't?
- What have we learned?

- What do we need to do to achieve this year's strategic objectives?
- How will these actions benefit us?

- Are there any unresolved issues?
- Do you need help with anything?
- Anything bothering you?

From the book, "Getting the Right Things done" by Pascal Dennis

To get excel spreadsheet templates such as this one, become a member of the Global OEM Consortium, http://lean101.ca/weboffice.htm.

There are three roles that I identify in the problem solving process; the owner, the deployment leader, and the team (or team members).

It is extremely important that the owner (owner of the company or manager) is your coach in this process. Your coach should know how to do A3 problem solving. If they don't and you do, coach the owner. The deployment leader (you) should be able to facilitate a meeting with your team. In order to do this, your most valuable trait is that you are a humble servant to your team.

For small companies of 50 people or less, the owner and the leader may be the same person. However, I highly suggest that you secure as a coach. You need a coach. Everyone needs a coach.

Steps to take in order to go through the A3 Problem Solving process (the owner's perspective);
1. Identify a goal, or a problem for a team to work on.
2. Identify a deployment leader, someone who competent, someone who is respected, and is going to be accountable to motivating the team and supporting them to get the problem solved.

3. Call weekly meetings with your deployment leader, and ensure that your leader understands the importance of accountability.
4. Perform a weekly check, and listen to the deployment leader's concerns, thank the deployment leader for his/her hard work, and ensure that you address all issues in the bottom right corner.
5. Only answer questions, try to learn.
6. Agree when you agree. Thank them for uncovering some insight that you also share.
7. Ask questions when you disagree to probe the deployment leader's understanding.
8. Ask questions to educate your leader.
9. Bring the project to a close, and celebrate the success with the entire team.
10. Give this deployment leader another problem to solve with a team.

Steps to take in A3 Problem Solving process (from the deployment leader's perspective);
1. Do the pre-planning work, identify all of the gaps related to the top left of the A3.
2. Privately with the owner, ensure that the owner agrees on the problem, and gaps to close.
3. With the team, review the gaps, and perform the reflection of what you did in the past to solve the same problem related to the gaps. Give an assessment of what you did, what worked, what did not, and judge its effectiveness (use - red, yellow, green)
4. With the team, perform root cause analysis to identify what you need to do in order to close the gaps identified in the top left corner. Don't forget what you failed at previously and why. Ensure that everyone agrees with at least one specific cause that is the biggest impact. Try to get 3 main causes at a minimum.
5. With the team, create an action plan for each root cause and assign owners to each action with deadlines for each action.
6. Ensure weekly meetings occur with the owner. Report on progress.
7. Observe what the situation is, go to the place where the problem exists
8. Plan to close the gap.
9. Do the activities to close the gap.
10. Check on your progress.
11. Adjust your activities accordingly.
12. Ask for an assessment on your progress.
13. Agree on the assessment, or educate the owner by asking questions.
14. Plan - Do – Check – Act – **Agree – Find a problem - Agree** - Plan – Do – Check – Act

Notice the deployment leader navigates through the A3 Problem Solving process. Applying the basics, and challenging your team to "think", makes all problems and goals achievable. You need to be humble enough to ask questions of your community, and global contacts. That is what lean is about. Lean is about the continual engagement with your peers in the process of problem solving. All you need to do is support your team and ask question of your lean community.

You have the easy job, and the most satisfying job of all. You get to see the most valuable resource in your company, not machines, but the people, deliver energy to the situation, and solve problems that you never thought possible. If you are doing this right your team is energized through the entire process.

Finally the How! This is the easiest and the hardest part.

 Trust in your people to do the work.

Trust is the most important value that you can exhibit to make your business run in the most efficient way possible. Trust is the glue that keeps everybody working together. Trust is what you give, not force other's to earn. If you don't trust someone, get them out of your organization. Obviously, the problem may be yours in not trusting them. But regardless, get them out of your business.

What are we going to focus on, people or process? For OEM, this represents the "sucker's choice". A sucker's choice is a choice that you might feel you need to make this choice. The way I described it requires an answer of one or the other. Don't let anyone try to influence you in this way. As soon as you hear a question that gives you a choice of one thing or the other, remember, you don't have to answer it. It is a sucker's choice, don't be a sucker. Consider this, why not both? Why not focus on people, and educate them to world's best processes, so that people can make improvements from there. Organizations are made up of people, and people develop systems, and systems are made up of processes, which can be categorized by the tools that they deploy.

In order to understand my perspective, I will share it with you in three words. Respect – Trust – Truthfulness. With each and every employee in your company, develop a bond of respect, a bond of trust and 100% truthfulness or 100% honesty (if you wish).

Perform a test if you are the owner of your company or even if you are an employee. With pen and paper, walk around your business, and talk to at least 10 people. During your exercise, identify whether you respect, trust, and can be 100% truthful with each of those employees. You see, it's not about them, it's about you. Not them, YOU.

 Can you trust?

If you find that you are not trustworthy, if the number of people you trust is 9 or less, and then consider getting to know yourself better. Get a coach. Do the things that make you a humble leader. Take Harada training. Do something for your own development as a leader. Only in this way will you be able to show the people around you, that you are a worthy leader.

know.

Every minute of every day that you spend with your ego in the way, you lose that minute forever.

Stop wasting time know that every individual in your company needs to know that you are actively pursuing perfection. Only in this way will they respect the fact that they must do the same. Setting the example is the only way those around you will learn.

Time is the currency of tomorrow.
George Trachilis

Step 6. Develop the Bond between Mentor/Mentee

I have to tell you that each time I meet great leaders; I take advantage and ask as many questions as possible. In the process, I learn so much and my understanding is elevated from where I was to one rung higher. In 2006, I met Masaaki Imai. For those of you that don't know of Masaaki, he is known as the "Lean Guru" and the "Father of Continuous Improvement".

We walked together through a company called E.H. Price one of the leanest organizations in my hometown of Winnipeg, Canada. I observed Mr. Imai and closely monitored his every move. I was very interested in his assessment of this company. I wanted to see what he would do, who he would talk to, and what his final assessment would be. I noticed a keen understanding of work flow analysis. We stopped in an area where this lady was pressing a pin through two parts. He stood there for about 10 minutes. He was watching this lady's hand movements as she picked up a part with one hand, placed the part on the machine and pressed the pin through both parts. I observed his keen assessment of the flow of the part. He even commented to the plant manager how the part travels backwards after it makes a forward motion. He said that this motion should be eliminated.

Masaaki Imai shares his knowledge with George and others as they tour E.H.Price

You see, process is what the observation was, not the people. However, he shocked me at the end of his plant tour when he did his report out to all of the consortium members that were there. He shocked me because his assessment, regardless of how he got to it was the same as mine. I will show you a visual of the PowerPoint presentation that he put together.

He said non-Lean companies are strong. They are like the Neanderthal man. He explained how many companies in North America are rigid, as he pointed with his stick to the upper back and shoulders of the middle monkey. These companies are made for strength and for fighting. He then focused his attention over to the right hand side is where he pointed his stick to the evolved human. He explained how Lean companies operate. They are more flexible, able to adjust quickly, nimble, and more importantly evolve. Non-lean companies cannot make this advancement too quickly to the right side of the picture. They need to start evolving slowly, get rid of the limitations that exist within their organizations before they can stand upright. He further explained that the Neanderthal man has an extra bone in his vertebrae; this prevents him from standing upright. This is exactly the same for non-lean companies. They are structured in a way that limits their performance. They need to become more flexible. Then they need to start standing more upright and then learn how to walk before they can run. Companies that are not lean must discard some structural limitations so that they can perform as lean companies do... without being limited.

The above was a response from Masaaki to the question that I raised. "What is the biggest difference between companies that are lean versus the ones that are not?". I guess that is the most popular question, because he had the PowerPoint slide ready.

In June 2012, I had the pleasure of meeting the owner of this company once again. I reminded him of the plant tour done by Masaaki. He recalled it immediately. He said, "You know George, the report that we got back was that we were 50% the way there." He later replied, "Now that is exciting! Considering the progress we have made so far, to have that much more to go is very exciting". I have to say, that is the right attitude to have. Problems are treasures.

An understanding of the meaning of Kaizen

Kaizen is a key to the success of a truly competitive organization. However, our interpretation of Kaizen is why we have accepted it as a process that we need to duplicate, and not a philosophy. You see, we don't really understand what Kaizen means. Maybe my communication should be a little clearer… You don't really understand what Kaizen means.

Here is a good definition of Kaizen;

Kaizen (改善$^?$), Japanese for "improvement", or "change for the better" refers to philosophy or practices that focus upon continuous improvement of processes in manufacturing, engineering, and business management. It has been applied in healthcare, psychotherapy, life-coaching, government, banking, and other industries. When used in the business sense and applied to the workplace, kaizen refers to activities that continually improve all functions, and involves all employees from the CEO to the assembly line-workers. It also applies to processes, such as purchasing and logistics…

Wikipedia

The essence of Kaizen is simple and straightforward: Kaizen means improvement. Moreover, Kaizen means ongoing improvement involving everyone, including both managers and workers. The Kaizen philosophy assumes that our way of life – deserves to be constantly improved.

Lean Organizations have developed a process-oriented way of thinking, which helps them guarantee continuous improvement with their people. This guarantees continuous improvement with their processes, because people create systems, and systems are made up of processes and tools.

Understanding why Kaizen does not happen in non-lean companies.

When companies that I know of look at Kaizen, they confirm that it is a "good thing do". Again, I point out the mistake, they try *to do* this. Kaizen is an output. What they see are tools like pull systems, andon lights, 5S, QC circles, Automation, TPM, Just-in-Time, Zero Defects, and a plethora of other techniques. These are the tools that are used to create processes that work. These processes work only to improve the company. But NONE of these tools improve your thought process. Your thought process can only be improved if you have a system of thinking that allows for improvement. The way most experts I know describe this is that they have removed the "ego" from conversations. Well, it really isn't anyone removing the ego. It is me and you not allowing it to get in the way of making improvement.

The OEM way is one of creating a bond of respect, trust, and truthfulness with all our customers, suppliers, partners, and yes, competitors. For OEM this is the only way that this is going to happen so that everyone we engage with feels safe. This is what I came up with about ten years ago. Well, it seems that I hit the nail on the head. Just a few months ago I was listening to a blog by Robert Porter Lynch (Proctor and Gamble), and he was describing some key understanding about the brain.

When you do the research virtually no one talks about the issue of trust when it comes to innovation. Do I trust the people that I am working with? Do I trust the process that I'm engaged in? Do I trust that I'll be taken care of after this innovation project is over? It's something you can't just bury but unfortunately most people don't talk about trust because they don't understand what it's really about. Until we understand what trust is about it's a great fuzzy hole, people abandon it and they go to something that they consider is more clear. My mission in life is to take this trust thing and turn it from fuzzy wuzzy into something that has a design, architecture, a science, strategy and best practices behind it.

Based on Robert's comments above, I will have to engage him in the future. He touches on the subject that has been preventing "innovation projects" or "Lean Thinking" from getting a good foothold in industry. He explains the following;

First of all, [the brain of] every human being on the planet has four drives. Those four drives are very simple and there's a simple pneumonic device to remember them.

A - Acquire B – Bond C - Create D – Defend

Every one of us has these built into our brains through millions of years of evolution. What ends up happening is that if you feel that innovation is threatening you then your drive to defend will create adrenaline. That will shut off the drives to create, acquire and bond with other people.

The key is revealed regardless of a complete understanding of the brain, since we can create a countermeasure.

You see, no one in this world will know you better than you. Unless you disagree with me, and in that case, I agree with you as well (Socrates). But, let's continue.

If an organization wants to put a countermeasure in place that strives to apply Lean Six Sigma to the human processes, then as far as I am concerned there is only one thing they need to measure as a defect. The defect would occur when the drive to Defend starts up. Each time the Defend drive starts we have someone, somewhere in our organization detached from the whole.

Their drive to acquire, bond, and collaborate is shut down. This is a defect. We are in jeopardy of losing this person. Energy must go back into engaging this individual again, and there could be damage done. Defending is not the way to go. Stated differently, forcing someone to defend his or her position is not the way to go. It immediately stops our need to bond, which is the main reason for OEM's existence.

How do we measure this defect? Well that is simple too. You need a daily diary. I suggest you create one for yourself. As a company, you cannot force anyone to create a daily diary, but you can encourage the process, by providing all of your new employees with a mentor when they arrive in your organization. The understanding that everyone in the organization should have, is;

Do not force anyone to defend their point of view. Just ask questions to learn from them.

The assumption should be made that you can learn from everyone around you. As a mentor you can learn, and definitely, as a mentee you should be learning. It does not have to be learning about this method of communicating, it can be anything. Learn about the products you sell, the services you sell, the customer.

Regardless of what you are learning, your daily diary should be filled out every day so that you can assess for yourself, where did your D drive kick in? What was the conversation about?

Why did you feel like you had to defend yourself? When are you going to mention this conversation to your mentor?

The mentors' job is to support the mentee, and encourage the right behavior.

A defect that causes the drive to Defend to kick in and shut everything down is of an interaction. This interaction can be analyzed. It does not need to be personalized. To understand the root cause, the first step is to collect information and DO NOTHING until you know what the problem is. Only through this method of identifying defects which stifle innovation, can a company go from being considered a Neanderthal man to the most evolved human being on the right hand side of the illustration shown earlier.

You as a company owner don't need to do anything more than create a continuous improvement system that starts encouraging the exposure of these defects. By encouraging the discussion of these crucial conversations, the number of times the "D" drive kicks in will decrease because you have developed countermeasures, and healthy discussion around the topic.

The OEM way is one that is measured by recognizing that someone else's "D" drive has kicked in. My measure of how well I am doing is simple.

If I create a situation where someone else's D-drive kicks in, I consider that a failure for me. I don't worry about the company not recording it. I am in an endless loop of improvement for myself. I get defensive, and I know the other person does not know my technique, because if they did, they would use it on me, and keep the relationship healthy and growing for a lifetime.

So, why do YOU think that Kaizen does not happen in non-lean companies?

This brings the most important chapter of the book to a close. I started my book with OEM Lean101-Principles the best training in the world. Insight from the Expert, Jeffrey K. Liker, wisdom from the "Godfather of Lean", Norman Bodek, experience from the "Lean Guru", Masaaki Imai, and then a discussion of neuroscience of the brain. This, coupled with the examples from James Bond, it should be obvious that I have instilled a process for myself to use.

My process is to;
- ✓ remove my ego from every conversation that I engage in.
- ✓ acquire knowledge from great teachers.
- ✓ bond as quickly as humanly possible with my colleagues.
- ✓ create custom-designed solutions with my chosen customers.

The only indicator I use regarding failure, is when I have forced someone to defend themselves, or their belief process. This is when I know that I have removed myself from their circle of trust.

The OEM way, is shown in the visual below.

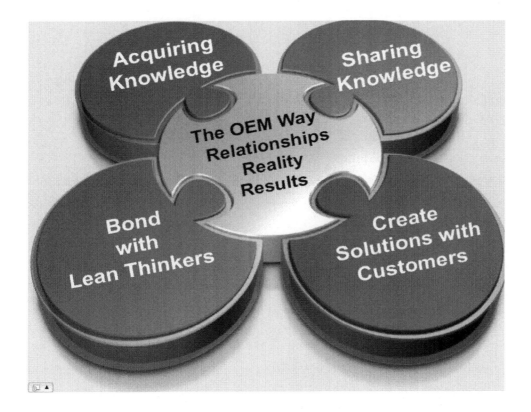

We are moving to a knowledge-based economy and as a result we must learn to become part of this knowledge-based world by creating a learning organization of OEM Lean Thinkers. Through innovation we will gain and then share our knowledge so that our organization will retain a competitive advantage over all other consulting firms – our belief system shown above.

The 100-Monkey Plan

One day I was visiting a company that was on the verge of a very exciting technology. I wanted to know their how they were planning on releasing information related to their grandiose claims. The CEO handed me a plan that had a lot of activities, but that really did not interest me after I got a glimpse of the title of the document.

The 100th Monkey Plan. I initially thought that it was disrespectful to talk about people as monkeys. But after you hear the story behind it, I think you will be as excited as I was. You see, this story is about social change. The company I visited had a story was about changing the way the world operates with their technology. And now, I must say, this story seems the most appropriate for me as well. I want my system for engaging people to be recognized by all of the relationships that I set up, then duplicated with my stakeholders, so that we create a great relationships between employees and their employer because the technique for learning and teaching is greatly improved using the OEM way.

The 100th Monkey

A story about social change.

By Ken Keyes Jr.

The Japanese monkey, Macaca Fuscata, had been observed in the wild for a period of over 30 years.

In 1952, on the island of Koshima, scientists were providing monkeys with sweet potatoes dropped in the sand. The monkeys liked the taste of the raw sweet potatoes, but they found the dirt unpleasant.

An 18-month-old female named Imo found she could solve the problem by washing the potatoes in a nearby stream. She taught this trick to her mother. Her playmates also learned this new way and they taught their mothers too.

This cultural innovation was gradually picked up by various monkeys before the eyes of the scientists. Between 1952 and 1958 all the young monkeys learned to wash the sandy sweet potatoes to make them more palatable. Only the adults who imitated their children learned this social improvement. Other adults kept eating the dirty sweet potatoes.

Then something startling took place. In the autumn of 1958, a certain number of Koshima monkeys were washing sweet potatoes -- the exact number is not known. Let us suppose that when the sun rose one morning there were 99 monkeys on Koshima Island who had learned to wash their sweet potatoes. Let's further suppose that later that morning, the hundredth monkey learned to wash potatoes.

THEN IT HAPPENED!

By that evening almost everyone in the tribe was washing sweet potatoes before eating them. The added energy of this hundredth monkey somehow created an ideological breakthrough!

But notice: A most surprising thing observed by these scientists was that the habit of washing sweet potatoes then jumped over the sea...Colonies of monkeys on other islands and the mainland troop of monkeys at Takasakiyama began washing their sweet potatoes.

Thus, when a certain critical number achieves awareness, this new awareness may be communicated from mind to mind.

Although the exact number may vary, this Hundredth Monkey Phenomenon means that when only a limited number of people know of a new way, it may remain the conscious property of these people.

But there is a point at which if only one more person tunes-in to a new awareness, a field is strengthened so that this awareness is picked up by almost everyone!

From the book "The Hundredth Monkey" by Ken Keyes, Jr.
The book is not copyrighted and the material may be reproduced in whole or in part.

CHAPTER 11 - The Harada Method

The Toyota Production System has its focus in two key areas. Just-in-Time and Jidoka. When I went to see Norman Bodek, "The Godfather of Lean", in March 2012 for one-week training course on the Harada Method. He explained how the recent recalls done by Toyota could have been greatly minimized through the practice of Zenjidoka. Had they practiced Zenjidoka, Toyota's customer service personnel and technicians would have raised a red flag, communicated with each other across dealerships, and solved problems much sooner. The Harada Method assists in establishing a Zenjidoka system.

At the heart of this system is Monozukuri & Hitozukuri. Monozukuri is "building excellent products" and Hitozukuri is "building excellence in people". Now here is the hard part... Hitozukuri is an organization's commitment to developing the skills and knowledge of all of their employees. Not many organizations can make this commitment. Here is an excerpt from Norman's new book (not yet printed as of June, 2012) on the Harada Method. After you read this, think about what you want to do with your life. Pick the most challenging goal you can. Then, follow each of these steps in sequence to get a quick understanding of the kind of insight you should be revealing for your employees. Remember, you are now developing a long-term philosophy for yourself, not your organization. This should drive your life from now on. Your long-term goal will take precedence over short-term goals that do not align with it. What a miraculous thought. We get out of the zombie like state by applying this long-term thinking.

The Harada Method is considered by many in Japan to be the world's best on day-to-day management to develop people to their fullest potential.

We normally consider senior managers to be fully self-reliant, to make the right decisions for the company, but this level of trust does not exist throughout the organization. When people are not viewed as self-reliant, they are closely monitored, and restricted. We found this amazing methodology *The Harada Method* that has been successfully applied in Japan these past fifteen years and it is our privilege to introduce it to the West.

Takashi Harada, a world-renowned coach, trainer and consultant, currently resides in Osaka, Japan. Takashi Harada initially was a junior high school track and field coach and he developed a method to transform a group of underachievers in one of the worst schools in Osaka into outstanding athletes. Thirteen students won gold medals, becoming the best in all of Japan in their age group, and the school became number one, out of 380 schools, for the next 12 years in a row. Many of these underachievers after learning from Mr. Harada achieved scholarships and went on to high school, college and into successful careers in industry.

Mr. Harada, after 20 years as a teacher, opened a consulting practice in 2002 and has taught over 55,000 people in 280 companies to use his training method to build both successful companies and successful lives.

Harada developed this marvelous technique to encourage students to excel and was able to take the same principles used to guide and build successful students into the world of business where thousands of people are improving their lives. The Harada Method leads people through a carefully thought out process, similar to a winning sport's team, to build a great company with outstanding employees.

Let us go through an example of the method:

Become an Astronaut

Imagine you want to be an astronaut, a person trained by a human spaceflight program to command, pilot, or serve as a crew member of a spacecraft. From where you are right now in life, what would you have to do to become an astronaut? :

1.   First, you can clearly define your goal and you can envision what it might take for you to become an astronaut. You believe in your ability to go through the rigorous steps and know that you have the willingness to overcome all obstacles to attain your goal. You can dream and see yourself in the future inside the space station. You have some real good knowledge of how to keep your spirits high, what kind of skills are needed for you to develop yourself, what would be needed to build your physical condition and also how it would require you to maintain a balance in your life style: relations with your family, friends, teachers, fellow astronauts and your community.

2.   You would then develop interim goals, building blocks, with specific measures and dates to monitor your progress. You would know when you have to be able to do certain key things that demonstrate your ability to be an astronaut.

3.   Then you would look deeply within yourself to discover the real purpose and value of becoming an astronaut and what the tangible and intangible benefits can be to yourself and to others.

4.   Clearly you understand what it means to be fully self-reliant where others will be fully supportive and know that you have the integrity, the knowledge, the skill, and the ability to make the right decisions and handle correctly all future responsibilities.

5.   You then analyze yourself, looking at your past successes and strengths with the thought on how to improve and repeat them in the future.

6.   You also analyze yourself again but this time you look at your past failures, the things you did not succeed at, with the thought on how you can prevent those failures from re-occurring again.

7.   Now try to anticipate any obstacles that might stand in your way of succeeding.

8.   You then write the potential countermeasures to those obstacles.

9.   It is time to create a list of detailed tasks, actions, and plans that you will have to take to build your skills and capabilities to become an astronaut. We call this the 64 chart.

10. Look at all of the above, closely noticing those habits, patterns and routines that prevented you from succeeding in your life and then write out a list of new routines that you need to do almost daily to set and keep you on the right path.

11. To gain the necessary confidence you will write down the kind of support you will need from others to attain your goals and who you know that you will give that support.

12. Lastly, you will keep a daily diary showing your schedule for each day with the tasks to be taken to insure that you will attain your goal.

The above items are a shortened version of the Harada Method. It might seem not too spectacular but when you fill in the details and proceed to follow them every day you will give yourself the greatest chance of succeeding and becoming an astronaut. The Harada Method is your guide. It does not tell you what to do. You pick your own goal but following the method is the best way for you to succeed.

When you play a sport, you primarily motivate yourself. The coach is there to help you, but you are the one that wants to succeed. You believe in yourself. You don't want to let your team down. You measure your own success. You establish the necessary steps or tasks to attain your goal.
The Harada Method is a well thought out process on how to take the concept of great sport's activities to help you plan how to be successful at work and in your daily life.
The Harada Method is the missing link to successful Lean efforts. It is the Human Side of Lean. It overcomes the Eighth Waste: the underutilization of people's creative talents. It empowers people to take charge of their own life to become highly skilled on the job. It teaches how the company and every employee can be successful at the same time.

The purposes of the Harada Method

- To teach managers to become leaders and coaches
- To help people develop their talents to their fullest
- To learn how to lead and motivate people to become high achievers
- To create a vision for long term personal success
- To raise your level of Self-esteem to help you achieve your vision
- To learn and understand how to communicate better within your organization
- To learn and understand the technique of goal setting
- How to be an independent person – self-reliant
- Setting both long term and short term goals and objectives
- How to build your skills and be trusted for making decisions
- Methods to enhance confidence
- How to solve problems to make your work easier and more interesting
- Why keeping a journal is important – write, write like crazy
- Everyone can work towards their personal success – success is a repeatable technique
- This is what I need to do my job better
- Unlimited growth is our target
- Why you need a coach and what are the coach's basic skills
- Attaining personal mastery
- How to be a mentor and set up a mentor/mentee process in your organization
- Self-improvement with management guidance
- To help you focus on value adding activities and to eliminate wasteful activities
- How to set new habits to lead you to success

The Method focuses on people breaking out of their constraining routine molds to achieve new levels of success.

As Mr. Harada says:

"Everyone can be successful"

When people can be empowered to pick their own goals and are taught how to achieve those goals, they come to work with a new level of enthusiasm and excitement. Throwing the javelin is not easy and takes many hours of practice, but athletes with clear goals are able to go beyond the pain and stay on course. You can do the same at work when you able to establish clear goals.

"If I decided to run the triathlon
And to do it six months from
Now; nothing will stand in the
Way of my practice!"

When you can pick your own growth goal, and deeply believe in your ability to attain that goal, virtually nothing can prevent you from attaining it.

Norman Bodek, the "Godfather of Lean"
Bodek@PCSpress.com

Norman Bodek (the Godfather of Lean) coaches George Trachilis on the Harada Method - March, 2012.

CHAPTER 12 – The Six Sigma Process

Six Sigma is one of the world's best quality techniques, and it is worth knowing. Drive the car by looking forward, not looking backwards. That is why most organizations who adopt the world's best practices will start by laying out a foundation of 5S, the system for workplace organization and standardization. This is so that consistency can be created in a process that you are trying to measure. There is enough variability in every process because of the people. And most of the implementations that I am involved in are people-based technology. Six Sigma falls into the category of being both, people based and process based.

Variation Reduction using the Six Sigma Process

Six Sigma is a process developed by Motorola in the early 1980's. It uses a broad set of statistical and analytical tools, interwoven into a business problem-solving process. Six Sigma uses statistical, lean and process tools in the five-step **DMAIC Process**. This methodology is used to design new products, improve current processes, decrease downtime, eliminate waste, improve customer satisfaction and reduce variation. When followed systematically, the process insures that variation, once uncovered and controlled, never returns.

Define
What is the defect, who does it affect, how big is the problem?

Measure
What is good enough, what is the current process?

Analyze
What is the cause of the problem and what can we change?

Improve
What improvements will optimize the product, process or service?

Control
Institutionalize the improvement and sustain the gain.

Developed by Motorola as a defect reduction concept in manufacturing, Six Sigma was then applied to other business processes. Motorola was spending between 5 to 10% of their annual revenue correcting concerns related to poor quality. This translated into approximately $900 million per year in lost profits.

In 1982, Motorola, in an effort to verify that their DMAIC Process actually worked, set the following internal goals:

- Achieve a 10x level of improvement in both quality and service by 1989.

- Achieve a 100x level of improvement by 1991.

- Achieve full 6-Sigma capability by 1992.

The results for Motorola were impressive. They validated that the Six Sigma Process worked:

- by 1989, Motorola had saved $2.2 billion using 6-Sigma

- by 1993, Motorola was operating at near 6-Sigma levels

Motorola's secret was combining a number of existing quality tools into something called Six Sigma:

Total Quality Management

Zero Defects

Statistical Process Control

Plan – Do – Check - Act

Lean Six Sigma is a synergized managerial concept of Lean and Six Sigma that results in the elimination of the seven kinds of wastes/muda (classified as Defects, Overproduction, Transportation, Waiting, Inventory, Motion and Over-Processing) and provision of goods and service at a rate of 3.4 defects per million opportunities (DPMO) . **Wikipedia.**

Everyone should know that they can't stay on any journey without the people side of Lean being addressed. Now for those companies who started off with Six Sigma initiatives, there is no point changing over completely. Six Sigma is the best system out there for reducing the variation in a process. So let's learn about LSS or Lean Six Sigma from our master black belt trainer.

"In the past 20 years, Motorola has documented over $17 billion in savings to their company through the use of the Six Sigma Process."

6-Sigma: The Overall Approach

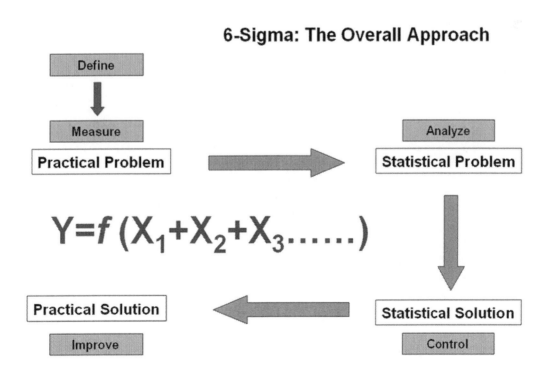

$$Y = f(X_1 + X_2 + X_3 \ldots \ldots)$$

The Six Sigma process is ....

A Methodology

- Define, Measure, Analyze, Improve, Control

- The 5 step process to identify a problem and prevent recurrence

A Philosophy

- Monitoring and controlling Inputs and Outputs

- **y = f(x)** The Output **y** is a function of **x**

- If you control the inputs, you can control the outputs

A Set of Statistical & Analytical Tools

- Qualitative and Quantitative

- Statistics, Flow & Control Charts, DOE, FMEA

- Lean, Kaizen

The Greek letter sigma **σ** is the mathematical symbol used to signify standard deviation.

- Standard Deviation is the measure of variation.

- Variation is how things change batch to batch, or over time.

- Variation is the distribution or spread of data from the target.

$$\sigma = \sqrt{\frac{\sum_{i=1}^{N}(X_i - \mu)^2}{N}}$$

So what is variation?

Variation is the difference found between similar or identical objects. It refers to the slight measurement difference that is detected within a batch or group of items. Statistically speaking, random variation places most data into a Normal Distribution; mathematically a Normal Distribution is defined by the Mean and Standard Deviation.

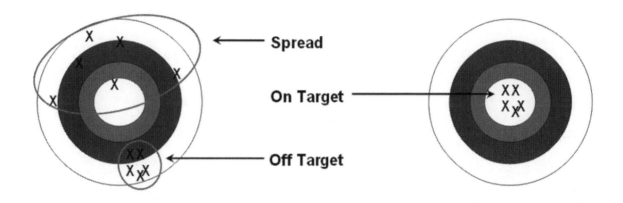

Mean and Standard Deviation are values calculated from the measured data. Mean is also known as the Average of a set of data

There is a mathematical or ""Empirical Rule"" in statistics that states:

• 68% of data is distributed within 1 standard deviation of the mean or average.

• 95% of data is distributed within 2 standard deviations of the mean or average.

• Almost 99.7% of data will fall within 3 standard deviations of the mean or average.

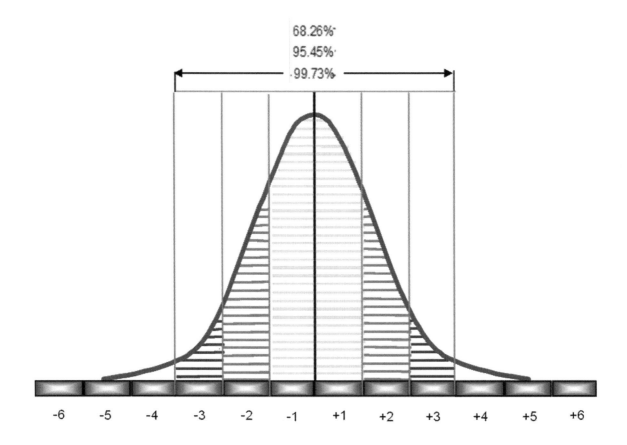

All of this merely indicates that when we have a bunch of measurement data, we can calculate some values (Standard Deviation) to determine how they disperse under the Bell Shaped Curve. So why is this all important?

Notice that the Bell Shaped Curve contains 99.73% of the data within plus or minus (+/-) 3 standard deviations. It is these Standard Deviations that we refer to as **Sigma** Levels. If the Sigma Level is +/- 6, then we have captured 99.99966% of the data"

Sigma = Standard Deviation

Whenever you measure something, it will fall into a distribution of data. This data can then be averaged, standard deviations determined and Sigma Values calculated. Knowing the Sigma Value, or Level of a process indicates if it is "***Just Good enough***" or whether we think we "***need it to be better.***"

Some companies are content with their operation or product if it performs satisfactorily 90% of the time. Others require a performance level of 99.9%. If your surgeon implanted a pacemaker in your heart, and the success rate of the device was 99%, then 1 in 100 of these pacemakers would fail. Would you want this pacemaker, or would you require one that performed at 99.99966%?

6 Sigma = 99.99966% Success Rate = 3.4 Defects per Million

Let's look at some common processes and see what the difference between 3.8-sigma and 6-sigma actually means to the consumer:

Process or Operation	3.8 Sigma Level 99% Good	6.0 Sigma Level 99.99966% Good
Pieces of Mail lost per hour	20,000	7
Minutes of unsafe Drinking Water	15 minutes/Day	1 Min. in 7 Months
Incorrect Surgical Procedures	5,000/week	1.7/week
Wrong Prescriptions per year	200,000	68
No Electricity	7 hours/month	1 hour in 34 years

One of the primary Six Sigma measurements is known as **DPMO**, or the number of "**D**efects **per** **M**illion **O**pportunities". When we begin to view defects on such a large scale, their presence is magnified as you'll soon see in their calculations.

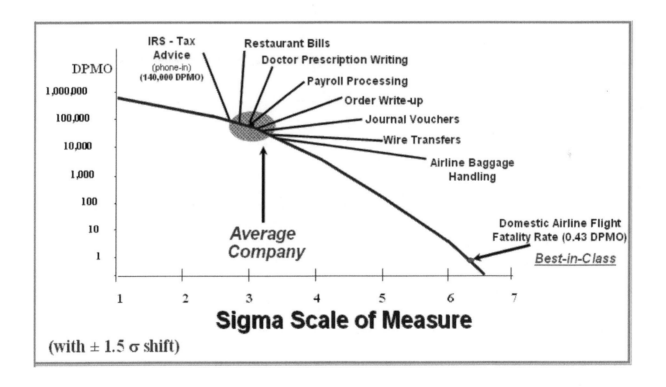

So why do we care about Sigma Levels and Variation?

The Six Sigma DMAIC Process can help you identify and quantify causes of variation, and develop solutions that will either eliminate or control those variables. As a Team Member of a problem resolution team, you have to ask yourself:

- Do we provide products or services that don't meet customer expectations, or fail to meet a particular specification?

- Do we produce products that are either scrapped or require rework?

Six Sigma allows you to compare your measurement or defect data with how well it meets a customer specification. The goal is to manufacture or produce products and services that are defect free. When the left and right hand tails of your Bell Shaped Curve exceed the defined specifications, then you just produced scrap.

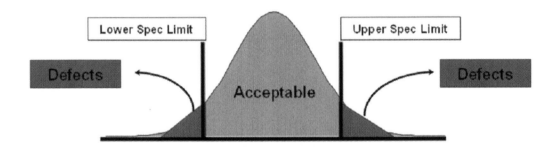

One method of insuring that you don't generate customer defects is by creating your own internal specifications for the product that does not exceed the customers. This however will require tighter control of your existing process to insure you haven't merely increased your scrap rate.

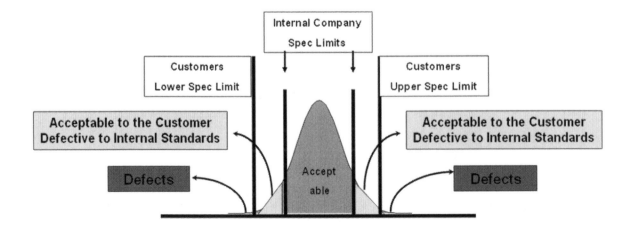

This section on Six Sigma is merely an introduction to the general concepts. To truly understand the Six Sigma Process, one needs to attend at a minimum, a 40 hour Greenbelt Training Seminar. This is where you become familiar with and begin to use many of the tools and applications of Six Sigma. One of the fundamental concepts of Six Sigma understands defect levels, as seen below.

How are Defects and Sigma Levels Related?

6-Sigma uses a number of calculations (metrics) to determine failure rates. The most common is DPMO, or Defects per Million Opportunities.

$$(DPU)\ Defect\ Per\ Unit = \frac{\#\ observed\ Defects}{\#\ Units}$$

> You make 10 Pizza's and 1 is bad: **DPU = 1/10 = 0.10**

$$(DPO)\ Defect\ Per\ Opportunity = \frac{\#\ Defects\ per\ Unit}{\#\ of\ opportunities\ for\ error\ per\ unit}$$

> It's not just the wrong Pizza, it has 5 chances to be the wrong Pizza

You make a Sausage Pizza with the wrong crust:

DPO = (1 Wrong Crust) / [(3 Crust Flavors) + (2 Sausage Types)]
= 1/5 = **0.20**

$$(DPMO)\ Defect\ Per\ Million\ Opportunities = \frac{\#\ Defects\ per\ Unit \times 1,000,000}{\#\ of\ opportunities\ for\ error\ per\ unit}$$

DPMO = [(1) x **1,000,000**] / 5 = 200,000

> 200,000 DPMO is basically 2.5 Sigma

Let's see a simple example of how Six Sigma actually works. The following occurred at Tyson Foods, incorporated in Buffalo, NY. The results are the benefits of implementing Six-Sigma Greenbelt Training for their employees.

Tyson Foods is a high quality manufacturer of processed meats. They were concerned that they couldn't always determine the root cause of a plant problem, so they utilized 6-Sigma Green Belt Training and saved over $300,000 in product yield and waste reduction during the first year of their program.

One of the areas the newly trained Greenbelts concentrated on was in the Cold Cut Slicing process. Here is what they found:

- Tyson slices over 300,000 pounds a week of cold cuts and puts them into 12 ounce packages.
- Many finished packages exceeded the 12 ounce weight minimum.
- Tighter weight controls allowed them to save approximately $140,000/year.

Other Six Sigma Green Belt Projects at this Tyson facility during the first year resulted in the following:

- $90,000 reduction in Kitchen Scrap due to change over improvements between different meat products.
- $70,000 increase in Ham yield due to process changes in the baking cycle.

Six Sigma is a very powerful process that concentrates on variation reduction. It has been said that program management solves problems with known solutions, while Six Sigma resolves concerns with no known solution. We highly encourage every company to send their employees to Six Sigma training to reap the benefits they truly deserve.

Daniel J. Stanley, Senior Leader, Six Sigma, Global OEM Solutions, Inc.

IQF Certified Six Sigma Master Blackbelt

Daniel@OEMsolutions.ca

CHAPTER 13 – Create and Collaborate

It is a weakness in companies that do not use their suppliers regarding innovation.

know.

Many suppliers are looking for customers to align themselves with in a strategic way.

There are so many examples in industry where a company that is selling their goods and/or services cut their supply base off from dealing with the end user. There are even more examples where a company has a large supply chain, and does not use them to their potential. This NxtNote is on a wonderful collaboration tool that has been used to implement a system of eliminating problems before they happen. That is Lean and Six Sigma put together. Any tool that is working the relationship side of the equation with employees should be promoted, adopted, and supported by upper management. Focus energy in the collaboration process, and watch as your team's productivity soar. NxtNote is being custom-designed to OEM customer requirements. It has just been molded to create a Value Stream Mapping process across global boundaries with a very high degree of flexibility. Get a NxtNote demonstration by emailing me, George@OEMsolutions.ca, and use OEM just as we use NxtNote to deliver value to our customers.

Lean Project Delivery

Can It Ensure a Project's BIG FIVE Metrics are achieved?

Ed Anderson, Senior Leader, Global OEM Solutions, Construction and Project Management. Ed@OEMsolutions.ca

It's one thing to say "Collaboration is King," but another to know HOW to accomplish effective collaboration. I site a couple of examples on the "How To" collaborate using a couple of powerful tools. These tools all but guarantee that the BIG FIVE metrics are met – safety, quality, schedule, cost, and sustainability (profitability).

Lean project delivery methods enable a win-win scenario for all stakeholders through a process of continuous collaboration from project conception through start-up.

The process promotes improving the project as a whole; the needs of teams come second.

This process is one that enables teams to collaborate immediately. All project members through resolve to work through process issues collaboratively. Many organizations let the "bright lights" of new technology blind them to the fact that it is of no value by itself. My good friend, Joe Morray, president of Trinity Technologies says it best: "Every project we embark on marries technology (tools) with work processes that enable people to achieve extraordinary results."

Solutions are negotiated at the lowest level in the organization with a "face-to-face" discussion. We talk to each other as opposed to sending emails back and forth. One case study details some of the results that can be achieved.

A Case Study and History of the use of Enabling Tools

Interestingly, introducing lean project delivery methods started with contractor stakeholders, not owners' legal departments. Contractors who wanted to deliver better products through a formalized "agreement of trust" among themselves. The tools that supported this process were 3D CAD (three-dimensional computer-aided design), ECM (enterprise content management) for visualization, and the most exciting of these tools is called NxtNote.

The overarching values that these tools bring are twofold:

1) **Improve collaboration and communication** among all project stakeholders to reduce project risk and maximize the BIG FIVE, and;

2) Deliver **a high quality information asset** (IA) as a by-product of the project.

Conventional projects that do not utilize these IT tools effectively require as much as 3% of the total installed cost be added to the project to deliver the IA for projects. This is a cost that our teams have eliminated through proper use of these tools.

The importance of 3D visualization and ECM is the ability for the casual end-user to create a work package that consists of both "pictures and lists."

While pictures have great intuitive value of comprehension, the details (lists) behind the pictures must also be available to put the pictures in explicit context.

"I didn't have to teach my kids how to watch TV"

Many owners believe that in order to get the benefits of 3D they must be proficient in 3D design software. This is not the case as there are many excellent 3D visualization software tools that are much easier to use than 3D design systems. Visualization includes the ability to view and redline documents, as well as generate 3D views.

Think of it this way: people want to watch TV with a smart remote and a selection device to pick what they want to see. They do not need to own the studios where the movies and TV shows are produced, do they? The same is true of 3D design software versus 3D/2D visualization software. It is why we classify visualization as a separate tool.

One case study completed in 1998, of which the author was an integral member, budgeted at $10 million, consisted of a major revamp of a chemical manufacturing facility. The plant project group employed three of the tools

A key requisite was that a full-time *change management team* was put in place to help the project team create and manage the new work processes that the tools enabled, and the evolution of those processes as the project progressed. You could think of this *change management team* as internal consultants. The senior management of this chemical manufacturer was ahead of its time in knowing that more money spent wisely up front would result in significant downstream benefits – the BIG FIVE *concurrently* improved.

An independent, third-party analysis group concluded that the performance of the project was "excellent." One key metric used was the MFL (Modified Lang Factor), an industry standard that quantifies cost comparisons between like projects. This project had an actual MFL of 3.7 vs. the industry average of 4.7, a 21% improvement over industry norms.

The coordination between engineering/design and operations allowed changes to be made early and virtually in the model as opposed to being made in the field. Coordination meetings were often conducted 2 or 3 times a week, both among individuals, as well as teams. While these were very effective they did not achieve what we can now achieve using NxtNote (more on this shortly).

And finally, the plant was restarted four days early, which provided a $1 million bonus for manufacturing. One new type of construction drawing that 3D enabled, shows what needs to happen before, during, and after a plant outage. It also advises the construction personnel of a key safety issue: where operations and maintenance will place the blinds to assure safe entry.

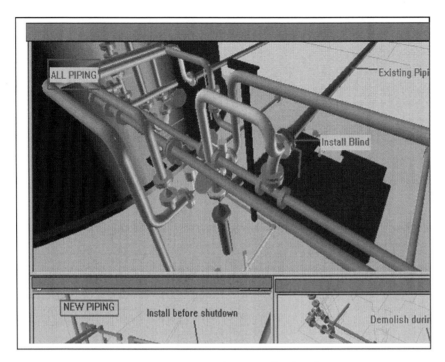

A New Type of Construction Drawing

The NxtNote Phenomenon

Let's skip ahead in time and consider how the results we achieved in 1998 could have been even more positive if we had a more effective tool to fill the gaps of what, at the time, we thought was the most effective method of collaboration.

In 1998 we did not utilize "sticky note collaboration" practices at all. We probably would have if we had known the value. Today, that practice is utilized globally with great effect as it allows every stakeholder to express their own opinion in their own words, and for those words to be posted on a wall where everyone can consider the combined effect of the individual ideas. It's another form of visualization that enables people to make better and faster decisions.

Even better, the sticky notes can be moved around to create, for instance, a much-improved plan since the stakeholders agree on the proper sequence. It is not just a to-do list. And the issue of "How do we get people to buy in to the plan?" is no more... People who co-create their own plan obviously buy into it.

The picture below is a standard sticky-note collaboration planning session where each team leader has their own colored stickies, and writes their own notes and places them on the planning wall.

Sticky Note Collaboration

NxtNote adds another dimension to the "sticky note collaboration process." The table below outlines the differences between conventional sticky note behavior and the enhanced NxtNote behavior.

Conventional "Sticky Note Collaboration"	NxtNote Collaboration
Handwritten notes are difficult to read as everyone has a different style – no standardization. The person doing the transposition can be easily confused and agitated.	NxtNotes are typewritten via computers, iPads, &/or smart phones to a central color printer. Look at the picture below to see the difference between hand-written notes and NxtNotes.
Color-coded notes tell us who proposed the item	Same with NxtNote, except anonymity is also possible.
The data input is freeform, and it is often difficult to separate the action from an adjective, making the note seem irrational in many cases, requiring further clarification by the owner. Rework is inherent.	NxtNotes puts every type of data into a specific location that is user definable. In Look at pictures to compare hand written notes with NxtNotes.

Transposition from the paper handwritten notes to a central report (spreadsheet, word, MS-Project) often takes hours, sometimes days as questions must be asked to get clarity about what the person meant.	With NxtNote, the data is readable and standardized. When the NxtNote is printed there is a 2D bar code imprinted in the upper center of the NxtNote. That data can then be scanned at 800 error-free words per minute into one or more computer applications. The scanner is inexpensive and standard in the industry.
Paper sticky notes can be used for any LOCAL collaborative process: brainstorming; problems solving via value stream mapping, Fish Bone diagrams, and many, many more.	NxtNotes are just as adaptable but can be used across global boundaries. You can now collaborate one-on-one, one-on-many, many-on-one, and many-on-many around the world, at the same meeting.

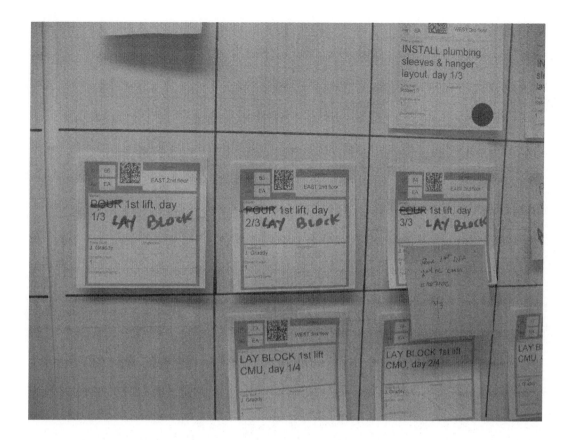

Handwritten Notes vs. NxtNotes

Additional "great" benefits are;

a. Notice that the craft foreman meant to say "Lay Block" but put "Pour" as he knew he had to lay block as part of the pre-pour. He did not see it as necessary to fully describe what he was doing, as he had never collaborated in this fashion before. His shorthand confused the other members of the team, thus the need for clarity, and that clarity was not evident until later when the transcriber, who was not a professional tradesman, tried to make sense of the data.

b. The NxtNotes are preconfigured so that specific data goes in specific places; there is both a standard and consistency to data capture. Some data fields are required, others are not.

c. The ground rules are followed to assure clarity. The 1st one is that the task description must start with a verb: Pour, lay, install, etc.

d. With conventional sticky notes the location of where the work is to be performed is often omitted. If locations are omitted, people often fail in their production commitments due to space conflicts.

For a demonstration of the NxtNote process, please join our Global OEM Solutions WebOffice group at http://lean101.ca/weboffice.htm, or email me directly.

The 1998 case study was completed based upon the project stakeholders agreeing that they wished to break the paradigm of "projects as usual." The same is true of the construction teams I have coached for the last 10 years in Pull Planning. But I have added NxtNote to my repertoire in the last two years as my standard practice because it brings so much more value and waste elimination to the process. It is the only technology like this in the world.

While the IT tools alone cannot enable a lean and collaborative system, they can enhance the results of a project because they contribute to the basic premise: improved collaboration, communication, and comprehension, and at the same time reducing risk.

Ed Anderson, Senior Leader, Global OEM Solutions, Construction and Project Management.

Ed@OEMsolutions.ca

CHAPTER 14 - The OEM Way – A Detailed Description

Lean implementations have been focused on improving processes, and doing it through the concepts of adding value, and eliminating waste. OEM's way of doing business is to focus on helping people to improve an organization. Our hoshin, or direction, is identified by three broad-brush goals.

Relationships, Reality, Results.

OEM believes that if it can attain relationships faster than any other consulting firm. It can define the reality and pain points of clients faster than any other business. OEM can engage the entire organization in moving towards a brighter Future State. By doing this and ensuring lasting results OEM will become the most trusted of consulting firms.

We will only grow by engaging our students to become teachers, our teachers to become students, and make the process of asking a lot of questions a business policy for all successful companies and organizations. We will encourage companies to make the switch between improving processes, and products to improving their people. Then it will be automatic that their people will make improvements to the services and products they create.

Why have 95% of the organizations failed their people?

People are very predictable. I shared a statistic earlier with you in which 3% of what we do is done through the thinking process, and 97% of what we do is sub-conscience. For change to happen in people need to be introduced to new routines. They need to perform these routines so that their thinking changes simply because they are performing actions that create new. Old habits are replaced with new ones. The company has enough leverage to do this, people will not do it on their own. Companies fail their employees because they expect that it will happen. Not a good expectation. Leadership starts at the top.

I particularly like this next chart on consequences. This completely resonates with me so I hope that it does with you too. I perform activities based on consequences just like the following graph shows. The consequences of things we do can be categorized by 3 categories;

- ✓ Impact
- ✓ Timing
- ✓ Certainty

The Impact can be positive (P), the timing can be immediate (I), and the certainty (C) can be 100%. The acronym would be PIC (positive, immediate, certain).

For example, in a lean organization a quick and easy kaizen being performed, is positive, the feedback from the team leader is immediate, and the certainty of this happening is 100%. This is very powerful. This is a PIC.

Types of Consequences

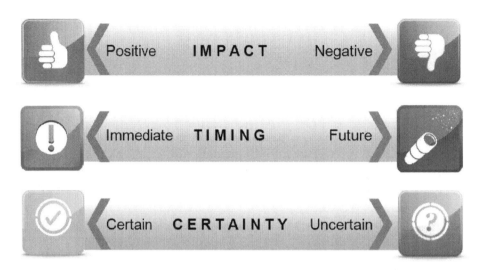

Source: Aubrey Daniels Group International   Graphic: The Rana Group Inc.

Looking at the graph below, there is a relationship on how powerful an impact this PIC is. You should know that PICs and NICs have the most powerful impact on people. People respond to this immediately. This is a most powerful way to persuade. From studies done say that there is a sweet spot of PICs over NICs, and that sweet spot is four to one.

Impact of Consequences

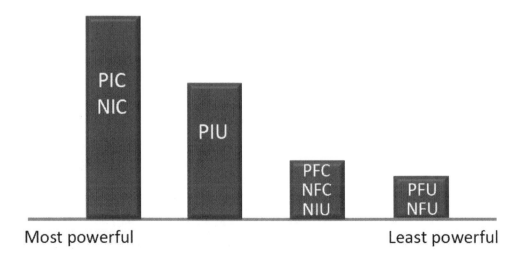

Source: Aubrey Daniels Group International   Graphic: The Rana Group Inc.

A company fails its employees because it does not convert the POSITIVE – FUTURE – UNCERTAIN gains of a Lean Implementation to POSITIVE – IMMEDIATE – CERTAIN activities that reward the employee right away. This is why "Quick and Easy Kaizen" works. It engages every employee immediately. It is a positive change, it is immediate (they make a good change in their area) and it is certain, their team leader gives them a thank you.

This brings us to the "thank you" discussion. This is assumed to happen. There is such a need for leader's standardized work for this reason. If the "thank you" comments were forthcoming, and positive reinforcement happened for the good things that people accomplish in the business, then one person would have an army follow them. Productivity would increase and alignment would happen by using the negative immediate consequence (NIC) appropriately. We may assume that doing kaizen, or implementing a future state map will give your company a good start towards implementing lean, and it does. Non-lean companies that have implemented lean tools also have to put in place the infrastructure that ensures these positive reinforcements happen. Otherwise Lean fails and it does so because people generally do not know how to handle other people. They end up missing the point that Lean is about people. Lean is a people-based process. Doing something to consistently hedge against people's old behaviors is what the leader's responsibility is. A company's responsibility is to create and share their Mission – why they exist, their Vision – Where they are going, and their Values – setting clear expectations of behavior that are to be reinforced.

So next time you speed in your car, ask yourself, "Why am I speeding?". The answer will most definitely contain the words, "I don't expect to get a speeding ticket". You see, it is not certain that there will be any negative consequences. So you take the chance. Stated more clearly, so I take the chance.

333

What is an OEM Lean Thinker?

An OEM Lean Thinker is one that applies Lean and Six Sigma to their own verbal communication process. It starts by making the statement; "If I cause any other human being to defend their belief system, then I have failed that person." An OEM Lean Thinker questions their own internal communication processes first, and assumes that they have something to learn. In this way, when they ask questions, they pull the other person into their world of thinking. They use words like, "Please help me understand what you mean", or "Am I interpreting what you said correctly, I think you meant this..., am I correct?" This is the ultimate Pull System, learning is endless for an OEM Lean Thinker. The technique of asking questions provides this endless opportunity to learn. In a way, we are pulling information when we want it or need it.

I have one last trick to share with you. For my organization, OEM, I have made it a rule that we only ask questions during our meetings. This is a rule that everyone must follow unless they are answering a question that someone asked. When I find that the conversation has slipped and is no longer focused, I ask, "Where is the question in that?" This brings everyone back to the topic at hand. Enjoy these techniques, and use them to make money and save time.

Alex Trachilis, George Trachilis, Kali Trachilis